James K. Baxter

New Selected Poems

Edited by Paul Millar

OXFORD
UNIVERSITY PRESS

OXFORD
UNIVERSITY PRESS

253 Normanby Road, South Melbourne, Victoria 3205, Australia

Oxford University Press is a department of the University of Oxford. It furthers the University's objective of excellence in research, scholarship, and education by publishing worldwide in

Oxford New York

Auckland Bangkok Buenos Aires Cape Town Chennai
Dar es Salaam Delhi Hong Kong Istanbul Karachi Kolkata
Kuala Lumpur Madrid Melbourne Mexico City Mumbai Nairobi
São Paulo Shanghai Taipei Tokyo Toronto

OXFORD is a trade mark of Oxford University Press in the UK and in certain other countries

First published 2001
Reprinted 2004

National Library of New Zealand
Cataloguing-in-Publication data:

ISBN 0 19 558429 5.

Typeset by Solo Typesetting, South Australia
Printed through Bookpac Production Services, Singapore

Contents

Acknowledgments

My sincere thanks to Jacquie Baxter for her encouragement, support, and friendship. Thanks also to my colleagues in Victoria University's School of English, Film, and Theatre who helped in ways both large and small, in particular Bill Manhire, Geoff Miles, David Norton, Vincent O'Sullivan, Roger Robinson, and Peter Whiteford. A number of academics from outside VUW specialising in New Zealand literature also made time to offer their opinions on the selection or assist in various ways, and I wish to thank Ken Arvidson, Patrick Evans, Mac Jackson, Lawrence Jones, Michelle Leggott, John Newton, Alan Riach, Terry Sturm, and Albert Wendt. At the end of the day, however, the selections are mine, and I absolve all those named above from any responsibility for the final product.

Jerusalem Daybook (1971), *Autumn Testament* (1972), and *The Tree House* (1974) were first published by Price Milburn, Wellington. Excerpts from these publications are gratefully acknowledged.

Particular thanks to my two excellent and highly professional research assistants, Charlotte Elder and Jan Cronin. Thanks also to John Baxter, Linda Cassells, Colin Durning, Greg O'Brien, Derek Melser, Peter Olds, Hugh Price, Peter Rose, and the editorial staff at Oxford University Press. The assistance and expertise of staff of the Hocken Library, especially Janine Delaney, and the Victoria University Library, especially Kathleen Coleridge, has been invaluable. The years of research done by Father J. E. Weir made my job less difficult—I appreciate more fully his achievement in editing Baxter's *Collected Poems*. Thanks to VUW's Internal Grants Committee and the Research Committee of the Faculty of Humanities and Social Sciences for the provision of a number of grants that were essential to the completion of this project. The book was finally completed while on a teaching exchange: thanks therefore to the Fulbright Foundation, the VUW FHSS Leave Committee, and the English Department of the University of Hawai'i at Manoa—mahalo!

Finally, I owe much to members of family. My parents Enid and Graham Millar have assisted as always—particularly my father, a friend and sounding board who went beyond the call of duty as my right arm in Wellington, scouring manuscripts and answering endless questions while I was overseas. And to those who lived with the book, thank you to my wife Kay for her insights, editing, and encouragement; and my small sons Aaron and Gareth for their frequent, sometimes welcome, usually loud, always interesting, interruptions.

Introduction

The poems in this selection place James K. Baxter among the major poets of the twentieth century. They show him emphatically as being more than a New Zealand poet. Yet New Zealand lies at the heart of his poems, the best of which constitutes an unparalleled, intensely personal engagement with the country, its people, and society.

As has often been the case with major literary figures in New Zealand and elsewhere, Baxter's reputation at home has waxed and waned since his death in 1972. Following a period of near beatification in the early 1970s, a climate of calculated scholarly indifference developed in New Zealand during the 1980s that continued in the 1990s, even while his work was being chosen for international anthologies and cementing its place as representing the finest among world literatures written in English. From the mid-1990s, however, new publications and original creative works in film, theatre, dance, and music have tapped a powerful and growing interest in Baxter. Usually the spotlight has been on the poet's colourful life, and only secondarily on his writing. This selection intends to place the focus back on Baxter's essential achievement: his poetry.

It has become something of a habit among critics to regard Baxter as a writer of great lines or phrases, rather than a writer of great poems. His prolific output contributed to the idea that poems came too easily and were not sufficiently polished; that his work habits were as scruffy as his later appearance. But the care Baxter lavished on his manuscripts, the reworking of numerous poems, often over a period of years, and the way successive versions of his final Jerusalem books were meticulously drafted, attest to the attention he paid to his craft and the high skill he attained. Few poets have approached their profession with such dedication or served so long an apprenticeship. Baxter read prodigiously and practised assiduously, experimenting with language and style, and developing a wide-ranging repertoire of technical tricks from which an entirely original type of poetry would ultimately develop.

The poetry covers a range of forms. Love lyrics like 'Let Time be Still' (p. 16); ballads and songs like 'Lament for Barney Flanagan' (p. 37)—the dramatic situations of which explain his interest in writing for the stage; and poems of protest like 'A Rope for Harry Fat' (p. 60) represent only a handful of the genres in which he wrote successfully. The largest single group of his poems are letters. Many of these are long verse letters personally addressing Noel Ginn (pp. 7 and 14), Sam Hunt (p. 241), or Max Harris (p. 248). Others are in series, like the 'Pig Island Letters' to Maurice Shadbolt (pp. 76 ff) or the *Jerusalem Sonnets: Poems for Colin Durning* (pp. 116 ff); then there is a range of intensely personal letters to his wife and family members. Devotional poems, like 'Song to the Lord God' (p. 270)—which relates Baxter to a long and rich tradition of devotional poetry in English—and some more generally addressed, like 'Ode to Auckland' (p. 154), also fall into this category. Just as often, Baxter's poems are letters to himself, many of them entries in a spiritual verse diary, or building blocks of a grand testamentary poem carefully crafted to connect backwards and forwards through metaphor and imagery.

It is in the best of the letter poems, when the language seems most natural and colloquial, the verse least structured, and the ideas fresh off the top of the mind, that Baxter's genius is most apparent. It is remarkable how exact and apt his use of language is, how carefully metaphor is used or extended, and how subtly a complex idea can be expressed through the barest articulation of a concept or experience.

To appreciate Baxter's poetry from a twenty-first-century perspective, the controversial aspects of both his life and his writing must be placed in some sort of context. These often put him at odds with a society unable to stomach its disturbing reflection in his work. Indifference was not something Baxter generated. His various manifestations—pacifist, poet, alcoholic, Catholic, commune leader, to name a few—elicited strong reactions, attracting devotees and provoking antagonists. His deficiencies have been extensively catalogued: he left a trail of broken friendships and relationships, his attitudes to women were problematic, his infidelities were legendary, his depictions of the middle classes were offensive to them, and his challenges to conventional morality were disturbing. How could the author of the deeply devotional 'Song to the Lord God' write at around the same time the scabrous 'Truth Song' from 'Ballad of Fire Trap Castle' (p. 264)? He became, by his own description, 'the nuns' devil and a bad smell in the noses of good churchgoing people' (p. 132).

Baxter classed as his most successful poems those containing a 'kernel of actual experiential knowledge', and emphasised the intimate connection between his life experiences and his verse: 'I know only a little about the world; and most of it is somewhere in the poems I have written.' But when biographical elements occur in the poems they are generally projected through a mythic lens. He once described each of his poems as 'part of a large subconscious corpus of personal myth, like an island above the sea, but joined underwater to other islands', and elsewhere commented that what 'happens is either meaningless to me, or else it is mythology'. The elements Baxter the poet valued in his own and others' lives were those that connect individuals to a wider mythical landscape of human experience. In the majority of his verse there are no individuals, only archetypes like the 'National Mum and Labour Dad' of the 'Ballad of Calvary Street' (p. 56).

Baxter's unusual ability to move between worlds, saying one thing while apparently doing another, was disconcerting, and has often been taken as evidence of personal duplicity for which the poetry must be held to account. Yet he never regarded himself as part of mainstream New Zealand society, and his poetry is written consistently from that position of principled self-marginalisation. From his teenage years as the son of pacifists in a world at war, he was a deliberate non-conformist who relished his description of the poet as the 'sore thumb of the tribe'. In practice he was the sore thumb of the dominant social order: the respectable citizens conforming to the dictates of a passionless central government that he characterises in 'The Bureaucrats' as 'Caesar' (p. 203). In Wellington, where he had done it 'hard/Carving stones in Caesar's graveyard' ('Ballad of Nine Jobs', p. 218), he was happy to leave his office desk to become a postman. To many in 1963 such a move would have seemed a retrograde step, but it was totally in keeping with his resistance to what he saw as a corrupting 'Calvinist ethos which underlies our determinedly secular culture like the bones of a dinosaur buried in a suburban garden plot'. Resistance to this ethos was his way of being a 'cell of good living in a corrupt society'.

Baxter was by nature tribal. He affiliated with small, tightly knit groups, whose cohesion was generally a function of persecution and alienation, and identified with various tribal manifestations. They ranged from the oppressed Highland clans of his Scottish forbears through pacifists, poets, alcoholics, and Catholics—a minority group in New Zealand—to the tribes of the Wanganui settlement called Jerusalem (where he ended his short life): the local Maori iwi, and Baxter's own commune, which he called Nga Mokai—the fatherless.

One of Baxter's intentions during the Jerusalem period was to present to other pakeha an entirely new way of relating to the tangata whenua—the people of the land. This aim, reflected in both his life and his writing, was the outcome of a steadily intensifying identification, over a number of years, with Maori culture, tradition, and spirituality. Through marriage to the Maori poet J. C. Sturm he had been drawn into participating in her activities among her own people. He also experienced the racial prejudice that she encountered. But she believed that not until his time in India in the late 1950s, and the experience of being the single white face in a throng of brown, did he truly understand her sense of alienation in the predominantly pakeha world they inhabited. It is an understanding that lies at the heart of poems like 'The Maori Jesus' (p. 220) and 'Tangi' (p. 107). At his death Baxter received the rare honour for a pakeha of being buried in the urupa at Jerusalem following a full tangi arranged by the elders of the local tribe, Ngati Hau.

For most of his life Baxter followed a double track, oscillating between the demands of correct society—where he played many roles—and his attraction to alienated tribes. This led to one of the key tensions in his life. The 'family man, teetotal, moderately pious, not offensive to sight or smell, able to say the right thing in a drawing room', was ever at odds with the clannish, anarchic other self, 'my collaborator, my schizophrenic twin, who has always provided me with poems'.

The paradoxes that are so evident, and to some so problematic, in Baxter's life produced a tension that assisted his creative process. During his teenage years he developed an enduring conception of the poetic self as a composite of opposites, dwelling within in a state of perpetual poem-producing tension. As he once explained, a 'kind of tension of belief often lies behind the poems, and it leads to a certain edge'. That type of tension would be for many years a necessary condition for producing poetry. Always at the locus of tension was some version of the 'gap' between the selves, a contradictory place where nothing existed but from which poems originated. Notions of this 'gap' are ubiquitous in Baxter's writing, but it is not a fixed symbol. It may be a paradoxical site of absence within which to discover the true self, or a place of stillness where the mind is silenced and God is experienced. In the later poetry it becomes 'Wahi Ngaro: the void out of which all things come. That is my point of beginning. That is where I find my peace.'

In the final decade of his life Baxter began exploring ways of practising the things he had been writing about. At first this occurred subtly in the plays he wrote in the 1960s, where the concerns of his verse were translated into the more externally dynamic medium of the stage. But ultimately the life became the poem. In the Jerusalem period, acting out beliefs on the importance of communality, poverty, and sacrifice, Baxter would come to describe himself as the man whose 'name is a way of saying—/"This gap inside a coat"' (p. 133).

There is not, as many have implied, any significant contradiction between Baxter's early and later years. Jerusalem was less a deviation than a natural progression. Baxter's poetry was the product of strong influences—parents, pacifism, war, and adolescence—that saw him break out in words. He began by reading the English poetic canon and writing in that tradition before gradually moving away from it. At around the same time as he was consciously deciding that he was a New Zealander rather than an Englishman (see 'Under the Dank Leaves', p. 176) his verse made its first concrete moves away from imitation and towards authenticity. Despite various attempts throughout his life to conform to the world around him, he remained outside the mainstream and its depersonalised way of living. Over time, impelled by recovery from alcoholism, conversion to Catholicism, and a life-changing few months in Asia, Baxter's conviction grew that simply writing about his beliefs was insufficient. Deprivation, which was little more than theoretical in New Zealand, was painfully real in India. He was forever changed by these experiences and moved inexorably towards Jerusalem and 'the Lord on his axe-chopped cross' (p. 146).

Eventually Baxter's art and life coalesced, and his move to Jerusalem was a way of actualising what he had until then only written about. Poetry, for so long the mainspring of his life, became his own cross. One of the features of Baxter's decision to abandon his old life so ostentatiously was his commitment to stop writing poetry, an activity that now seemed at odds with his new vocation of poverty. Yet he could no more stop writing than he could cease breathing. The Jerusalem period produced some of his most significant poetry and something entirely new. Whereas the earlier verse might, with ponderous metre and latinate diction, move towards a final grand, sonorous phrase, now unrhymed run-on couplets (increasingly the unit of choice in his later work) create a tone both direct and personal, moving closer to a synthesis of Baxter's various selves that had for so long operated in tension.

If, at times, Baxter appears to evaluate New Zealand society harshly, his judgments are always from the perspective of one intimately involved in the social process. His criticisms of national life and his ultimate decision to step out of the mainstream seemed to develop naturally from the preoccupations of a lifetime of verse. Yet these preoccupations were, as a rule, neither negative nor despairing. Rather, the deliberately mythological cast of mind that underpinned his poetry sought to place the individual (and the nation) within a wider frame by directing attention towards universal elements of human experience. The Baxter who, writing shortly before his death, found the Medusa's head of present-day urban global civilisation—with its 'depersonalisation, centralisation, [and] desacralisation'—intolerable could still find reason for hope 'in the hearts of people'.

Paul Millar
Victoria University of Wellington, New Zealand
Te Whare Wananga o te Upoko o te Ika a Maui, Aotearoa

About the text

This book is very much a selection; one that endeavours to give a sense of the range of Baxter's achievement, not merely its peaks. Consequently some poems that I and others consider outstanding have, when others of a similar kind are included, been forced out in favour of work that is to me of particular interest or importance, even if in a few cases of lesser quality. My most difficult decision has been to include in full only a very few of Baxter's poem sequences, which should ideally be read as complete poems in their own right. But as all of these sequences are currently available in print, I have again elected to reserve some space for less readily accessible material.

This selection is divided into two parts: part 1 comprises a range of poems from books published during Baxter's lifetime, or over which he had significant editorial input shortly before he died (see the more detailed description in the introduction to part 1); part 2 moves away from the careful structuring of the first section to present a range of posthumously published, published but uncollected, and unpublished poems ordered chronologically by date of composition (see the more detailed description in the introduction to part 2).

As far as possible this book is intended to be a companion to the much larger *Collected Poems* edited by J.E. Weir. Because Weir took considerable pains to present the texts as accurately as possible, poems in this selection that also appear in the *Collected* follow Weir's text (with some very minor exceptions). These poems have a single date—the estimated year of composition—appended (a firm date is indicated by the addition of the day and month). Where a poem is published but uncollected, the Hocken Library's manuscript reference number (if available), the approximate date of composition, and the details of first publication are appended. These poems are read against the manuscript versions, but in cases of textual variation I have not observed any hard and fast rules about which version to favour, preferring to make judgments based on the content and context of the available versions. Previously unpublished poems are followed by the Hocken manuscript reference number and approximate date of composition. In the rare case that Baxter did not supply a poem with a title, I have followed Weir's or supplied my own in square brackets. A very small amount of commentary is included in the text, generally to clarify points that might now be becoming obscure.

Part 1

Part 1 comprises a selection of poetry (and a small amount of prose) from all of Baxter's books and most of his broadsheet publications either published during his lifetime or over which he had significant editorial control. Many of these poems form the core of the Baxter canon; they are ordered according to the sequence of publication so as to convey a sense of the way he was received as a poet. It is on the basis of these poems, in this order, that Baxter's reputation was established. Four brief biographical pieces on the 1940s, 1950s, 1960s, and the Jerusalem period place the poetry in context.

The 1940s

James Keir Baxter was born in Dunedin in 1926, the second son of Archibald Baxter, an Otago farmer and notorious pacifist, and Millicent Baxter (née Brown). His middle name—after the Scottish socialist, Keir Hardie—signified his parents' left-leaning politics. Because of Baxter's stated tendency to mythologise his life in verse, biography is important in any study of his work. His parents' socialist and pacifist beliefs profoundly influenced him, as did their strikingly contrasting backgrounds: Archie was a quiet, self-educated man, whose ancestors had been small farmers in the Scottish Highlands; and Millicent was the strong-minded eldest daughter of a noted Christchurch professor, John Macmillan Brown.

Apart from brief periods in Wanganui, England, and Europe, Baxter grew up in Brighton, a small settlement on the Otago Coast south of Dunedin. A lifelong suspicion of education systems developed as he attended first Brighton Primary School and later Quaker schools in Wanganui and the English Cotswolds and Dunedin's King's High School.

The early 1940s was not a good time for pacifists: the family was suspected of spying, James was bullied, and his older brother Terence was sent into detention as a military defaulter. James's adolescence was therefore a solitary time, but he felt that his experiences 'created a gap in which the poems were able to grow'. Indeed, between 1942 and 1946 he would draft some 600 poems.

An able, although unmotivated, student, Baxter matriculated a year early, with unspectacular results, applying himself meanwhile to reading and emulating almost the entire English poetic canon. The moderns, particularly Auden, Spender, MacNeice, and Day Lewis, inspired him with the voice they were giving to the social battles of the time. By his late teens he was developing a discernible voice out of adolescent imitation.

In 1944 Baxter began a 'long, unsuccessful love affair with the Higher Learning' when he enrolled at Otago University. 'Incipient alcoholism' soon became a problem, but in 1944 he also won the Macmillan Brown literary prize (for 'Convoys') and Caxton Press published his first collection, *Beyond the Palisade*, to critical acclaim.

This remarkable debut volume is a selection of thirty-four poems from some 500 written between the ages of 15 and 18. Allen Curnow selected six poems from it for his groundbreaking anthology *A Book of New Zealand Verse, 1923–45*, in which he described Baxter's poems as 'a new occurrence in New Zealand: strong in impulse and confident in invention, with qualities of youth in verse which we have lacked'. His endorsement established Baxter's reputation before most New Zealanders had read his work.

Critics commented on Baxter's style and tone, with its mix of imitation and assimilation of numerous major poets of the English canon—Yeats, Auden,

MacNeice, Keats, Blake, and Shelley, to name a few. No one, however, disagreed with Curnow's observation that Baxter had also written 'some poems which could only be his and only a New Zealander's'. Despite this praise, Baxter privately acknowledged a certain unevenness in the volume and described it as a sort of 'poet's progress'. A second collection, *Cold Spring*, considered by Baxter to be somewhat better than his first, remained unpublished (see part 2, p. 175).

Abandoning university study, Baxter worked in factories and on farms from 1945 to 1947. Part of this period is fictionalised in his novel *Horse* (1985). His struggle with alcoholism was both cause and consequence of the failure of his first significant love affair, which was with a young medical student. Her enduring effect, however, is evident in three poem sequences: 'Songs of the Desert' (see part 1, p. 42), 'Cressida' (see part 2, p. 177), and 'Words to Lay a Strong Ghost' (see part 1, p. 157). An even more important relationship began in 1947 when he met Jacqueline Sturm.

In late 1947 Baxter moved to Christchurch, ostensibly to renew his university studies, but actually to visit a Jungian psychologist. He began incorporating Jungian symbolism into his poetic theory and practice. His behaviour, thanks to the 'irrigating river of alcohol', could be erratic as he sporadically attended lectures and took jobs as a sanatorium porter, copy-editor for the Christchurch Press, and freezing worker. He began associating with the poets Curnow and Glover, and his reading remained copious.

Blow, Wind of Fruitfulness (1948) confirmed Baxter as the pre-eminent poet of his generation. Where *Beyond the Palisade* is occasionally uneven and too obviously imitative, and the unpublished 'Cold Spring' dense with personal symbolism, the poems of *Blow, Wind of Fruitfulness* have more control and assurance. Curnow was moved to describe Baxter as 'the most original of New Zealand poets now living'. He argued that if 'these poems are full of echoes, they are not the echoes of mimicry but the true, if altered, accents of other voices, inherited by right of a natural eloquence'.

The New Zealand landscape plays an important role in the poems of *Blow, Wind of Fruitfulness*, as it did in *Beyond the Palisade*. Its spaces are again sparsely peopled, and consequently a tone of solitude and alienation recurs. What is new is what Curnow called a 'welcome gain in irony and detachment'. The pompous and laboured 'University Song' (p. 12), for example, is delightfully subverted in 'Envoi' (p. 13), the final lines of which encapsulate Baxter's reservations about 'the higher learning': 'Lost one original heart and mind/Between the pub and the lecture room.'

Baxter's interest in religion led to his baptism as an Anglican, and, despite considerable parental concern, he and Jacquie were married in St John's Cathedral, Napier, in 1948. That same year they moved to Wellington, where their daughter Hilary—dedicatee of the broadsheet *Charm for Hilary* (p. 20)—was born in 1949.

from *Beyond the Palisade* (1944)

The First Forgotten

O fons Bandusiæ!
The green hill-orchard where
My great-granduncle lived
Is overgrown. No cache and no reprieve

The chilly air holds. They came from the
Old lands, for hunger, or fearing the young
Would shoot from thicket a keeper,
Be transported or hung.

So beholding the strange reeds,
Arrogant flax and fen,
They saw release, eventual and ancestral peace,
Building the stubborn clans again:

Bee-hives along an elderberry fence . . .
The land is drained. Gorse
Only will grow. To the towns now
Their sons' sons gone, expanding universe:

A light and brittle birth.
I would glorify
Innumerable men in whose breasts my heart once beat,
Is beating. They were slow to die.

One who drove a bullock-team
In the gold-rush on an upland track.
One smiling and whistling softly
With a horseshoe behind his back.

Steel mutilates: more, the hollow
Facade, the gaudy mask
On a twisted face. Clay-shut, forgetful, shall
They answer? we ask?

Only the rough and paper bark peeling
From young bluegums, while undergrowth
Among stunted apple-trees coiling
Trips the foot. Sods grass-buried like antique faith.

1944

The Mountains

In this scarred country, this cold threshold land,
The mountains crouch like tigers.   By the sea
Folk talk of them hid vaguely out of sight.
But here they stand in massed solidity
To seize upon the day and night horizon.

Men shut within a whelming bowl of hills
Grow strange, say little when they leave their high
Yet buried homesteads. Return there silently
When thunder of night-rivers fills the sky
And giant wings brood over loftily and near.

The mountains crouch like tigers. Or they wait
As women wait.   The mountains have no age.
But O the heart leaps to behold them loom!
A sense as of vast fate rings in the blood. No refuge,
No refuge is there from the flame that reaches

Among familiar things and makes them seem
Trivial, vain.   O spirit walks on the peaks!
Eye glances across a gorge to further crags.
There is no desire. But the stream, but the avalanche speaks,
And their word is louder than freedom, the mountain embrace
Were a death dearer than freedom or freedom's flags.

I will go to the coastline and mingle with men.
These mountain buttresses build beyond the horizon.
They call. But he whom they lay their spell upon
Leaves home, leaves kindred.   The range of the telescope's eye
Is well, if the brain follows not to the outermost fields of vision.
I shall drown myself in humanity. Better to lie
Dumb in the city than under the mountainous wavering sky.

The mountains crouch like tigers.
They are but stone yet the seeking eyes grow blind.

1942

Hill-Country

White sky, mountains mount
High: near, terraced, clear
Groined, shouldered

Black-bouldered. Sallow flats lie
Dry.
Yellow broom blooming
Pollen-heavy. Bees hum
Come from air there—
Bare, bleak, blue-peak
Towers over mountain flower—
Bees come, hum home
Home to hive in house-wall
Fall.
All heard, small bird;
Wind strums over plain
Same dry, high plain:
Thin grass sounds in winds
As winds pass.

Rock-face, clay fallen away
Gravel sluices loose for gold
Travels down, silts over
Old boulders. Land-lover
Here stand, stay.

Sallow flat, yellow flat, willow-flat
Pass. Let pass hill-wind, hill-grass:
Here stay: lay aside
Dry brick, sun-dried.
Here stay, deep in clay
Sun-clay, water-clay
Gouged-out, gaping clay
Clay.

1942

Rain-Ploughs

Rain-ploughs rend the interstices of hills
  And serpents grey-jawed drift and raven;
  Sodden cadaver the earth, identity unproven;
Based granite-galleons probe eroded hulls
Teeth from earth's withered gum; and split sky spills
  Her world-enveloping waters winter-riven—
  Sun by insane poltergeist gashed from heaven
Gives outer demons room to wreak their hells.

World crumbles, warped and wan: in talon
Of shackle-broken djinn: how exorcise? O where
Is the bottle black-stone whence wound he jail-break felon?
. . . upheaval, twisted rock: gigantic there
Jar hurled to prone resisting sea-bottom; and sullen
Monsters guard, waiting till water oust air.

Yet hope stays for him who dare.
Dost see yonder the angel-Archer stand?
Frail-veined twig in hand
By blinding sky fire-tipped he doth bear:
Fire-feathered arrow-thought to set new sun on flare
Brave djinn and monster, green again the land.

1942–44

Letter to Noel Ginn

They can admire the empty lion-skin
The heart skewered by print, who will admire:
But from you, Noel, I wish more—
The friend's stance, confessor for my sin
Which is pride alone: yet pride alone will win
Niche of immortal marble despised and hungered for.

As a child I was childish . . . an intuitional ease;
Had missed the vice of sensitivity;
Waded the flood-race of a century;
But felt capacity for pain increase
Till each day no longer a wood of peace
Held larks of Shelleyan song, tigers of poetry.

When I saw Europe . . . a kaleidoscope
Fluttered, flashed elusive in place of the grave
Time-wading fortitude:—oil-weighted wave
Feathering bows forever; blind seascape;
Nights of storm, screw thudding; Gibraltar cape—
Peered through field-glasses, played chess till nausea claimed her slave.

Or earlier: in Australia the hot days;
Mast-cracking Sydney bridge; golden Colombo
With fishing-fleets on estuaries to show
A bird's plumage, a bird's surf-shadowing ways;
A camel scrubbed upon the banks near Suez;
Crete's iron citadel; and Plymouth bitter with snow.

London claimed me: she was heavy and huge;
Her barges, and her dank wharves flecked with soot;
Placarded Tubes; and fog at Christmas; mute
Paling and palace. The Cotswolds were a refuge:
Leaf-mould . . . stone . . . thatched roofs . . . blackberry hedge;
Lanes, willows . . . snow-slush; bells; homesickness; running the gauntlet.

Europe claimed me: then she did not bleed.
Flat Danish fields, yellow sky spun by the rocking
Express; and at Copenhagen seabirds flocking
Along quays. The rock Rhine towered and treed;
Clean Berlin; at Eisenach sycamore seed;
Rothenberg . . . dungeons; friendly Storm Trooper . . . the wind is mocking.

France: where the Rhône ran under concrete;
Sewer at bridge-base. Out of the violent sun
I wrote poems, scrapped poems half-begun
On clouds and comets. A tower seen from the street:
Skeletons found there. Bats. Snake at my feet.
The castle . . . Terry's arm broken; when set, he sweated with pain.

And Scotland was my spiritual home,
Or so it seemed. The tide ancestral swung
Over rock-weed. I plucked the bells of ling;
Saw bald Glencoe . . . and watched the red-coats come.
Old Edinburgh . . . were the cobbles dumb?
England again: Boscastle . . . crags and a blowhole spouting.

——Here once more I walk in the troubled water.
Our hills call: but what shall I learn from them?
Pride bids me stare upon the broken time
Of lies and high explosive; prompts this letter.
With pride for armour men in their abattoir slaughter.
Pride holds me from like hells: pride makes me what I am.

What land shall receive me save as a stranger?
Sea-blown Ulysses said: and Ithaca
More alien was than Troy. Nor could Minerva
Content him long: aged he craved for danger
For withered fame. So Time was Troy's avenger.
Slight parallel . . . yet seek I *res habita*.

The same inhuman cataclysm that set
You weeding flax upon a worthless ground
Both truth and talent to a treadmill bound

Leaves me upon a waiting Ararat:
(The flood may not subside): no marionette
Jerked by the city string, nor in her rubble drowned.

Both clouds and houses are a frozen tide
Till poetry inhabit them with fire.
Men only stay, their masque and their desire;
Thus among men I move my tap-roots wide
The roots of verse, the roots of life beside;
Leave empty lion-skin for dullards to admire.

Women as flowers: they are embodiment
Of the gross earth and the rhetorical cloud;
But shaped as bird, as flower to strange and loud.
. . . A span of threescore and the heart is spent:
This word invades, but I have armament—
The gift of ancestry, the armour of the proud.

The backward groping of a tree of blood
Coils in the dark: but from its mountain springs
Brings mountain pride, and brings
Each impulse of the evil and the good,
With something of a Celtic hardihood:
The pain and poetry . . . I did not dream these things.

Those who grew old: those who were shrewd and hardy;
As children wondered and as men grew sure:
They are but painted figures insecure
Upon a tattered backcloth tamed and tardy.
And we their unreflecting progeny
Forget, inherit: thus their deeds, their deaths endure.

My son, at first a knocking in the womb
Can speak beyond the thundering gates of war,
Symplegades: it is his voice I hear;
And my son's son; braving the storms of time
The storms and sultry shallows—vortex, storm,
They beat on us, they break: pride is the saviour.

1944

from *Blow, Wind of Fruitfulness* (1948)

High Country Weather

Alone we are born
    And die alone;
Yet see the red-gold cirrus
    Over snow-mountain shine.

Upon the upland road
    Ride easy, stranger:
Surrender to the sky
    Your heart of anger.

4 October 1945

Returned Soldier

The boy who volunteered at seventeen
At twenty-three is heavy on the booze.
Strafed in the desert and bombed out in Crete—
With sore dark eyes and hardened by the heat
Entitled now to call himself a man
And in the doll's-house walk with death at ease:
The Cairo women, cobbers under sand
A death too great for dolls to understand.

Back to a city bed or station hut
At maelstrom centre falling through the night
To dreams where deeper than El Alamein
A buried childhood stirs with leaves and flowers
Remembered girls, the blurred and bitter waters.
Wakes to the midnight rafters and the rain.

1946

Blow, Wind of Fruitfulness

Blow, wind of fruitfulness
        Blow from the buried sun:
Blow from the buried kingdom
        Where heart and mind are one.

Blow, wind of fruitfulness,
    The murmuring leaves remember;
For deep in doorless rock
    Awaits their green September.

Blow from the wells of night:
    The blind flower breathes thy coming
Birds that are silent now
    And buds of barren springing.

Blow from beyond our day.
    The hill-born streams complain;
Hear from their stony courses
    The great sea rise again.

Blow on the mouth of morning
    Renew the single eye:
And from remembered darkness
    Our immortality.

19 January 1946

Sea Noon

The grey smoke of rain drifts over headlands
And clear drops fall on the paper as I write.
Only the light thunder and murmur
Of ebbing and flowing furrows is endlessly repeated
And the rapid gulls flash over without sound.

Where is a house with windows open to the afternoon?
With light beer on tables and tobacco smoke
Floating; with a fire in the grate;
With music and the mind-filling pleasure of easy company.
Lying back in a chair to laugh or standing and smiling
One would accept all fates, and even the gold
Melancholy leaves of late autumn
Would seem as natural as a child's toy.

But labour and hunger strides the year
In seasonal repetition, more harsh than tidal waters.
The very rocks are cold: and they were lava once.

So stand the dull green trees bearing the weather
On solitary boughs; so the grey smoke of rain
Drifts on a painted verge of sea and air.

The fisherman casts his net to hold the tide.
Chilly the light wind blowing. And dark the face of noonday
As at the inconsolable parting of friends.

10 June 1946

The Bay

On the road to the bay was a lake of rushes
Where we bathed at times and changed in the bamboos.
Now it is rather to stand and say:
How many roads we take that lead to Nowhere,
The alley overgrown, no meaning now but loss:
Not that veritable garden where everything comes easy.

And by the bay itself were cliffs with carved names
And a hut on the shore beside the Maori ovens.
We raced boats from the banks of the pumice creek
Or swam in those autumnal shallows
Growing cold in amber water, riding the logs
Upstream, and waiting for the taniwha.

So now I remember the bay and the little spiders
On driftwood, so poisonous and quick.
The carved cliffs and the great outcrying surf
With currents round the rocks and the birds rising.
A thousand times an hour is torn across
And burned for the sake of going on living.
But I remember the bay that never was
And stand like stone and cannot turn away.

1946

University Song

Among these hills our fathers came.
By strength of eye and hand alone
They built: and murmur loud as flame
Their voices from the living stone.

Forget not those whom Scotland bred
Above whose bones our cities stand.
Forget not them! nor the unknown dead
Whose broken veins flow through our land.

As streams in wildernesses rise
And green the desolate shingle plain:
So under windy southern skies
Peace flowered and Wisdom shall remain.

The generations rouse and pass
Like falling birds to well of night,
Or like the windsown summer grass
Now tall, now withered in our sight.

But our sons' sons alike shall find
Perpetual, though nations cease,
Within these walls the quiet mind
The storm-unshaken rose of Peace.

1945

Note: MS Book has '*Tune:* Jerusalem'.

Envoi [to 'University Song']

And blackened by the early frost
Leaves beat upon the window pane
Like paper mouths—an image lost
Between the eyeball and the brain.

Above, about, on either hand
Their multitudinous seven wings
The uncreated winds expand
In sufferance of created things.

Where evening darkening in dejection
Can hear, monotonous, profound
The too long dead for resurrection
In suspiration from the ground—

Attenuate ghosts expound their lean
Philosophies of When and If;
And oft on that enchanted green
Chimera mates with hippogriff.

The classics student feels an urge
To emulate Empedocles
But rides upon the lava surge—
Oh forest of the bloody trees—

Per ardua ad astra: blind
Inscription from a catacomb.
Lost, one original heart and mind
Between the pub and lecture-room.

1946

Letter to Noel Ginn II

Two years of silence—I take pen again
To write a rhyming letter. You'll forgive
The interim, and knowing how we live
From hand to mouth, a certain thread of pain
And bitterness that blurs the narrative.
My last was in a more romantic vein.

Our dreams take refuge from the men we are
And hide as flies do from the winter chill.
The lost traveller's dream under the hill
Remains with me when propping up a bar
Or in strange beds I do the body ill
To gratify a merciless guiding star.

'Th' expense of spirit . . .' Yet the spirit grows
By grieving for the sensual heart in chains.
Birth-pangs that we mistake for burial-pains
Give promise of the everlasting rose
Where bitter Loss consolidates its gains.
This is the answer that no question knows.

I have the letters that you wrote from camp
(Defaulters' camp, in case this should be read
By other men) where living men grew dead
In grey monotony. I was a lamp,
A kind of beacon to you then, you said—
Since then the wick has grown a trifle damp.

No man can play Aladdin all his life.
The oil is blood, although the flame be clear,
And world-annihilating djinns appear

Unasked-for at the falling of a leaf.
Or else the heart becomes a cinder—Fear
Is Art's companion, and the hermit Grief.

So poets learn to live like other men
For money, lovers, or the friends with whom
Music can animate a sunless room
And rouse the rumour of a different Sun
That shines the same though endless night draw on
And wakes the dead heart from its numbered tomb.

Perhaps I overstate the case—but I
Live by extremes. The madman and the saint
Have both (I fear) the same extremist taint,
And both are mad to Madame Butterfly.
Being no Francis, I can scarcely paint
A halo—'poet's licence' is my cry.

It was my dearly held delusion once
That labouring men were better than their betters
And needed only to throw off their fetters
For Eden to return to Adam's sons.
Since then I've worked with them; and they're go-getters
Just like the Rev. Fraser—bless his bones.

An 8 hour day is not conducive to
The exercise of one's imagination.
So I have found alas that my true station
Is still among the academic crew
Whom I despised for undue cerebration
That leads to withering of the heart and thew.

No doubt I'll find a niche where I can grumble
About the clique that pay me for my pen,
And drink with other intellectual men,
And gain some slight prestige, however humble,
With a little bitter poem now and then
Until the first apocalyptic rumble:

And that will be the Bomb. I often think
Of the climb we made like beetles up a drain
From neanderthal, to be washed down again
In a flood of dirty water from the sink.
Lions and horses also sport a brain
But do not pine for a celestial stink.

From this high window I can see the swells
Roll in with their incessant cannonade
Upon that shore where once, a lonely child, I made
My own mythology of weeds and shells
And dreamed I heard from the green water shade
The pealing of sea drowned cathedral bells.

(While in bombed Germany the violent dream
Grew flesh and blood and tore a city down
Whose dazed survivors searching among stones
Can find the lichen hunger or the scream
Of mandrake pain, but never that first sun-
Flower of peace upon a lucid stream.)

And it is good to walk upon the sand
In winter when the dunes are hard and dry
With frost that binds an iron earth and sky.
Bone of my bone, the stubborn rocks withstand
The ebb and surge of grief. The ocean I
Once feared, I love more than the frozen land.

There is a kind of reconciliation
With buried selves and seasons, so to walk
And listen to the arrogant seabirds' talk
Who have no interest in our damnation,
And feel beyond those frosty hillocks the
Thunder of an obliterating sea.

1946–48

Let Time be Still

Let Time be still
Who takes all things,
Face, feature, memory
Under his blinding wings.

That I hold again the green
Larch of your body
Whose leaves will gather
The springs of the sky.

And fallen from his cloud
The falcon find
The thigh-encompassed wound
Breasts silken under hand.

Though in a dark room
We knew the day breaking
And the rain-bearing wind
Cold matins making.

Sure it seemed
That hidden away
From the sorrowful wind
In deep bracken I lay.

Your mouth was the sun
And green earth under
The rose of your body flowering
Asking and tender
In the timelost season
Of perpetual summer.

1946

Haast Pass

In the dense bush all leaves and bark exude
The odour of mortality; for plants
Accept their death like stones
Rooted for ever in time's torrent bed.

Return from here. We have nothing to learn
From the dank falling of fern spores
Or the pure glacier blaze that melts
Down mountains, flowing to the Tasman.

This earth was never ours. Remember
Rather the tired faces in the pub
The children who have never grown. Return
To the near death, the loves like garden flowers.

1946

Tunnel Beach

The waist-high sea was rolling
Thunder along her seven iron beaches
When we climbed down to rocks and the curved sand,

Drowned Lyonesse lay lost and tolling
Waiting the cry of the sun's phoenix
From the sea-carved cliffs that held us in their hand.

Forgotten there the green
Paddocks we walked an hour before,
The mare and the foal and the witch-tormented wood
And the flaked salt boughs, for the boughs of flame were seen
Of the first garden and the root
Of graves in your salt mouth and the forehead branded fire.

Through the rock tunnel whined
The wind, Time's hound in leash,
And stirred the sand and murmured in your hair.
The honey of your moving thighs
Drew down the cirrus sky, your doves about the beach
Shut out sea thunder with their wings and stilled the lonely air.

But O rising I heard the loud
Voice of the sea's women riding
All storm to come. No virgin mother bore
My heart wave eaten. From the womb of cloud
Falls now no dove, but combers grinding
Break sullen on the last inviolate shore.

1946

The Cave

In a hollow of the fields, where one would least expect it,
Stark and suddenly this limestone buttress:
A tree whose roots are bound about the stones,
Broad-leaved, hides well that crevice at the base
That leads, one guesses, to the sunless kingdom
Where souls endure the ache of Proserpine.

Entering where no man it seemed
Had come before, I found a rivulet
Beyond the rock door running in the dark.
Where it sprang from in the heart of the hill
No one could tell: alone
It ran like Time there in the dank silence.

I spoke once and my voice resounded
Among the many pillars. Further in
Were bones of sheep that strayed and died
In nether darkness, brown and water-worn.
The smell of earth was like a secret language
That dead men speak and we have long forgotten.

The whole weight of the hill hung over me.
Gladly I would have stayed there and been hidden
From every beast that moves beneath the sun,
From age's enmity and love's contagion:
But turned and climbed back to the barrier,
Pressed through and came to dazzling daylight out.

1948

Farmhand

You will see him light a cigarette
At the hall door careless, leaning his back
Against the wall, or telling some new joke
To a friend, or looking out into the secret night.

But always his eyes turn
To the dance floor and the girls drifting like flowers
Before the music that tears
Slowly in his mind an old wound open.

His red sunburnt face and hairy hands
Were not made for dancing or love-making
But rather the earth wave breaking
To the plough, and crops slow-growing as his mind.

He has no girl to run her fingers through
His sandy hair, and giggle at his side
When Sunday couples walk. Instead
He has his awkward hopes, his envious dreams to yarn to.

But ah in harvest watch him
Forking stooks, effortless and strong—
Or listening like a lover to the song
Clear, without fault, of a new tractor engine.

1948

from *Charm for Hilary* (1949)

Charm for Hilary

May the Pleiads seven
And the powers of Heaven
Keep thee night and day
From harm and disarray.
In thy body neither
Cough, nor colic either;
Fume of woodsmoke leave thee
Whole; nor chill wind grieve thee.
Spider black and hairy
Nowhere lurk to scare thee,
Whining midge to bother,
Prowling cat to smother.
Lie on pillows white
Through the rainy night;
No opossum leaping
Stir thee from thy sleeping,
Nor the mouse's laughter
Chittering on the rafter.
And ever, while thou
Like young wood dost grow—
By thy bed and board,
Hand on burning sword
Holy Michael guard thee,
From ill demons ward thee.

1949

The 1950s

In 1950, following the move to Wellington with his new family, Baxter enrolled at Victoria University College. He also began associating with a generation of writers—among them W.H. Oliver, Alistair Campbell, and Louis Johnson—that would become known as the Wellington Group.

In 1951, now attending Wellington Teachers' College, Baxter enthralled the New Zealand Writers' Conference with his lecture '*Recent Trends in New Zealand Poetry*', which was subsequently published by Caxton Press. One reviewer described him as 'the profoundest critic we have'. A selection of poems in a collaborative volume, *Poems Unpleasant*, was published in 1952.

Having completed his teachers' college course, Baxter studied full-time at Victoria University in 1953, also publishing *The Fallen House*, a collection that exhibited greater confidence and maturity through the evenness of its tone and the less emphatic echoes of Baxter's many adolescent influences. A few poems exhibit an uncharacteristic simplicity more common in later collections. But usually, when Baxter writes about natural features or everyday events, he develops his themes to communicate a hidden meaning, or connect images of the landscape to the wider landscapes of human experience.

In 1954 he was assistant master at Lower Hutt's Epuni School. An able teacher, but no disciplinarian, his major contribution was a series of children's poems published posthumously in 1974 as *The Tree House* (see part 2, p. 180). Also in 1954 he gave three Macmillan Brown lectures on poetry at Victoria University, which were published, to mixed reviews from critics concerned by his simplification of issues and reliance on anecdote, as *The Fire and the Anvil* (1955).

In late 1954 Baxter joined Alcoholics Anonymous, espousing its principle of helping others in a course of counselling and prison visitation that continued for the rest of his life. Greater stability—personal, financial, and domestic—was also achieved through a substantial legacy with which the family purchased a house in the Wellington suburb of Ngaio. He received his BA in 1955 and published a long poem in pamphlet form, *Traveller's Litany*. He left Epuni School in 1956 to work for School Publications, a period that provided material for numerous attacks on bureaucracy.

Baxter discovered the pitfalls of parody when his skilful imitations of seventeen New Zealand poets, *The Iron Breadboard: Studies in New Zealand Writing* (1957), was received with acrimony by some of his peers. Fourteen more serious poems appeared in a collaboration, *The Nightshift: Poems on Aspects of Love* (1957), a collection that, to quote Howard McNaughton, 'established a position of alienation that would recur in his work for two decades'. The following year Baxter received international recognition when Oxford University Press published *In Fires of No Return*. Despite this recognition and the book's selection as the Poetry Book Society's Choice, the collection was not judged successful by critics. The book is divided into three sections. Section 1—some stronger early poems—and section 2—a number of previously uncollected pieces—received little criticism. However, section 3—Baxter's more recent work—was censured for its many poems that contain superb lines or phrases yet fail to achieve wholeness.

Baxter's greatest success in 1958 was the radio play, broadcast in September, *Jack Winter's Dream*. Domestically, things were less successful. Jacquie was astonished by Baxter's unheralded decision to convert to Roman Catholicism, and in October 1957 they separated. He was received into the Church in 1958.

A UNESCO fellowship to study educational publishing in Japan and India gave Baxter and Jacquie a chance to reconcile. He left for Japan in September 1958, and the family joined him later in India. Baxter was overwhelmed by India's poverty and the situation of its ethnic minorities. The Indian poor would haunt his imagination and his poetry.

Returning to New Zealand wasted by dysentery, he showed increasing disillusionment with New Zealand society. Drama became a vehicle for such criticism. *The Wide Open Cage*, which was staged in 1959 by Richard Campion, explored such themes as guilt and alienation in relationships.

from *Poems Unpleasant* (1952)

Never No More

Oh the summer's afloat on spindrift beaches
Brown as bread in a holiday heaven:
The same sweet lie the lupin teaches
As always dropping her gay pollen
On a girl's print frock leg shoulder bare
Never no more never no more.

The boys climb to their branch-high houses
Under a black bridge dive for pennies
The noon cloud like a bird's breast downy
Night come cool as a hawthorn berry
Kite tails tied on a telephone wire
Never no more never no more.

Cigarette stink from a hole in the rushes
Dark as a dunny the under-runner
The green flax plaited for whiplashes
Cockabully finned with the fire of summer
Jack loves Jill on the garage door
Never no more never no more.

The trodden path in the brambles led
Sweet and sure to a lifted frock
To the boathouse spree and the hayloft bed
A hamstrung heart and no way back:
Like a toi-toi arrow shot in the air
Never no more never no more.

1952

The Surfman's Story

On such a day as this
When breakers bay on the reef like a minutegun
Or up the tall beach grind and hiss
Like flattened snakes—we hauled out
Tackle and lifeline, at the run,
For two swept seaward, bathers, caught in the current's rout.

(There by the Maori Rock
A narrow rip runs out, rapid as death,
Each tide, regular as the clock:
Nothing to fear, once known—but a few
Fool bathers drowned there a bad name bequeath
Till it grows to a gorgon myth, a cud for gossips to chew.)

I stood by the reel
And Jake plunged in a smother of surf and sand.
He could swim, that boy, like a river-eel;
It was hard going even for his crawlstroke—
I cursed the mad bathers, you'll understand.
Over his head the flurry of waves battered and broke.

He told us after how
They beat him off; or rather the man did (she
Was near sinking). He warded the blow,
Trod water, waited; then by the hair
Hauled her, a dead weight, from the treacherous sea
Back through the hurly-burly of breakers to earth and air.

We worked for an hour to keep
The spark in her body alive; then gave her rum,
Wrapt her in blankets to lie and sleep
In the shed down there (the lupin and swordgrass
Half hide it). But when she had come
To her senses it was only to yammer and cry *Alas*.

Like a dove that has lost its mate,
Or an eagle maybe (she had more that look
In the full lip and nose knife-straight,
Great cavernous eye): she'd have run back
To the brawling sea if I hadn't took
Her by the arms and held her—the bruises stayed blue-black.

It seemed they had made a pact
To drown together, impatient of Love's slow
Guttering to death, and what life lacked
For two fettered in wedlock, wild
To wound each other—the undertow
Of passion drew them till it seemed the blind sea smiled.

Well—he was washed ashore
Some weeks after, eaten by fishes, foul
With tangleweed. She cried no more.
We were married within the year: that house
By the river's ours, with the climbing cowl
Of woodsmoke, the paddock behind, in a nest of orchard boughs.

1950–52

The Homecoming

Odysseus has come home, to the gully farm
Where the macrocarpa windbreak shields a house
Heavy with time's reliques—the brown-filmed photographs
Of ghosts more real than he; the mankind-measuring arm
Of a pendulum clock; and true yet to her vows,
His mother, grief's Penelope. At the blind the sea wind laughs.

The siege more long and terrible than Troy's
Begins again. A love demanding all,
Hypochondriacal, sea-dark and contentless:
This was the sour ground that nurtured a boy's
Dream of freedom; this, in Circe's hall
Drugged him; his homecoming finds this, more relentless.

She does not say, 'You have changed'; nor could she imagine any
Otherwise to the quiet maelstrom spinning
In the circle of their days. Still she would wish to carry
Him folded within her, shut from the wild and many
Voices of life's combat, in the cage of beginning;
She counts it natural that he should never marry.

She will cook his meals; complain of the south weather
That wrings her joints. And he—rebels; and yields
To the old covenant—calms the bleating
Ewe in birth travail. The smell of saddle leather
His sacrament; or the sale day drink; yet hears beyond sparse fields
On reef and cave the sea's hexameter beating.

1952

from *The Fallen House* (1953)

Wellington

Time is a frown on the stone brow
Of a monument, a gale shaking the quay.
There is never time to let the whole day sink
Into the heart, and hold it sheltered there.

Power breeds on power in labyrinthine hives
Nested under the daylong driving cloud;
Stale breath of suburb dawn hazing the harbour,
Tiring the eye, stripping the nerve to fever.

City of flower-plots, canyon streets and trams,
O sterile whore of a thousand bureaucrats!
There is a chasm of sadness behind
Your formal giggle, when the moon opens

Cold doors in space. Here on the dark hill
Above your broken lights—no crucifix
Entreats, but the gun emplacements overgrown
And the radio masts' huge harp of the wind's grief.

1949

Elegy for an Unknown Soldier

There was a time when I would magnify
His ending; scatter words as if I wept
Tears not my own but man's. There was a time.
But not now so. He died of a common sickness.

Nor did any new star shine
Upon that day when he came crying out
Of fleshy darkness to a world of pain
And waxen eyelids let the daylight enter.

So felt and tasted, found earth good enough.
Later he played with stones and wondered
If there was land beyond the dark sea rim
And where the road led out of the farthest paddock.

Awkward at school, he could not master sums.
Could you expect him then to understand
The miracle and menace of his body
That grew as mushrooms grow from dusk to dawn?

He had the weight though for a football scrum
And thought it fine to listen to the cheering
And drink beer with the boys, telling them tall
Stories of girls that he had never known.

So when the War came he was glad and sorry,
But soon enlisted. Then his mother cried
A little, and his father boasted how
He'd let him go, though needed for the farm.

Likely in Egypt he would find out something
About himself, if flies and drunkenness
And deadly heat could tell him much—until
In his first battle a shell splinter caught him.

So crown him with memorial bronze among
The older dead, child of a mountainous island.
Wings of a tarnished victory shadow him
Who born of silence has burned back to silence.

1948

To My Father

Today, looking at the flowering peach,
The island off the shore and waves that break
Quiet upon the rocks and level beach—
We must join forces, you and I, remake
The harbour silted and the city bombed
And all our hopes that lie now fire-entombed.

Your country childhood helped to make you strong,
Ploughing at twelve. I only know the man.
While I grew up more sheltered and too long
In love with my disease; though illness can
Impart by dint of pain a different kind
Of toughness to the predatory mind.

There is a feud between us. I have loved
You more than my own good, because you stand
For country pride and gentleness, engraved

In forehead lines, veins swollen on the hand;
Also, behind slow speech and quiet eye
The rock of passionate integrity.

You were a poet whom the time betrayed
To action. So, as Jewish Solomon
Prayed for wisdom, you had prayed
That you might have a poet for a son.
The prayer was answered; but an answer may
Confound by its exactness those who pray.

Finding no fault in you, I have been tempted
To stay your child. But that which broke
(Nature) the navel-cord, has not exempted
Even your light and sympathetic yoke.
It is in me your own true mettle shows;
Nor can we thus be friends till we are foes.

This you know well, but it will bear repeating—
Almost you are at times a second self;
Almost at times I feel your heart beating
In my own breast as if there were no gulf
To sever us. And you have seemed then rather
An out-of-time twin brother than a father.

So much is true; yet I have seen the time
When I would cut the past out, like a cancer,
Which now I must digest in awkward rhyme
Until I move 'in measure like a dancer'.
To know an age where all our loves have scope:
It is too much for any man to hope.

You, tickling trout once in a water-race;
You, playing cards, not caring if you lost;
You, shooting hares high on the mountain face;
You, showing me the ferns that grow from frost;
You, quoting Burns and Byron while I listened;
You, breaking quartz until the mica glistened.

These I remember, with the wind that blows
Forever pure down from the tussock ranges;
And these remain, like the everlasting snows,
Changeless in me while my life changes;
These, and a thousand things that prove
You rooted like a tree in the land's love.

I shall compare you to the bended bow,
Myself the arrow launched upon the hollow
Resounding air. And I must go

In time, my friend, to where you cannot follow.
It is not love would hope to keep me young,
The arrow rusted and the bow unstrung.

We have one aim: to set men free
From fear and custom and the incessant war
Of self with self and city against city—
So they may know the peace that they were born for
And find the earth sufficient, who instead
For fruit give scorpions and stones for bread.

And I sit now beside the wishing-well
And drop my silver down. I will have sons
And you grandchildren yet to tell
Old tales despite the anger of the guns:
Leisure to stroll and see Him unafraid
Who walked with Adam once in the green shade.

1947

Virginia Lake

The lake lies blind and glinting in the sun.
Among the reeds the red-billed native birds
Step high like dancers. I have found
A tongue to praise them, who was dumb,
And from the deaf morass one word
Breaks with the voices of the numberless drowned.

This was the garden and the talking water
Where once a child walked and wondered
At the leaves' treasure house, the brown ducks riding
Over the water face, the four winds calling
His name aloud, and a green world under
Where fish like stars in a fallen heaven glided.

And for his love the eyeless statues moved
Down the shell paths. The bandstand set
On fire with music blazing at its centre
Was havened in his love.
The lichened elm was rafters overhead;
Old waves unlocked their gates for him to enter.

Who now lies dumb, the black tongue dry
And the eyes weighed with coins.
O out of this rock tomb

Of labyrinthine grief I start and cry
Toward his real day—the undestroyed
Fantastic Eden of a waking dream.

1947–48

Poem by the Clock Tower, Sumner

Beside the dark sand and the winged foam
Under the shadow of the naked tower
Play the wild children, stranger than Atlanteans.
For them the blazed rock hieroglyph burns clear:
Bear dance and bull dance in the drenched arena
To the sun's trumpet and the waves' cryring.

They are the terrible mirrors where our time
Stares back with gorgon eyes. An Ice Age lies
Between us; for they know
The place and hour of the young phoenix' nest
On the bare dune where we can see only
Worn glacial stones and terminal moraine.

And for them rises yet
From earth's still centre the heaven-bearing
Immortal Tree. The ponds and hollow groves
Peopled with fish and speaking birds receive them,
Teach them the language in which stones converse,
Show them the arrows of the toi-toi plume.

We in the murdering city hug our death
Closer than jewels; to the mud-stained sky
Daylong expectant turn one questioning face.
Or in the long night frozen the caress
Of flesh on flesh and stone on stone are one
Suspending rainbow in the lost abyss.

Where is the white stone that shall transmute
Our average day to gold?
The green lane that leads to the wishing well
The secret house the fertile wilderness
Where grief and memory are reconciled.
Angels of fire and ice guard well that garden.

And yet the tower stands, four-square and casting
A sundial shadow on the dancing sand.
The blown cloud blares with trumpets. And the wind

Beyond the Cave Rock scatters birds and spume,
Strikes out an echo from the ringing stone,
Strikes where the boat is tugging at its chain.

These images disturb our human night
With joy, and promise of prodigious noon:
Childhood and age in one green cradle joined.
Again from this blind rock of time I know
In heart of lethargy a drowned sun rising;
Again the dark Dove nestles in my breast.

1948

Rocket Show

As warm north rain breaks over suburb houses,
Streaming on window glass, its drifting hazes
Covering harbour ranges with a dense hood:
I recall how eighteen months ago I stood
Ankle-deep in sand on an Otago beach
Watching the fireworks flare over strident surf and bach,
In brain grey ash, in heart the sea-change flowing
Of one love dying and another growing.

For love grows like the crocus bulb in winter
Hiding from snow and from itself the tender
Green frond in embryo; but dies as rockets die
(White sparks of pain against a steel-dark sky)
With firebird wings trailing an arc of grief
Across a night inhuman as the grave,
Falling at length a dull and smouldering shell
To frozen dunes and the wash of the quenching swell.

There was little room left where the crowd had trampled
Grass and lupin bare, under the pines that trembled
In gusts from the sea. On a sandhillock I chose
A place to watch from. Then the rockets rose,
O marvellous, like self-destroying flowers
On slender stems, with seed-pods full of flares,
Raining down amber, scarlet, pennies from heaven
On the skyward straining heads and still sea-haven.
Had they brought death, we would have stood the same,
I think, in ecstasy at the world-end flame.

It is the rain streaming reminds me of
Those ardent showers, cathartic love and grief.
As I walked home through the cold streets by moonlight,
My steps ringing in the October night,
I thought of our strange lives, the grinding cycle
Of death and renewal come to full circle,
And of man's heart, that blind Rosetta stone,
Mad as the polar moon, decipherable by none.

1949

Wild Bees

Often in summer, on a tarred bridge plank standing,
Or downstream between willows, a safe Ophelia drifting
In a rented boat—I had seen them come and go,
Those wild bees swift as tigers, their gauze wings a-glitter
In passionless industry, clustering black at the crevice
Of a rotten cabbage tree, where their hive was hidden low.

But never strolled too near. Till one half-cloudy evening
Of ripe January, my friends and I
Came, gloved and masked to the eyes like plundering desperadoes,
To smoke them out. Quiet beside the stagnant river
We trod wet grasses down, hearing the crickets chitter
And waiting for light to drain from the wounded sky.

Before we reached the hive their sentries saw us
And sprang invisible through the darkening air,
Stabbed, and died in stinging. The hive woke. Poisonous fuming
Of sulphur filled the hollow trunk, and crawling
Blue flame sputtered—yet still their suicidal
Live raiders dived and clung to our hands and hair.

O it was Carthage under the Roman torches
Or loud with flames and falling timber, Troy!
A job well botched. Half of the honey melted
And half the rest young grubs. Through earth-black smouldering ashes
And maimed bees groaning, we drew out our plunder.
Little enough their gold, and slight our joy.

Fallen then the city of instinctive wisdom.
Tragedy is written distinct and small:
A hive burned on a cool night in summer.

But loss is a precious stone to me, a nectar
Distilled in time, preaching the truth of winter
To the fallen heart that does not cease to fall.

1941–49

Song for an Old Soak

For why should I remember
The unimagined good
The promise of September
The bird song in the wood,
When these have passed me by
Like morning from the sky.

Before the winter ditches
Grew cold as charity,
The little strolling bitches
Would turn and smile at me
For the eyes of devil-may-care
And the curling coal-black hair.

The face in the mirror changes
Changes and grows old:
It's farewell to the ranges
And the upland rivers cold
Where I was herding sheep
In a world as wide as sleep.

As many brave ships founder
Upon the Goodwin Sands
(Or a belly that grows rounder)
And perish with all hands,
So in the same pit lie
Love, grief, and memory.

Jesus and Mary, make
The springtime come again
Somewhere sometime, or take
The burden of my pain.
I seek the green inn
Where life and death begin.

20 June 1946–48

The Morgue

Each morning when I lit the coke furnace
Unwillingly I passed the locked door,
The room where Death lived. Shadowless infection
Looked from the blind panes, and an open secret
Stained even the red flowers in the rock garden
Flesh-fingered under the sanatorium wall.

And each day the patients coming and going
From light jobs, joking below the sombre pines,
Would pass without looking, their faces leaner
As if the wintry neighbourhood of Death
Would strip the shuddering flesh from bone. They shouted,
Threw clods at one another, and passed on.

But when at length, with stiff broom and bucket,
I opened the door wide—well, there was nothing
To fear. Only the bare close concrete wall,
A slab of stone, and a wheeled canvas stretcher.
For Death had shifted house to his true home
And mansion, ruinous, of the human heart.

1949

Poem in the Matukituki Valley

Some few yards from the hut the standing beeches
Let fall their dead limbs, overgrown
With feathered moss and filigree of bracken.
The rotted wood splits clean and hard
Close-grained to the driven axe, with sound of water
Sibilant falling and high nested birds.

In winter blind with snow; but in full summer
The forest blanket sheds its cloudy pollen
And cloaks a range in undevouring fire.
Remote the land's heart. Though the wild scrub cattle
Acclimatized, may learn
Shreds of her purpose, or the taloned kea.

For those who come as I do, half-aware,
Wading the swollen
Matukituki waist-high in snow water,

And stumbling where the mountains throw their dice
Of boulders huge as houses, or the smoking
Cataract flings its arrows on our path—

For us the land is matrix and destroyer,
Resentful, darkly known
By sunset omens, low words heard in branches;
Or where the red deer lift their innocent heads
Snuffing the wind for danger,
And from our footfall's menace bound in terror.

Three emblems of the heart I carry folded
For charms against flood water, sliding shale:
Pale gentian, lily, and bush orchid.
The peaks too have names to suit their whiteness,
Stargazer and Moonraker,
A sailor's language and a mountaineer's.

And those who sleep in close bags fitfully
Besieged by wind in a snowline bivouac—
The carrion parrot with red underwing
Clangs on the roof by night, and daybreak brings
Raincloud on purple ranges, light reflected
Stainless from crumbling glacier, dazzling snow,

Do they not, clay in that unearthly furnace,
Endure the hermit's peace
And mindless ecstasy? Blue-lipped crevasse
And smooth rock chimney straddling—a communion
With what eludes our net—Leviathan
Stirring to ocean birth our inland waters?

Sky's purity; the altar cloth of snow
On deathly summits laid; or avalanche
That shakes the rough moraine with giant laughter;
Snowplume and whirlwind—what are these
But His flawed mirror who gave the mountain strength
And dwells in holy calm, undying freshness?

Therefore we turn, hiding our souls' dullness
From that too blinding glass: turn to the gentle
Dark of the human daydream, child and wife,
Patience of stone and soil, the lawful city
Where man may live, and no wild trespass
Of what's eternal shake his grave of time.

1949

The Fallen House

I took the clay track leading
From Black Bridge to Duffy's farm,
In no forefarer's footmark treading,
Thus free, it would seem, from any harm
That could befall me—the kind of ill-luck charm
That clings to a once-fair steading—

When South the sky thickened
And rain came pelter on the hill-scurf:
So in a grove (where the wind quickened
Their young leaves like the mile-off surf)
Of gums I sheltered, whose roots had drained the turf
Of life till a starved soil sickened.

But an older grief spoke plainly
From the green mound where thistle strewed
Her bearded gossamer. Ungainly
The sprawled stones fire-blackened could
Recall man; though where the house stood
Stands ragged thistle only.

It was not Woe that flaunted
Funereal plume and banner there,
Nor an Atridean doom that daunted
The heart with a lidless gorgon stare;
But darker the cradling bluegums, sombre the air,
By the wraith of dead joy haunted.

There once the murk was cloven
By hearthlight fondly flaring within:
Adamant seemed their hope and haven.
O Time, Time takes in a gin
The quick of being! Pale now and gossamer-thin
The web their lives had woven.

1950

Lament for Barney Flanagan (1954)

Lament for Barney Flanagan

Licensee of the Hesperus Hotel

Flanagan got up on a Saturday morning,
Pulled on his pants while the coffee was warming;
He didn't remember the doctor's warning,
  'Your heart's too big, Mr Flanagan.'

Barney Flanagan, sprung like a frog
From a wet root in an Irish bog—
May his soul escape from the tooth of the dog!
  God have mercy on Flanagan.

Barney Flanagan R.I.P.
Rode to his grave on Hennessey's
Like a bottle-cork boat in the Irish Sea.
  The bell-boy rings for Flanagan.

Barney Flanagan, ripe for a coffin,
Eighteen stone and brandy-rotten,
Patted the housemaid's velvet bottom—
  'Oh, is it you, Mr Flanagan?'

The sky was bright as a new milk token.
Bill the Bookie and Shellshock Hogan
Waited outside for the pub to open—
  'Good day, Mr Flanagan.'

At noon he was drinking in the lounge bar corner
With a sergeant of police and a racehorse owner
When the Angel of Death looked over his shoulder—
  'Could you spare a moment, Flanagan?'

Oh the deck was cut; the bets were laid;
But the very last card that Barney played
Was the Deadman's Trump, the bullet of Spades—
  'Would you like more air, Mr Flanagan?'

The priest came running but the priest came late
For Barney was banging at the Pearly Gate.
St Peter said, 'Quiet! You'll have to wait
  For a hundred masses, Flanagan.'

The regular boys and the loud accountants
Left their nips and their seven-ounces
As chickens fly when the buzzard pounces—
        'Have you heard about old Flanagan?'

Cold in the parlour Flanagan lay
Like a bride at the end of her marriage day.
The Waterside Workers' Band will play
        A brass goodbye to Flanagan.

While publicans drink their profits still,
While lawyers flock to be in at the kill,
While Aussie barmen milk the till
        We will remember Flanagan.

For Barney had a send-off and no mistake.
He died like a man for his country's sake;
And the Governor-General came to his wake.
        Drink again to Flanagan!

Despise not, O Lord, the work of Thine own hands
And let light perpetual shine upon him.

1953

from *The Iron Bread Board: Studies in New Zealand Writing* (1957)

The Last Hero

(R.A.K.M. [R.A.K. Mason])

Hemmed in with swords daggers scimitars
        under the last thornbush he hauled out
        the breadboard marked smeared with his blood's gout
        and to the invincible night where were no stars
        offered what remained after so many wars
        of him still living, a green onion sprout
        and half a loaf near mouldy . . . Still the knout
        waited his coming and none wept his scars

Where he lay smitten, save one gathered up
the breadboard relic of the hero's doom
and took it off with her for bite and sup
after the sad event, in her little room
drank weak tea and wept into her cup
lamented long his strength cut down in bloom.

1956

Any Poet to a Breadboard

(A.R.D.F. [A.R.D. Fairburn])

Let others write of heaven and hell;
there's just one theme that I know well
and now after my fifteenth beer
I'll tell it to your wooden ear.
A poet in his Indian summer
prefers a woman slightly dumber
than you, easy to get as bread,
who'll never never read in bed;
for brains and beauty ill assort,
I only want one who's a sport.
My ancient verses I will trot
out as if minted on the spot,
changing meanwhile from 'dark' to 'fair'
the lines that praise her 'naiad's hair'
and ending what's begun by flattery
with unreproved assault and battery.
Love is a word that poets rhyme with
and idle children pass the time with;
a woman's wit can never fail,
her intellect is in her tail.
Let her be calm, and kind and gay,
accessible by night and day,
in my poor wandering Arab tent
a breadboard and an ornament.
If she be termagent, instead
I'll hug a breadboard in my bed.

1956

Sings Clarry

(D.G. [Denis Glover])

Hagley Park on a Sunday
Or Auckland's One Tree Hill,
I have worn my boots out walking
And I still will,
sings Clarry.

You think you're pretty smart,
But a cat has nine lives.
The barman's fart
Smelt of onion and chives,
sings Clarry at the beer pump.

They wouldn't give it to me
Though she left it in her will,
But my mother's kauri breadboard
Belongs to me still,
sings Clarry.

That's One-Legged Clarry,
He'll go to hell and back.
Take a look at the breadboard
Tied on to his pack.

'I feel sorry for him,'
Flossie the barman said.
'What use is a breadboard
If you haven't any bread?'

I knew when I was coming round the bend
That I would find a breadboard in the end,
sings Clarry.

1956

Woman with Breadboard

(from the picture by Juniper Magwort)

(A.C. [Allen Curnow])

She stands at the breadboard. What does she want?
What must I do? We have heard
The sound of surf pounding on the absurd
Reef of an island age: the noise will haunt

Till all time in the end-all fog is ended.
Our own face looks back
From every mirror, like a closed book
Receding, interceding. Who looks? The candid

Eyes at the breadboard tell us what we know,
Our human weakness. The breadboard smiles;
Dust closing Helen's eye, the four mud walls
Of a room enclosing sorrow.

What shall I say? I feel more ill
Than a breadboard or a word could ever tell.

1956

The Breadboard

(J.K.B.)

This is the breadboard that my father found
In a corner of the woodshed once, where lean
Spiders had wrapped their cerements around
It, and for long it had lain there unseen
Recalling days of fruitfulness now gone
When mother, man and child, about it fed
And in their porridge dipped their homely bread.

No one can tell what grief lies locked within
Another's breast. We only know our own.
It is the memory of ancestral sin
Which turns the moon to blood, the heart to stone.

The breadboard preaches loss which love alone
Can soothe—my love, when warm in bed she lies
And offers to the night her breadboard thighs.

Drink up, my friend—the nights are growing longer,
And even porridge scarcely has the power
To fill the void within, the spirit's hunger.
Perhaps I should have written somewhat more
About the breadboard, but my heart is sore
For other reasons; and I save my breath
To blow my porridge cool, though in the gates of death.

1956

Poem to a Small Flower

(A.C. [Alistair Campbell])

When you, my sweet, are near me,
Your small hands like daffodils on green
Stalks, your forehead wet with dew,

I think incessantly of the breadboard
In your mother's kitchen, smooth grained
Wood simple on stillness.

In the grace of your appearing
And your gentle tears full of rainbows
Astonishing the grave and intrepid swans,

I am reminded continually of the breadboard
And of Rodin's *The Kiss* where simple bodies
Intertwined are more than twined bodies.

Each moment of your presence, when you stand
Before me with small eyes downcast
Full of tears, I find my thought of you

Inseparable from my thought of the breadboard
So simply, gently giving, like you who rest
Like a small flower on the surface of my mind.

1956

from *The Night Shift: Poems on Aspects of Love* (1958)

from *Songs of the Desert*

9

Though usage and oblivion do us part
And your womb be barren, from no fault
Of nature but our own devising art
Like labourers that sow the field with salt,
Yet I go heavy from our naked bed
With that quick child fathered by grief and you
Which shall endure, as amber, being dead
Outlasts the living forest where it grew.
Having no heart, these words cannot decay
As your young body shall and tender eyes,
Nor like true children go their careless way
Forgetting us for an obscure sunrise—
But men shall murmur, 'These are his and hers,'
When we both lie in our foul sepulchres.

1947

from *Chosen Poems* (1958)

My Love Late Walking

My love late walking in the rain's white aisles
I break words for, though many tongues
Of night deride and the moon's boneyard smile

Cuts to the quick our newborn sprig of song.
See and believe, my love, the late yield
Of bright grain, the sparks of harvest wrung

From difficult joy. My heart is an open field.
There you may stray wide or stand at home
Nor dread the giant's bone and broken shield

Or any tendril locked on a thunder stone,
Nor fear, in the forked grain, my hawk who flies
Down to your feathered sleep alone

Striding blood coloured on a wind of sighs.
Let him at the heart of your true dream move,
My love, in the lairs of hope behind your eyes.

I sing, to the rain's harp, of light renewed,
The black tares broken, fresh the phoenix light
I lost among time's rags and burning tombs.

My love walks long in harvest aisles tonight.

1953–56

Song of the Years

When from my mother's womb I came
Disputandum was my name.

Weeping hoping threatening
Beyond myself I had no king.

I drew in with each hour's breath
The grey dust of the second death.

When my childhood days were spent
To Venus I grew suppliant.

Little tremors woke and died
Within the mountain of my pride.

Singing on the gallows cart
Created beauty held my heart.

The aardvark and the onager
Were stabled at my sepulchre.

In that deep den the King of bliss
Broke my heart and gave me His.

'This for your doom and penance take,
Be merry always for My sake.'

He gave me a white stone to bear
With my true name written there.

Without end I will say,
Laus tibi, Domine!

1958

from *In Fires of No Return: Selected Poems* (1958)

Elegy at the Year's End

At the year's end I come to my father's house
Where passion fruit hang gold above an open doorway
And garden trees bend to the visiting bird:
        Here first the single vision
Entered my heart, as to a dusty room
Enters the pure tyrannical wind of heaven.

The coal burns out; the quiet ash remains
That tired minds and coarsened bodies know.
        Small town of corrugated iron roofs
Between the low volcanic saddle
And offshore reef where blue cod browse,
From husks of exile, humbled, I come to your fond prison.

At an elder uncle's deathbed I read the graph
Of suffering in the face of country cousins.
        These have endured what men hold in common,
The cross of custom, the marriage bed of knives;
Their angular faces reflecting his
Whose body lies stiff under the coverlet.

One may walk again to the fisherman's rock, hearing
The long waves tumble, from America riding
Where mottled kelpbeds heave to a pale sun,
        But not again see green Aphrodite
Rise to transfigure the noon. Rather the Sophoclean
Chorus: *All shall be taken.*

Or by the brown lagoon stand idle
Where to their haunted coves the safe flocks go,
And envy the paradise drake his brilliant sexual plumage.
        For single vision dies. Spirit and flesh are sundered
In the kingdom of no love. Our stunted passions bend
To serve again familiar social devils.

Brief is the visiting angel. In corridors of hunger
Our lives entwined suffer the common ill:
Living and dying, breathing and begetting.
Meanwhile on maimed gravestones under the towering fennel
Moves the bright lizard, sunloved, basking in
        The moment of animal joy.

1953

Eleven O'Clock Blues

King Solomon he loved a lass
        crowed the black booze rooster
rattle them bones and fill your glass
Solomon he lies dead and deep
ten gin bottles at his feet
at his head a broken vase
        and the world's love weeping.

Jack Larry Kate and Lou
        crowed the black booze rooster
before my father ever crew
thc course was laid the bed was made
and there within the inmost glade
the bog-eyed serpent wet with dew
        and the world's love sleeping.

Adam had a good estate
        crowed the black booze rooster
but the bum bailiff's at the gate
Adam rode off in the furniture van
with a million brats and a bun hat on
with a pound of apples and a whisky crate
        and the world's love weeping.

Climb climb the crooked stair
        crowed the black booze rooster
you will find green Asia there

pint pots blooming on every tree
and the Himalayas at her knee
granny Time in her rocking chair
        and the world's love sleeping.

Fire and ice fire and ice
        crowed the black booze rooster
rattle them bones roll them dice
a time and a time and half a time
till the doorknob twists at the midnight chime
lets in the walking corpse of Christ
        and the world's love weeping.

1953

The Bad Young Man

'Oh summer is a beggar's feast,'
        Cried the rumbustious bad young man,
'And Nobodaddy cares in the least
If we two make the two-backed beast—
So lie you down, lie you down!'
'I think my maiden aunt would frown,'
        She said under the yellow lupin.

'Gulls are tumbling on the wing,'
        Cried the rumbustious bad young man,
'And the little fishes have their fling:
So why should a scruple keep us waiting?
And O my dear, I love you so.'
'You'll tell a different tale tomorrow,'
        She said under the yellow lupin.

'O cover me with your tent of hair,'
        Groaned the rumbustious bad young man.
'Milk and honey, your breasts are bare,
My sucking dove, my silken mare—
Wherever you learnt it you have the knack.'
'Gentlier, or you'll break my back,'
        She moaned under the yellow lupin.

'Ah Love's joy was not made to last,'
        Sighed the rumbustious sad young man.
'The world's mill is grinding fast
And the sky, the sky is overcast—

But still, I thank you for your kindness.'
'I fear the sand has soiled my dress,'
        She said under the yellow lupin.

1951

In Fires of No Return

While bluegum fables burn
To summer's ash
In fires of no return
Above the farms and crying folds
That house the doom of flesh,
To Barney's pulpit rock I climb
Where the sea aisles burn cold
In fires of no return
And maned breakers praise
The death hour of the sun.
To wave and bird I open wide
The bible of my rimrock days,
To salt-grey ngaio boughs that cross
The forehead of the west,
To Venus' holy star who smiles
Upon the lives she cannot save,
Man, beast, bird, lover
In orchards of a spring desire,
Hermit old on his wintry pyre,
All flesh wound in the bright snare,
In fires of no return
Wrung by the power of the prince of the air.

My country fathers laid
Under angel and cold urn
In fields of silence burn,
From folds of ngaio and strong fern
Turn their immortal eyes on mine,
Tell me this day the world was made.
I hear in frond and shell
The voice of the drowned sailor
Tossed on the black bar, with a winy breath
Shout from the feast of Cana.
How love has raked the embers of his death.
And hermit from a holy cell

I watch my brother
King shag dive
Down from his windy
Rock to the humble tide
Where the sea poor, old crab and limpet,
Sigh to the resurrection thunder.
Among night dunes the moony lovers
In lupin shade far and near
Twined under Venus' carnal star
Mock the power of the prince of the air.
Their doomed flesh answers an undying summer.

1956

Crossing Cook Strait

The night was clear, sea calm; I came on deck
To stretch my legs, find perhaps
Gossip, a girl in green slacks at the rail
Or just the logline feathering a dumb wake.

The ship swung in the elbow of the Strait.
'Dolphins!' I cried—'let the true sad Venus
Rise riding her shoals, teach me as once to wonder
And wander at ease, be glad and never regret.'

But night increased under the signal stars.
In the dark bows, facing the flat sea,
Stood one I had not expected, yet knew without surprise
As the Janus made formidable by loveless years.

His coat military; his gesture mild—
'Well met,' he said, 'on the terrestrial journey
From chaos into light—what light it is
Contains our peril and purpose, history has not revealed.'

'Sir—', I began. He spoke with words of steel—
'I am Seddon and Savage, the socialist father.
You have known me only in my mask of Dionysus
Amputated in bar rooms, dismembered among wheels.

'I woke in my civil tomb hearing a shout
For bread and justice. It was not here.
That sound came thinly over the waves from China;
Stones piled on my grave had all but shut it out.

'I walked forth gladly to find the angry poor
Who are my nation; discovered instead
The glutton seagulls squabbling over crusts
And policies made and broken behind locked doors.

'I have watched the poets also at their trade.
I have seen them burning with a wormwood brilliance.
Love was the one thing lacking on their page,
The crushed herb of grief at another's pain.

'Your civil calm breeds inward poverty
That chafes for change. The ghost of Adam
Gibbering demoniac in drawing-rooms
Will drink down hemlock with his sugared tea.

'You feed your paupers concrete. They work well,
Ask for no second meal, vote, pay tribute
Of silence on Anzac Day in the pub urinal;
Expose death only by a mushroom smell.

'My counsel was naïve. Anger is bread
To the poor, their guns more accurate than justice,
Because their love has not decayed to a wintry fungus
And hope to the wish for power among the dead.

'In Kaitangata the miner's falling sweat
Wakes in the coal seam fossil flowers.
The clerk puts down his pen and takes his coat;
He will not be back today or the next day either.'

With an ambiguous salute he left me.
The ship moved into a stronger sea,
Bludgeoned alive by the rough mystery
Of love in the running straits of history.

1947–56

At Hokianga

Green floating mangrove pods reveal,
Plucked from the lagging tide, their small
Man-in-a-boat, kernel and clitoris:
Set free to sail, they climb a hundred beaches,
Germinate in night-black mud. Tell,
Historian, how the broken tribes were healed

In a land of exhausted wells, north
From that great ragged capital
Flung like a coat to rot on garden earth.

In houses thatched with nikau palm,
Fearing the dead, riding bareback
On hill stallions, those who learned before us
The secret of survival, to be patient,
Suffer, and shut no doors,
Change all things to their habit, bridge
The bogs with branch laid to branch:
Nourished at compliant breasts, wish only
To drink with friends, own a launch.

To scrape the bones of the dead, how needful,
Lest they should walk, undo forgetfulness
With blight on crops, sickness at home.
In packed ground the missionary fathers
Drowned at river crossings, rest in one bed,
While a boy cuts from flax a spirit boat
Perfect, lightly as a bird's wing
Riding the void of waters
Untaught, a full hour floating.

1957

At Akitio

Consider this barbarian coast,
Traveller, you who have lost
Lover or friend. It has never made
Anything out of anything.
Drink at these bitter springs.

Fishing at river mouth, a woman
Uses the sea-drilled stone her mother used
For sinker, as big kahawai come,
As tides press upward to time's source.
This coast is shelter to the shearing gangs
Who burn dead matai in their kitchen.

Squirearch, straight-backed rider, built
An ethos of the leisured life,
Lawn, antlered hall and billiard room,

Glass candelabra brought from Paris,
The homestead foundered among fields.
Unhorsed they sleep.

A girl with a necklace of mako teeth
They dug from a sandcliff facing south,
Axe and broken needle.
Stay good under slab and cross
Thin bones of children burnt by cholera,
Made tidy by the last strict nurse.
As tributary of a greater stream
Your single grief enlarges now
The voice of night in kumara gardens,
Prayer of the bush pigeon.

One drowned at the cattle crossing,
One tossed and kicked by a bucking horse—
Who died without confession, wanting
No wafer in their teeth—
Does the toi-toi plume their altar?
Are they held safe in the sea's grail?
This gullied mounded earth, tonned
With silence, and the sun's gaze
On a choir of breakers, has outgrown
The pain of love. Drink,
Traveller, at these pure springs.

Remember, though, the early strength
Of bull-voiced water when the boom broke
And eels clung to the banks, logs
Plunged and pierced the river hymen.
Remember iron-coloured skulls
Of cattle thrown to the crab's crypt,
Driftwood piled by river flood
On the long beach, battered limb
And loin where the red-backed spider breeds,
By a halcyon sea the shapes of man,
Emblems of our short fever.

Pluck then from ledges of the sea
Crayfish for the sack. Not now but later
Think what you were born for. Drink,
Child, at the springs of sleep.

1957

The 1960s

The success of *The Wide Open Cage* in the late 1950s inspired Baxter to write two further plays: *Three Women and the Sea* (1961) and *The Spots of the Leopard* (1962). His first major poetry publication of the 1960s was a broadsheet that would come to be one of his most enduring social critiques, *Ballad of Calvary Street*. It was followed in 1961 by *Howrah Bridge and Other Poems*, a collection that symbolises the tremendous changes—personal and poetic—he went through in the late 1950s; changes brought into focus by the months he spent in Asia in 1958–59. The poems in India mark this change. Stylistically, the Indian poems reflect the strong influence of Lawrence Durrell.

Becoming a postman in 1963, Baxter produced a number of polemical poems; many protesting against the Vietnam War. Themes inherited from his pacifist parents and explored in his unpublished adolescent verse were reworked to satiric effect in such poems as 'A Bucket of Blood for a Dollar' and 'The Gunner's Lament'. *Poetry Magazine* published *A Selection of Poetry* in 1964, but Baxter's next major collection was the widely praised *Pig Island Letters* (1966).

Pig Island Letters' title sequence, dedicated to his friend the author Maurice Shadbolt, identifies with Shadbolt's despondency at an apparent loss of creativity before taking gloomy inventory of his own failed undertakings. Typically, lost youth is mourned and death looms large in the future, yet the poems also achieve a new, less censorious, realism—of which 'Pig Island', Baxter's colloquial, amiably caustic name for New Zealand, is emblematic. The collection fully anticipates the Jerusalem poetry as Baxter further develops his notion of the 'gap'—that paradoxical site of absence within which one discovers one's true self—and prefigures a full adoption of the role of social prophet by diagnosing society's maladies through a rehearsal of the dramas of his own life. Critic C.K. Stead, who savagely criticised *The Fire and the Anvil*, was won over by this volume, describing its 'total effect [as] richer than anything Baxter had achieved before'.

In 1966–67 Baxter was Burns Fellow in creative writing at the University of Otago. It was a triumphant homecoming for the man who had left twenty years earlier under a cloud of failure. Baxter took an active part in university life, protesting against Vietnam and satirising the university prohibition against student cohabitation in his pamphlet *A Small Ode on Mixed Flatting*. Through all this his creative output was staggering: he wrote numerous poems and published a selection, *The Lion Skin: Poems* (1967), through the university's Bibliography Room.

Revisiting the site of his painful but formative adolescence also impelled Baxter to revisit in his poetry the themes and locales of the verse of that period. Family memories and Otago landscapes again feature but always with the presence of death, at times subtly, at other times looming, within the poetic frame. A marked change in style accompanied these variations on earlier themes. Whereas the youthful poetry might, with ponderous metre and latinate diction, move towards a final grand, sonorous phrase, now unrhymed run-on couplets (increasingly the unit of choice in Baxter's later work) create a tone both direct and personal. Baxter's later poetry becomes stripped of artifice and abstraction until all that remains is a personal voice described by Vincent O'Sullivan as 'almost ostentatiously matter of fact'.

In 1967 Baxter also published two volumes of criticism—*Aspects of Poetry in New Zealand* and *The Man on the Horse*—and saw a number of his plays and mimes staged by Dunedin director Patric Carey, among them *The Band Rotunda*, *The Sore-Footed Man*, *The Bureaucrat*, and *The Devil and Mr Mulcahy*. Just as Baxter's verse supplied several of the characters for these dramas, so his experiences as an alcoholic and working with alcoholics supplied a usefully emblematic 'tribal' context within which human frailties were examined through a mythical, or archetypal, lens. The majority of Baxter's drama is in Howard McNaughton's edition of his *Collected Plays* (1982).

In 1968 Dunedin's Catholic Education Office employed Baxter to prepare catechetical material and teach at Catholic schools, and his articles for the Catholic periodical *The Tablet* were collected and published in *The Flowering Cross* (1969). Yet the Burns Fellowship appeared to have drained him of energy and refilled him with doubt. He struggled in his marriage, fearing the trap of domesticity; found difficulty relating to his children; and was dogged by the feeling that words had become impotent and should be replaced by actions.

Around April 1968 'a minor revelation' led him to think of Jerusalem (in Maori 'Hiruharama')—'the mission station on the Wanganui river'. He thought he might go to this small Maori settlement, bordered by a Catholic church and a convent, and 'form the nucleus of a community where the people, both Maori and pakeha, would try to live without money or books, worship God and work on the land'. Following the family's return to Wellington in December, Baxter left home to put his beliefs into practice.

Auckland was his initial stop. There he failed to hold down a job found for him by the poet Hone Tuwhare at the Chelsea sugar refinery. He discovered his Auckland niche in a cluster of run-down squats in the suburb of Grafton. Number 7 Boyle Crescent, where he settled in Easter 1969, became a drop-in centre for drug addicts. Baxter, adopting the Maori transliteration of his first name, 'Hemi', set about counselling and attempting to establish a Narcotics Anonymous organisation similar to AA. His appearance—barefoot, bearded, and shabbily dressed—attracted the attention of both media and police, who suspected his motives and morality. He put the drug users' side of the story in 'Ballad of the Junkies and the Fuzz', and published a selection of twenty years' verse in *The Rock Woman* (1969).

The Rock Woman's fifty-three poems were largely chosen by Baxter's London publisher, Oxford University Press. Baxter approved the choices, which were intended to provide an overview of his achievements during the preceding two decades, but critics have commented on a certain unevenness in the book. The title poem refers to a rock, found on the coast, that resembles a woman. The drops of sea water that cover her are reminiscent of the rosary beads found on a medieval statue. For Baxter, the Rock Woman also symbolised New Zealand's bare, stony landscapes, which were for him as familiar as a lover—alone with her, he experienced peace.

But poetry was not Baxter's main focus at this time. By August 1969 the Boyle Crescent period had ended and he was heading for Jerusalem, to begin his commune.

Ballad of Calvary Street (1960)

Ballad of Calvary Street

On Calvary Street are trellises
Where bright as blood the roses bloom,
And gnomes like pagan fetishes
Hang their hats on an empty tomb
Where two old souls go slowly mad,
National Mum and Labour Dad.

Each Saturday when full of smiles
The children come to pay their due,
Mum takes down the family files
And cover to cover she thumbs them through,
Poor Len before he went away
And Mabel on her wedding day.

The meal-brown scones display her knack,
Her polished oven spits with rage,
While in Grunt Grotto at the back
Dad sits and reads the Sporting Page,
Then ambles out in boots of lead
To weed around the parsnip bed.

A giant parsnip sparks his eye,
Majestic as the Tree of Life;
He washes it and rubs it dry
And takes it in to his old wife—
'Look Laura, would that be a fit?
The bastard has a flange on it!'

When both were young she would have laughed,
A goddess in her tartan skirt,
But wisdom, age and mothercraft
Have rubbed it home that men like dirt:
Five children and a fallen womb,
A golden crown beyond the tomb.

Nearer the bone, sin is sin,
And women bear the cross of woe,
And that affair with Mrs Flynn
(It happened thirty years ago)
Though never mentioned, means that he
Will get no sugar in his tea.

The afternoon goes by, goes by,
The angels harp above a cloud;
A son-in-law with spotted tie
And daughter Alice fat and loud
Discuss the virtues of insurance
And stuff their tripes with trained endurance.

Flood-waters hurl upon the dyke
And Dad himself can go to town,
For little Charlie on his trike
Has ploughed another iris down.
His parents rise to chain the beast,
Brush off the last crumbs of their lovefeast.

And so these two old fools are left,
A rosy pair in evening light,
To question Heaven's dubious gift,
To hag and grumble, growl and fight:
The love they kill won't let them rest,
Two birds that peck in one fouled nest.

Why hammer nails? Why give no change?
Habit, habit clogs them dumb.
The Sacred Heart above the range
Will bleed and burn till Kingdom Come,
But Yin and Yang won't ever meet
In Calvary Street, in Calvary Street.

1960

from *Howrah Bridge and Other Poems* (1961)

Perseus

Leaving them, children of the Sun, to their perpetual
Unwearying dance about the ancient Tree,
Perseus flew east, the bird-winged sandals beating
Smooth and monotonous; sauntered above
Fens peopled by the placid watersnake,
Flamingo, crocodile—

And those unfallen creatures, joyful in
Their maze of waters, watched; with reedy voices
Praised the oncoming hero; cried
And coupled in his path. But he felt only
Scorching his shoulders, the shield, Athene's lovegift—and the first
Wind of foreboding blow from Medusa's home.

So entered the stone kingdom where no life
Startled, but brackish water fell
Like tears from solitary beds
Of sphagnum moss, or spray from cataracts
Sprinkled the grey-belled orchid, feathered grass
And spider's coverlet.

Till by the final cleft precipitous
At a blind gorge's end he lighted, stood,
Unslung the heavy shield, drew breath, and waited
As the bright hornet waits and quivers
Hearing within her den the poisonous rustle
And mew, for battle angry, of tarantula.

Fair smote her face upon the burning shield,
Medusa, image of the soul's despair,
Snake-garlanded, child of derisive Chaos
And hateful Night, whom no man may
Look on and live. In horror, pity, loathing,
Perseus looked long, lifted his sword, and struck.

Then empty was the cave. A vulture's taloned body
Headless and huddled, a woman's marble face
With snakes for hair—and in the wide
Thoroughfares of the sky no hint of cloudy fury
Or clanging dread, as homeward he
Trod, the pouched Despair at his girdle hanging,

To earth, Andromeda, the palace garden
His parents bickered in, plainsong of harvest—
To the lawgiver's boredom, rendering
(The task accomplished) back to benignant Hermes
And holy Athene goods not his own, the borrowed
Sandals of courage and the shield of art.

1952

The Giant's Grave

Some heavens ago, when the wind blew from a calmer
Airt, and stood yet Atlas, benignant Titan,
At the winged horizon's gate, his locks of cloud unshorn,
Heaving the sky on his shoulders—there deep in memory's glass,
Free of the torturer's hand, I and my elder brother
Walk the green riverbank in the land where I was born.

On one side, high ground ridged by cattletracks
Where our careering sledges would often whip from grassheads,
Before sunrise, a soaking dew; the beer-brown somnolent wave
Of the brackish river, cattleflats beyond it,
Brimmed sluggish under gorsepods; between them, a narrow tumulus,
Manuka-groved, broom-feathered, we called *The Giant's Grave*.

The horned beasts roared, ponderous at their crossing,
Dewlap-plunged in the dark stream; all night the reedy voices
Cried, *Aqua! Aqua!*, breaking the skin of sleep,
From ditch and bog; at noon the swampgrass flared
Smoke-pillared sacrifice, burned back to a stump of ashes
Beside Antaeus' bones in the grave-mound bedded deep.

In its rock flank a ngaio tree gave foothold,
Flesh-leaved, whose tarry buds breaking in flower sprinkled
Dust on an ageless mirror. There my brother laid
Lines for the basking eels, brutes thicker than a forearm,
Sailed his flaxstick navy, twig-masted on rough ripples
Flogged by desire's crosswind. Nothing made us afraid.

No, not fear of drowning, drawn down in weedy arms,
Nor any ghost dragging the eyes unwilling
To gaze on Adam's wound. Yet once, in a safe bed,
Sweating, chilled by nightmare, I saw a pyre kindled
On the river mound, and stark there, her face in anguish smiling,
Ablaze and unconsumed, my loved grandmother, dead.

1951–55

Evidence at the Witch Trials

No woman's pleasure did I feel
Under the hazel tree
When heavy as a sack of meal

The Black Man mounted me,
But cold as water from a dyke
His seed that quickened me.

What his age I cannot tell;
Foul he was, and fair.
There blew between us both from Hell
A blast of grit and fire,
And like a boulder is the babe
That in my womb I bear.

Though I was youngest in that band
Yet I was quick to learn.
A red dress he promised me
And red the torches burn.
Between the faggot and the flame
I see his face return.

1956–60

A Rope for Harry Fat

Oh some have killed in angry love
And some have killed in hate,
And some have killed in foreign lands
To serve the business State.
The hangman's hands are abstract hands
Though sudden death they bring—
'The hangman keeps our country pure,'
Says Harry Fat the King.

Young love will kick the chairs about
And like a rush fire burn,
Desiring what it cannot have,
A true love in return.
Who knows what rage and darkness fall
When lovers' thoughts grow cold?
'Whoever kills must pay the price,'
Says Harry Fat the old.

With violent hands a young man tries
To mend the shape of life.
This one used a shotgun
And that one used a knife.

And who can see the issues plain
That vex our groaning dust?
'The Law is greater than the man,'
Says Harry Fat the just.

Te Whiu was too young to vote,
The prison records show.
Some thought he was too young to hang;
Legality said, *No*.
Who knows what fear the raupo hides
Or where the wild duck flies?
'A trapdoor and a rope is best,'
Says Harry Fat the wise.

Though many a time he rolled his coat
And on the bare boards lay,
He lies in heavy concrete now
Until the Reckoning Day.
In linen sheet or granite aisle
Sleep Ministers of State.
'We cannot help the idle poor,'
Says Harry Fat the great.

Mercy stirred like a summer wind
The wigs and polished boots
And the long Jehovah faces
Above their Sunday suits.
The jury was uncertain;
The judge debated long.
'Let Justice take her rightful course,'
Said Harry Fat the strong.

The butcher boy and baker boy
Were whistling in the street
When the hangman bound Te Whiu's eyes
And strapped his hands and feet,
Who stole to buy a bicycle
And killed in panic blood.
'The parson won his soul at length,'
Said Harry Fat the good.

Oh some will kill in rage and fear
And some will kill in hate,
And some will kill in foreign lands
To serve the master State.

Justice walks heavy in the land;
          She bears a rope and shroud.
'We will not change our policy,'
          Says Harry Fat the proud.

1956

Eioko

That one should suffer for a nation,
Small folded hands, blackcurrant eyes
Alive with character among the sequins:
Eioko, sold in Choshi by her father
(Leg sores and all) for thirty thousand yen,
As if with stakes of split bamboo
To bank one paddy field against the river.

Her templebones pierced for the blood to flow
Lest she should die untimely
(By God transfusèd thence to graceless souls)
Eight days head down above a charcoal pit . . .
For Eioko, a deadlier martyrdom,
At drunken midnight tables
Displayed like butcher's meat, unable
To yawn at will, or smoke or frown or sit,

Becomes a stupid mask, an aching cistern.
The granite maxim: One must always please
Tourist, soldier, ape and boor,
With courtesy more durable than love.
Great dolls like captives nod above her bed.
In Tokyo's ashy dawn she gently touches
A chopstick-holder carved like a green fish,
Sharing her rice bowl with a child more poor.

1958

Howrah Bridge

(To my wife)

Taller than the stair of Qtub Minar
These iron beams oppress the eagle's town.
Bare heels will dint them slowly.
And swollen Gunga's muscles move
Beneath, with freight of garbage,
Oar and sail, the loot of many lives.

In the unsleeping night my thoughts
Are millet falling from an iron pan,
While you, my dear, in Delhi lying down
Enter the same room by another door.
The rupee god has trampled here;
The poor implore a Marxist cage.
Dragon seed, the huddled bundles lying
In doorways have perhaps one chilli,
A handful of ground maize.
King Famine rules. Tout and owl-eyed whore
Whose talons pluck and stain the sleeve,
Angels of judgement, husk the soul
Till pity, pity only stays.

Out of my wounds they have made stars:
Each is an eye that looks on you.

1958

This Indian Morning

This Indian morning brown as Icarus
Flows guiltless to the vault of noon
Not influenced by cent per cent,
Obediences baggy at the seams,
Outside the Cretan labyrinth
Of money, conscience, work, glum dreams.

Now from the Muslim quarter rise
Dissolving cries and arabesques of fire
From braziers heated with dry cattle-dung.
Tomb-dwellers, women in black shawls,
With pots of dirty brass
Pad to the well, and chatter in the sun.

Eagles have bathed their wings at the ocean streams.
In a cold taxi coming from the mass
With Bertha in her blue silk dress
I think of money. Lepers in the gateway
Hold out their cups and bandaged palms.
Their eyes like desert cisterns burn.
Each soul a moonless oubliette
Waiting for the last great Key to turn.

1959

Night in Delhi

The moon's vast geometric nimbus
Includes the town, the tombs, the heavy eaves
As cold as Rome and twice as foreign.
At night the cages of the past open,
Love shakes the safe dwelling.
Bar the thin door to keep out thieves.

I want simplicity and lightness
To break these daily fetters and
Thoughts that move like Delhi oxen
Gaunt-ribbed, with gold-painted horns,
Hauling the load of endless noon.
The empire of a poem gladly
Would hide beneath your hand.

We broach the midnight of the Kama Sutra
(Mare's hold, spear-thrust, split-bamboo,
Crab and blossoming lotus)
Nudging from the earth of many wishes
While under flowered quilts the children sleep.
Unbind your dark hair. Seas of the heart
Drawn by the nearness of the moon
Into prodigious waterspouts. These
Were our familiar proud catastrophes
That spilt upon the rock a rain of fishes.

I saw where in a wilderness did lie
The royal spirits of our burdened age.
Some slept; some roared, and shook the walls in rage;
Crowned beasts in cages open to the sky.

The lucky ones are mated. O my queen,
Here is your mortal canopy and throne.
We are two eagles in an equal gyre
Rising above the wilds of sense
In the sun's eye and freedom of his grove.
Such love seems to the world indifference.

1959

Elephanta

Accordion and sweet brisk drum
Waken a lounging passion

Outside the wooden teashop where a young
Black-trousered androgynous dancer

Trounces the dust, crooking a maggot's finger,
While pockmarked queers applaud and smoke.

Great hawks like monoplanes
Above the bony tamarind,

Above the quarried rock sail high, high,
And Shiva like a business uncle watches

The village girls with cans to fill
File through the temple to a covered cistern.

Consider. Seasnake, white cloud minnow,
Octopus and moray eel,

Lovely in their lit aquariums
Breathe water as we do,

Have the advantage that they cannot feel.
Yet I have seen, across an angry tide-rip,

The narrow coffin-boat, the catamaran,
Go simply as a girl, with forward-leaning

Mast and torn triangular sail,
Leaving a crowded net behind.

1959

A Prospect of Old Age

Suppose a nest of bees, their honey staining
Brown brittle paper on the wall:
A sundried hut of bricks, bone-dry
Kiln for the hermit years remaining.

Let this man work entirely to recapture
The aerial music of his youth,
Or talk with angels as the carnal
Agony subsides. A stony rapture

This would be. Revengeful, as if joking,
Cheat Caesar by apparent death,
Deny his relatives their pound of flesh,
To criticise his smell, his cough, his smoking.

Let that sweet corrosive dream
More dangerous than Simeon Stylites'
Take shape: an old man at his prayers,
Self-gutted, tugged from the human stream,

An old grey gander with no goose
Who wakes in moonlight groaning for
The dead to answer. Hears above his head
The cranky shutter clatter loose.

1959

She who is like the moon

I do not know another beauty
Like what your face has shown
Silently, silently,

Pure as the moon in fences of torn cloud
Who floods the earth and sky and troubled water
With light like music for one man alone:

Beauty you possess, time's daughter,
Lamp of my life, O hidden one,
You who are the song you sing,

Silently, silently,
From faithful pillows on a night of love
Pouring in my heart's gulf

Your light, your song, your cataract of beauty.

1960

On the Death of her Body

It is a thought breaking the granite heart
Time has given me, that my one treasure,
Your limbs, those passion-vines, that bamboo body

Should age and slacken, rot
Some day in a ghastly clay-stopped hole.
They led me to the mountains beyond pleasure

Where each is not gross body or blank soul
But a strong harp the wind of genesis
Makes music in, such resonant music

That I was Adam, loosened by your kiss
From time's hard bond, and you,
My love, in the world's first summer stood

Plucking the flowers of the abyss.

1960

Election 1960

Hot sun. Lizards frolic
Fly-catching on the black ash

That was green rubbish. Tiny dragons,
They dodge among the burnt broom stems

As if the earth belonged to them
Without condition. In the polling booths

A democratic people have elected
King Log, King Stork, King Log, King Stork again.

Because I like a wide and silent pond
I voted Log. That party was defeated.

Now frogs will dive and scuttle to avoid
That poking idiot bill, the iron gullet:

Delinquent frogs! Stork is an active King,
A bird of principle, benevolent,

And Log is Log, an old time-serving post
Hacked from a totara when the land was young.

1960

The Sixties

(for Louis Johnson)

'The icy dawn of the sixties'—
Yes, you have it there.
Today I saw a black sperm whale
Rolled on the rocks at Pukerua Bay.

The stench grew loud as I came near,
Gulls were grabbing at the kill.
From that sleek projectile body
Jutted a gigantic reddened phallus
Mauled by the Cook Strait squid.

Under the sunset fires it seemed to be
The body of our common love
That bedrooms, bar rooms never killed,
The natural power behind our acts and verses
Murdered by triviality.

1960

To Our Lady of Perpetual Help

Mother, below my life you live,
Nurse of the unlucky ones:
Some old square-headed cabbage-eating priest

Bedragoned by arthritis, or a girl
Who has not found a single trusty man,
All who howl in the rusty frying pan.

Mother, I have no hope unless
You bring me in your holy apron
Clean to the garden gate. Mary, raise
Us who walk the burning slum of days
Not knowing left from right. I praise
Your bar room cross, your star of patience.

1960

from *A Selection of Poetry* (1964)

Mother Crawford's Boarding House

In Mother Crawford's boarding house the company is grand,
There's bludgers, thieves and con men, who will take you by the hand,
A bloody sight more human than the company outside,
And very very seldom are you taken for a ride.

In Mother Crawford's boarding house the food is extra good,
Though the medical attention is at times a little crude.
I told a bloody demon, though he didn't understand,
I thought their hospitality the finest in the land.

In Mother Crawford's boarding house when metho boys arrive
They lay a great red carpet down and welcome them inside.
There's a pigsty and an orchard where we wander in the sun,
And the screws are always helpful as a father to a son.

In Mother Crawford's boarding house you've time to meditate
Upon the good advice you've had from many a magistrate,
And if you stay a year or two, you needn't do it hard,
The only disadvantage is the fact the door is barred.

1960

Note: the poem refers to Wellington's Mount Crawford Prison;
'demon' is prison slang for detective.

For a Child at Nagasaki

Having seen an ocean of fire and then
An ocean of ashes, her mother's head
On the ground in the pumpkin field, Eioko lies
Under a stone in Akagi. Not yet ten
She liked bean jam. You guardians of the dead,
Comfort this child, so young in your mysteries.

1958–62

To a Samoan Friend

[Albert Wendt]

As those cold waters rise at Rainbow Springs
Endlessly from the underworld
(So deep a fountain that the divers cannot
Find its beginning in the groins of earth;
So strong a current that the coins they drop
Spin sideways onto ledges)—

As those fish-breeding waters flow
Under tidy bridges,
Over white choking roots, through ditches
Where willows trail their leaves in shallows
For fretful girls on holiday—

So the creative current of your mind
Rises and flows in this dry land
Bringing to one or two the taste of peace.

1961

A later version of this poem is included in the sequence 'Words to Lay a Strong Ghost' as poem no. 10 'The Friend'. See the *Collected Poems*, p. 361.

A Bucket of Blood for a Dollar (1965)

A Bucket of Blood for a Dollar

(A conversation between Uncle Sam and the Rt Hon. Keith Holyoake, Prime Minister of New Zealand)

'You'll have to learn,' said Uncle Sam,
'The Yankee way of work
Now that you've joined in our crusade
Against the modern Turk;
The capital of the Commonwealth is
Not London, but New York.'

'Don't tell them that,' cried Holyoake,
'In Thames or Dannevirke.'

'Then use your loaf,' said Uncle Sam,
'Newspapers hit the eye;
If you get trouble from the men
That you can't bluff or buy,
Just spread the word that they're all Reds
And let the rumours fly.'

'I'll bang the drum,' said Holyoake—
And yet he heaved a sigh.

'Tell them straight,' said Uncle Sam,
'That it's a dirty war;
Mention the Freedom of the West
That we are fighting for;
But keep the money side of it
Well tucked behind the door.'

'I'll make it sound,' said Holyoake,
'Just like a football score.'

'Between the fights,' said Uncle Sam,
'They'll need some exercise;
There's a thousand brothels in Saigon
Where they can fraternize.
The peasants send their daughters there
When they have no rice.'

'Let's not be coarse,' said Holyoake,
Turning up his eyes.

'I fried a village,' said Uncle Sam,
'With the new phosphorus bomb
The day a Yankee Army nurse
Was killed by the Viet Cong;
A white dame's worth a million gooks—
In Asia, *we* belong.'

'Your chivalry,' said Holyoake,
'Puts angels in the wrong.'

'The newest way,' said Uncle Sam,
'To interrogate the brutes
Is a wet wire on the private parts
That half-electrocutes—
Though I do hate having to wash
Their vomit from my boots.'

'Don't talk so loud!' groaned Holyoake—
'We'll want the churches' votes.'

'I'm a simple chap,' sighed Holyoake,
'Politics hurt my head;
But why do you scrap with China
To the tune of a million dead
And sign a Pact with Russia,
When both of them are Red?'

'Get with it, Keith,' said Uncle Sam,
'We need the East for trade.'

'I'm a simple chap,' said Holyoake,
'Politics frighten me;
But whether it's frozen meat or men
We send across the sea,
We want good prices for our veal—
What can you guarantee?'

'Just name your price,' said Uncle Sam,
'And leave the rest to me.'

1965

The Gunner's Lament (1965)

The Gunner's Lament

(For my wife, Te Kare)

A Maori gunner lay dying
In a paddyfield north of Saigon,
And he said to his pakeha cobber,
'I reckon I've had it, man!

'And if I could fly like a bird
To my old granny's whare
A truck and a winch would never drag
Me back to the Army.

'A coat and a cap and a well-paid job
Looked better than shovelling metal,
And they told me that Te Rauparaha
Would have fought in the Vietnam battle.

'On my last leave the town swung round
Like a bucket full of eels.
The girls liked the uniform
And I liked the girls.

'Like a bullock to the abattoirs
In the name of liberty
They flew me with a hangover
Across the Tasman Sea,

'And what I found in Vietnam
Was mud and blood and fire,
With the Yanks and the Reds taking turns
At murdering the poor,

'And I saw the reason for it
In a Viet Cong's blazing eyes—
We fought for the crops of kumara
And they are fighting for rice.

'So go and tell my sweetheart
To get another boy
Who'll cuddle her and marry her
And laugh when the bugles blow,

'And tell my youngest brother
He can have my shotgun
To fire at the ducks on the big lagoon,
But not to aim it at a man,

'And tell my granny to wear black
And carry a willow leaf,
Because the kid she kept from the cold
Has eaten a dead man's loaf,

'And go and tell Keith Holyoake
Sitting in Wellington,
However long he scrubs his hands
He'll never get them clean.'

1965

The Old Earth Closet (1965)

The Old Earth Closet

(A tribute to regional poetry)

Oh some will sing of Dannevirke
And some will sing of Troy
And some of girls on Lambton Quay,
But since I was a boy
A genuine earth closet
Is my peculiar joy.

The one my Grandad dug when first
He reached this island shore
Was sunk into volcanic rock
For thirty feet or more—
He kept the family Bible
Nailed up behind the door.

From Genesis to Amos
He had travelled ere he died
(A frugal Scottish farmer

Whose potatoes were his pride)
And they laid its tattered pages
In the coffin by his side.

The old earth dyke was standing
In my father's day and mine
With its seat of polished hardwood
And its door of knotted pine—
To a faithless generation
It remaineth as a sign.

And to that seat of refuge
In my boyhood I would come
To meditate for hours and hear
Aeolian voices drum
In the cave of the Delphic oracle,
Till my backside was numb.

There in the drowsy summer light
My first bad verse was made,
My first experiments in Yoga
Conducted in its shade—
May none disturb that hallowed spot
With an unreverent spade!

Across the hills of manuka
I watched the cows come home,
And as they wandered up the track
It turned my heart to stone
That I was a New Zealander
And therefore Man Alone.

And that is why my verses plod
So deep in our native clay—
To regional environment
This tribute I must pay
Lest an earth closet swallow me
Upon the Judgement Day.

1954–65

from *Pig Island Letters* (1966)

In the original volume Baxter notes: 'The term "Pig Island" is used to refer to the South Island in New Zealand vernacular [but here] it is used more generally to refer to the whole country.'

from *Pig Island Letters*

(to Maurice Shadbolt)

1

The gap you speak of—yes, I find it so,
The menopause of the mind. I think of it
As a little death, practising for the greater,
For the undertaker who won't have read
Your stories or my verse—
Or that a self had died
Who handled ideas like bombs,

In that bare southern town
At a party on a cold night
Men seen as ghosts, women like trees walking,
Seen from the floor, a forest of legs and bums
For the climbing boy, the book-bred one.

And this, the moment of art, can never stay.
Wives in the kitchen cease to smile as we go
Into the gap itself, the solid night
Where poor drunks fear the icy firmament:
Man is a walking grave,

That is where I start from. Though often
Where the Leith Stream wandered down
Its culvert, crinkled labia of blossom
On the trees beside the weir
Captured and held the fugitive
From time, from self, from the iron pyramid,

These were diversions. Give my love
To Vic. He is aware of
The albatross. In the Otago storms
Carrying spray to salt the landward farms
The wind is a drunkard. Whoever can listen
Long enough will write again.

21 September 1963

Note: 'that bare southern town' is Dunedin. Baxter wrote: 'Shadbolt was down there on a Burns Fellowship. The place has for me the morgue-like attraction of the place one began to grow up in' (MS Book 24).

2

From an old house shaded with macrocarpas
Rises my malady.
Love is not valued much in Pig Island
Though we admire its walking parody,

That brisk gaunt woman in the kitchen
Feeding the coal range, sullen
To all strangers, lest one should be
Her antique horn-red Satan.

Her man, much baffled, grousing in the pub,
Discusses sales
Of yearling lambs, the timber in a tree
Thrown down by autumn gales,

Her daughter, reading in her room
A catalogue of dresses,
Can drive a tractor, goes to Training College,
Will vote on the side of the Bosses,

Her son is moodier, has seen
An angel with a sword
Standing above the clump of old man manuka
Just waiting for the word

To overturn the cities and the rivers
And split the house like a rotten totara log.
Quite unconcerned he sets his traps for 'possums
And whistles to his dog.

The man who talks to the masters of Pig Island
About the love they dread
Plaits ropes of sand, yet I was born among them
And will lie some day with their dead.

1963

Note: Baxter wrote, in MS Book 24, 'Her antique horn-red Satan'—'The concept of a phallic devil is one of the glories of the theology of the Church of Geneva. The intuition of believers has naturally attributed to Satan, the Arch-Enemy, the faults of incontinence, one of the chief signs of a state of reprobation.'

3

That other Baxter the Sectarian
Said that the bodies of the damned will burn
Like stubble thrown into a red-hot oven
On Judgement Day. In Calvin's town
At seventeen I thought I might see
Not fire but water rise

From the shelves of surf beyond St Clair
To clang the dry bell. Gripping
A pillow wife in bed
I did my convict drill,
And when I made a mother of the keg
The town split open like an owl's egg
Breaking the ladders down. It was
Perhaps the winter of beginning:

Frost standing up like stubble in the streets
Below the knees of Maori Hill,
Looking for the last simplicity
And nothing to explain it in the books,
In a room where the wind clattered the blind-cord
In the bed of a girl with long plaits
I found the point of entry,
The place where father Adam died.

Meanwhile a boy with dog and ferret
Climbed up the gorse track from the sea
To the turn at the top of the gully
Twelve paces past the cabbage tree,
And saw from the crest of the hill
Pillars of rain move on the dark sea,
A cloud of fire rise up above Japan,
God's body blazing on damnation's tree.

Thank you for the letter. I read your book
Five days ago: it has the slow
Imperceptible wingbeat of the hawk
Above the dry scrublands. The kill is there
In the Maori riverbed below
Where bones glitter. I could tell
Of other matters, but not now.

11 October 1963

Note: Baxter wrote, in MS Book 24, ' "That other Baxter"— one of the prophets of the Puritan Revolution . . . he stressed justice more than mercy.'

4

The censor will not let my lines reveal
Pig Island spinning on the potter's wheel.

A skinny wench in jeans with a kea's eye:
The rack on which our modern martyrs die.

I prophesy these young delinquent bags
Will graduate to grim demanding hags.

Our women chiefly carry in their bones
The curse that stuck to the scattered oven stones.

How often Remuera girls abort
Has not been mentioned in the Hunn Report.

Holyoake yammering from a kauri stump—
God save us all! I need a stomach pump.

Sea-eggs, puha, pork, and kumara:
The Maori owned the land. I have a camera.

Though Freud and God may bless the marriage vow
You must know how to work the hillside plough.

The sun is warm, the nosebag smells of hay,
The wind is blowing from the north today.

You who were pulled apart by four draught horses,
Saint Hippolytus, pray for us!

1963

Note: Baxter wrote, in *Pig Island Letters*, 'The Hunn report is a negative and officious statement on Maori social conditions, which some Maori leaders have ironically called their Bible. Remuera, referred to by contrast, is a suburb of the city of Auckland, socialite by reputation.'

8

When I was only semen in a gland
Or less than that, my father hung
From a torture post at Mud Farm
Because he would not kill. The guards
Fried sausages, and as the snow came darkly
I feared a death by cold in the cold groin
And plotted revolution. His black and swollen thumbs
Explained the brotherhood of man,

But he is old now in his apple garden
And we have seen our strong Antaeus die
In the glass castle of the bureaucracies
Robbing our bread of salt. Shall Marx and Christ
Share beds this side of Jordan? I set now
Unwillingly these words down:

Political action in its source is pure,
Human, direct, but in its civil function
Becomes the jail it laboured to destroy.

1963

Note: Baxter wrote, in MS Book 24, 'The torture was No. 1 Field Punishment administered by soldiers who were keen on their job.'

9

Look at the simple caption of success,
The poet as family man,
Head between thumbs at mass, nailing a trolley,
Letting the tomcat in:
Then turn the hourglass over, find the other
Convict self, incorrigible, scarred
With what the bottle and the sex games taught,
The black triangle, the whips of sin.
The first gets all his meat from the skull-faced twin,
Sharpening a dagger out of a spoon,
Struggling to speak through the gags of a poem:
When both can make a third my work is done.

Nor will the obituary ever indicate
How much we needed friends,
Like Fitz at the National
Speaking of his hydatid cyst,

A football underneath the lung,
Or Lowry in Auckland: all who held the door
And gave us space for art,
Time for the re-shaping of the heart:
Those whom the arrow-makers honour least,
Companions to the manbeast,
One man in many, touching the flayed hide gently,
A brother to the artist and a nurse.

The trees rustle as October comes
And fantails batter on the glass,
Season when the day nurse tuts and hums
Laying out pills and orange juice
For one who walks the bridge of dread
As oedema sets in,
While through the bogs and gullies of Pig Island
Bellies are beaten like skin drums
In pup tents, under flax or lupin shade,

As if the sun were a keg. And this man
On the postman's round will meditate
The horn of Jacob withered at the root
Or quirks of weather. None
Grow old easily. The poem is
A plank laid over the lion's den.

12 October 1963

11

Tonight I read my son a story
About the bees of Baiame, who tell the east wind
To blow down rain, so that the flowers grow
In dry Australia, and the crow *wirinun*
Who jailed the west wind in a hollow log:

My son who is able to build a tree house
With vine ladders, my son
In his brown knitted jersey and dungarees,
Makes clowns and animals, a world of creatures
To populate paradise,

And when he hands me easily
The key of entry, my joy must be dissembled
Under a shutter of horn, a dark lantern,
In case it should too brightly burn,

Because the journey has begun
Into the land where the sun is silent
And no one may enter the tree house
That hides the bones of a child in the forest of a man.

1963

13

Stat crux dum volvitur orbis: I will sing
In the whale's belly.
'Great Mother of God
Sweeten my foul breath. I wait for a death.
Cradle me, Lady, on the day they carry
My body down the bush track to the road
To the rollers of the decorous van.
The leper's stump, the thick voice of the drunk,
Are knocking at Nazareth. I am a naked man.'

'How can I let you in?
The time for talk has gone;
A mountain is the threshold stone.'

'Mother, I come alone.
No books, no bread
Are left in my swag.'

'Why are your hands not clean?'

'There was no soap in the whole damned town.'

'God's grace has need of man's apology.'

'Your face is my theology.'

'Yes; but I gave you a jewel to bring.'

'In the thick gorse of the gully
I lost your signet ring.'

'Why should I listen then?'

'On Skull Hill there was none,
No scapular, no sign,
Only the words, *I thirst*,
When the blood of a convict burst
From the body of your son.'

'You may come in.'

Is it like that? At least I know no better;
After a night of argument
Mythical, theological, political,
Somebody has the sense to get a boat
And row out towards the crayfish rocks
Where, diving deep, the downward swimmer
Finds fresh water rising up,
A mounded water breast, a fountain,
An invisible tree whose roots cannot be found;

As that wild nymph of water rises
So does the God in man.

13 October 1963

Note: Baxter wrote, in MS Book 24, 'I conceive of the dying man as a swagger looking for a night's lodging. Our Lady traditionally offers hospitality to those who have only a death to count on.'

East Coast Journey

About twilight we came to the whitewashed pub
On a knuckle of land above the bay

Where a log was riding and the slow
Bird-winged breakers cast up spray.

One of the drinkers round packing cases had
The worn face of a kumara god,

Or so it struck me. Later on
Lying awake in the verandah bedroom

In great dryness of mind I heard the voice of the sea
Reverberating, and thought: As a man

Grows older he does not want beer, bread, or the prancing flesh,
But the arms of the eater of life, Hine-nui-te-po,

With teeth of obsidian and hair like kelp
Flashing and glimmering at the edge of the horizon.

1962–63

At Taieri Mouth

Flax-pods unload their pollen
Above the steel-bright cauldron

Of Taieri, the old water-dragon
Sliding out from a stone gullet

Below the Maori-ground. Scrub horses
Come down at night to smash the fences

Of the whaler's children. Trypots have rusted
Leaving the oil of anger in the blood

Of those who live in two-roomed houses
Mending nets or watching from a window

The great south sky fill up with curdled snow.
Their cows eat kelp along the beaches.

The purple sailor drowned in thighboots
Drifting where the currents go

Cannot see the flame some girl has lighted
In a glass chimney, but in five days' time

With bladder-weed around his throat
Will ride the drunken breakers in.

1961

The Cold Hub

Lying awake on a bench in the town belt,
Alone, eighteen, more or less alive,
Lying awake to the sound of clocks,
The railway clock, the Town Hall clock,
And the Varsity clock, genteel, exact
As a Presbyterian conscience,
I heard the hedgehogs chugging round my bench,
Colder than an ice-axe, colder than a bone,
Sweating the booze out, a spiritual Houdini
Inside the padlocked box of winter, time and craving.

Sometimes I rolled my coat and put it under my head,
And when my back got frozen, I put it on again.
I thought of my father and mother snoring at home

While the fire burnt out in feathery embers.
I thought of my friends each in their own house
Lying under blankets, tidy as dogs or mice.
I thought of my med. student girlfriend
Dreaming of horses, cantering brown-eyed horses,
In her unreachable bed, wrapped in a yellow quilt,

And something bust inside me, like a winter clod
Cracked open by the frost. A sense of being at
The absolute unmoving hub
From which, to which, the intricate roads went.
Like Hemingway, I call it *nada*:
Nada, the Spanish word for nothing.
Nada; the belly of the whale; *nada*;
Nada; the little hub of the great wheel;
Nada; the house on Cold Mountain
Where the east and the west wall bang together;
Nada; the drink inside the empty bottle.
You can't get there unless you are there.
The hole in my pants where the money falls out,
That's the beginning of knowledge; *nada*.

It didn't last for long; it never left me.
I knew that I was *nada*. Almost happy,
Stiff as a giraffe, I called in later
At an early grill, had coffee, chatted with the boss.

That night, drunk again, I slept much better
At the bus station, in a broom cupboard.

1961–62

The Hollow Place

On the waste low headland
Below the road, above the plunging sea,
I would climb often round the crumbling face
Where flax bushes precariously
Gave something to grip: then I'd stand
Alive in the hollow place
That meant . . . well, I must describe it: a bent cleft
In limestone rock above a pool
Of fluttering scum; bushes to the left,
And an overhang. The passage was dark and cool,

Three yards long perhaps, hidden from any eye
Not acquainted; and the air
Tainted by some odour as if the earth sweated
In primeval sleep. I did nothing there;
There was nothing to do but listen to some greater I
Whose language was silence. Again and again I came
And was healed of the daftness, the demon in the head
And the black knot in the thighs, by a silence that
Accepted all. Not knowing I would come again,
My coat of words worn very thin,
Knocking, as if lame,
With a dry stick on the dumb
Door of the ground, and crying out:
'Open, mother. Open. Let me in.'

1962

A Takapuna Business Man Considers his Son's Death in Korea

Your sailboat yawns for you in the spidery shed
Among the mangrove trunks; I watched you build it
Before they hid you under stones in a pit
In North Korean ice. Your mother's head,

High cheekbones, hard black eyes! At Cherry Farm
She waits for God, a tube-fed schizophrene
With the unwrinkled forehead of eighteen.
The harbour's death-mask sweats in summer calm.

In my wall safe I keep the fir tree cone
You gave me once. You liked your whisky-mad
Iron-gutted killjoy of a Dad;
Too well perhaps. Why did I let you groan

That rugged year, when you reached out to me
For help, down South? I thought, 'The lion's whelp
Must learn to fight the jackals without help'—
And you became a prefect. Sodomy

Is what they teach. I heard that little slut,
Your stepmother, after she'd piled me drunk
Under a blanket in my dogbox bunk,
Creep out to join you in the garden hut;

I never whispered of it. Muskets blazed
From the hunched snipers of pohutukawa
The day you stole my wallet and my car
And drove to Puhoi. Now I fumble dazed

Outside the door. O Absalom, the beast
Of anger, time and age will grind my skull
To powder! Spiders web your sailboat's hull.
The sword of Joab rages in the East.

1961

Thoughts of a Remuera Housewife

The tranquillizers on my
glass-topped table, black-and-green
pomegranate seeds, belong to
Pluto, that rough king—so I
have eaten six, to go in
quietly, quietly through

the dark mirror to his world
of chaos and the grave—'Ann,
how strong you are!' my mother
said yesterday when the wild
pony all but threw Robin
under its hooves; I got her

to mount again. They don't know
I am Pluto's Queen . . . Oh yes,
I kept your letter saying
it was no good—what did you
mean by that? The drugged clouds race
over the gun-pit facing

all storm, where you stopped the car
and undid my jersey—now
my husband is undressing
and jerking at his collar
with the Bugs Bunny grin I
hated so . . . Our sort of dying

kept me young—my love, how high
the cocksfoot was! our own bed
walled in by soldier stalks of

grass—no one else could touch me,
among the lions' dens—mad,
happy, lost! In Pluto's cave

from granite thrones we watch the
ghosts whirling like snaking fog
quietly, quietly down
to their own urn, not to see
ever the sun's sweat-streaked flag
thunder again . . . In London

do they play Schubert or Brahms
in asbestos rooms? Do girls
bite your throat? When you turned me
into a violin (dreams
are what I go by) that pulse
in your neck . . . My Satan, why

did you not stay where flames rise
always up? You said no one
can fight the world . . . No; it's not
a world at all, but Pluto's
iron-black star, the quiet
planet furthest from the sun.

1962–65

from *The Holy Life and Death of Concrete Grady*

1 The Ballad of Grady's Dream

One clink black night in June
Concrete Grady sat
Between the knees of the pines
With Old Jack Flynn his mate,

And through the harbour fog
The guts of Wellington
Glowed like a great morgue
Where even the cops had gone.

'I had a dream,' said Grady—
Flynn said, 'Stuff your dream!
I'd give my ballocks now
For a bucket of steam.'

'I had a dream,' said Grady,
'When I slept in Mulligan's woodyard
Under a wad of roofing iron;
I was a white bird,

'And then a gale caught me
And threw me north;
There was nothing left standing
On the bare-arsed earth,

'And I thought of the time in Crete
When we jammed the Bren gun
And the paratroops came over
Like washing on a line,

'And you'll remember, Jack,
Because you were there,
We shot twelve prisoners
In Imvros village square;

'Because the wind blew me
To the door of a stone barn,
And the Nazi lads were sitting
At a table playing cards—

'*Sergeant, come in,* they said,
We've kept you a place—
And when they turned I saw
The red-hot bone in each one's face,

'So I let the wind carry
Me out past Kapiti
In the belly of the storm above
A thousand miles of sea,

'Till I came to a blind cliff
That got no sun,
Deep as the cunning of Hell
And high as the trouble of man.

'There was one gap in it
Where only a bird could fly;
I said the Hail Mary
And threaded the needle's eye,

'And there in a green garden
I saw the Tramways Band
And a crowd of people walking
With flagons in their hands,

'And on a bullock wagon
The Host Itself with seven nuns,
And one of them had the face
Of Rose O'Rourke when she was young.'

'You've struck it there,' said Flynn,
'She'd be a bit of all right;
But I'd give old Rose the go-by
For a bottle of steam tonight.'

1965

Note: 'steam' is New Zealand drunks' slang for methylated spirits.

Henley Pub

(a traveller's soliloquy)

Brown-bellied curtains, blood-beat of
The radiogram . . . I'll not forget
Your flat in Royal Terrace where the wet
Tom-kitten squealed at the porch door: you'd smile
And call him grizzle-guts . . . I drove
Drunk as a crocodile
At eighty round the bends to Henley
Under an asphalt moon. It's morning. Look:
The Taieri flood, Jehovah's book,
Ruffles its page, does not untwist our sin
Which is itself, the triple snarling grin
Of Cerberus. The barman's heel
Crushes a hot butt, and I
Burn. The vacillations of the sky
Shine through the brandy glass.
Hail, holy Queen!
Beyond the serpent waves they glitter green,
Your willows on the far bank. Mother, my dream
Of God has died. The bog-black stream
Swallows time. Trout and eel

Are sliding through my rib-cage. They will eat
The self no fire could touch, your faithful deadbeat
Altar boy. One room
Contains the bandaged glory and the doom
Of Israel. In Father Hogan's box
I gripped the lion by the jowls,
Splitting her sin from mine to feed the fowls
Of judgement. Then wild bees among the rocks
Loaded miraculous honey in the white
Carcass.
          I loved you well,
Delilah; and I lost my hold on life
The day you burnt that letter from my wife.
Your body is my Hell.

The waves of the Taieri are bending bright;
A car and a man could go down
Easily under it. Last night in town,
The gin-glass empty on the floor,
I felt the rustle of the hunter's net—
A Swedish novel on the coverlet,
Your window open to the Leith Stream's roar,
Your head thrown back like one about to die,
Your body plump and bare—
I thought, shoving my muscle through black hair,
'What is a man, this glittering dung-fed fly
Who burrows in foul earth?'
                                        And that is all,
All; Jehovah's sky
And earth like millstones grind us small.

1961–65

At Days Bay

To lie on a beach after
looking at old poems: how
slow untroubled by any
grouch of mine or yours, Father
Ocean tumbles in the bay
alike with solitary

divers, cripples, yelling girls
and pipestem kids. He does what
suits us all; and somewhere—there,

out there, where the high tight sails
are going—he wears a white
death flag of foam for us, far

out, for when we want it. So
on Gea's breast, the broad nurse
who bears with me, I think of
adolescence: that sad boy
I was, thoughts crusted with ice
on the treadmill of self-love,

Narcissus damned, who yet brought
like a coal in a hollow
stalk, the seed of fire that runs
through my veins now. I praise that
sad boy now, who having no
hope, did not blow out his brains.

New Year, 1965

Tomcat

This tomcat cuts across the
zones of the respectable
through fences, walls, following
other routes, his own. I see
the sad whiskered skull-mouth fall
wide, complainingly, asking

to be picked up and fed, when
I thump up the steps through bush
at 4 p.m. He has no
dignity, thank God! has grown
older, scruffier, the ash-
black coat sporting one or two

flowers like round stars, badges
of bouts and fights. The snake head
is seamed on top with rough scars:
old Samurai! He lodges
in cellars, and the tight furred
scrotum drives him into wars

as if mad, yet tumbling on
the rug looks female, Turkish-
trousered. His bagpipe shriek at

sluggish dawn dragged me out in
pyjamas to comb the bush
(he being under the vet

for septic bites): the old fool
stood, body hard as a board,
heart thudding, hair on end, at
the house corner, terrible,
yelling at something. They said,
'Get him doctored.' I think not.

1960–64

A Wish for Berries

Today the waves of bright lead
lift rubbish, driftwood, in each
high bending wall: a good day
for gulls or dogs. The worn touch
of air and sun unkindly
like a dull whore tames the blood

offering only sleep. Yes . . .
I think of a friend who took
poison lately. Being dead,
he has gone into the dark
sheaf of truth and shares a word
with me just as my eyes close—

'Pity all things'—Do the tough
kids need pity who wrestle
under the bathing shed wall?
or the girls whose broad muscles
slide in bermuda shorts, all
intent on a thunder-proof

world of knowledge? I cannot
pity what is; but look up
at the karaka tree whose
thick wide leaves contain such ripe
yellow berries, their clusters
would take a fortnight to eat.

14 February 1965

from *The Lion Skin: Poems* (1967)

The Lion Skin

The old man with a yellow flower on his coat
Came to my office, climbing twenty-eight steps,
With a strong smell of death about his person
From the caves of the underworld.
The receptionist was troubled by his breath
Understandably.
                    Not every morning tea break
Does Baron Saturday visit his parishioners
Walking stiffly, strutting almost,
With a cigar in his teeth—she might have remembered
Lying awake as if nailed by a spear
Two nights ago, with the void of her life
Glassed in a dark window—but suitably enough
She preferred to forget it.
                              I welcomed him
And poured him a glass of cherry brandy,
Talked with him for half an hour or so,
Having need of his strength, the skin of a dead lion,
In the town whose ladders are made of coffin wood.

The flower on his coat blazed like a dark sun.

1965

from *The Man on the Horse* (1967)

The Origins of Art

(From the Journal of Truthful James)

Here comes the mirror-gazing multitude,
Bureaucrat, yahoo, statistician, prude;
And who's that standing at the corner pissing?
Why—old Utrillo with a brain-lobe missing!

1960

On Possessing the Burns Fellowship 1966

(to Nicholas Zissermann)

Trees move slowly. The rain drops arrows
As on the Spartans from the Persian bowstring
Some while ago, across the tennis court
Behind the convent they hope to pull down,

And I who wrote in '62,
Dear ghosts, let me abandon
What cannot be held against
Hangmen and educators, the city of youth!—

Drink fresh percolated coffee, lounging
In the new house, at the flash red kitchen table,
A Varsity person, with an office
Just round the corner—what nonsense!

If there is any culture here
It comes from the black south wind
Howling above the factories
A handsbreadth from Antarctica,

Whatever the architect and planner
Least understand—not impossibly the voice
Of an oracle rising from that
Old battered green veranda

Beyond the board fence: a blood transfusion
From the earth's thick veins! As if
Caesar had died, and clouds, leaves, conspired to make
A dark mocking funeral wreath.

1962–66

The Girl in Yellow Jeans

'Let's Love' said the poster in the Tourist Bureau,
And the man behind the desk was nice;
He didn't ask if she was a virgin, or
Offer all kinds of prissy advice. No;
He complimented her on her yellow jeans
And took her sixpence and swung the poster back

And showed her a funny round stone door
(*Like a safe*, she thought)—well, there could be no harm
In paying a visit. The tunnel was black;
(*Soon*, she thought, *I'll know what it means*,
But she would have cried if he hadn't held her arm
Very tight) . . . Out into a coffee bar
That she knew already. The band struck up.
Harry tooted his horn and gave her a grin
And Wally was tuning a new guitar.
Her companion had gone. She settled herself in the far
Corner; the Dutch waitress was very slow;
The band stopped. She felt the silence grow;
Wondered, *How soon does the telly show begin?*—
Looked down; and suddenly screamed at the blood in her cup.

1962

At Aramoana

Boulders interrupt the long
jetty from whose black asphalt
tongue the godwits fly to their
Siberian lakes, or—*Abba,*
father!—melt like ash or salt
in the void white thundering

wilderness. Yet on the spit
sheaves of water bow as if
to the sickle, and boys make
from earth, air, a goatskin ark,
each watching the same girl of
blood and fibreglass go out

into the surf and shake back
the hanging gardens of her
sun-bleached hair. I turn also
to my dream, in nooks below
the sandhill cone, where Gea
speaks in parables of rock,

wordless, unconnected with
the acedia of a tribe
never *once* happy, never
at peace . . . There is no other
rest for the heart, but these drab
mats of cutty-grass, no truth

outside her changing and austere
testament of sand. Beyond
her breast, though, I must walk on
to where the black swells begin
Abba, father—to swamp, pound
and hurt the land—on further,

where the serpent current flows
out of the harbour gates, long-
flowing, strongly tugging at
the roots of the world. The night
sky tells that after singing
silence is the only voice.

1966

Ode

Soon I will go South
To my birth land,
Island and river mouth
Under the sun's face,
From whose body, as if damned,
I fled towards the night,
Burnt black—till the axe of dawn
Rise up from a hidden place
To show our flesh, burnt white,
That the furious Christ is born

Among straight candles in
Some church or pre-fab shack;
And where all wars begin,
On His anvil reconciled
We will kneel down, deaf rock,
To eat the God of Bread
Whose flesh received our scorn,
In the nail-struck hands of a child
Perceiving the hope of the dead
And the sorrow of all men born.

Speak from the chains of the sea,
Mother of martyrs! Teach
Your sons by the mystery
How they, burnt black, may learn

The vowels of human speech,
Lest we achieve damnation
In the fields of untilled corn
Where souls, uprooted, spurn
The stable of contemplation
Where the midnight sun is born.

I imagine a limestone cave
Under the green bush wall
That was a Maori grave
That the pioneering men
Had used as a cattle stall.
To the desecrated earth
Under hooked lawyer thorn
We come—like a beast to its den—
Desiring no second birth
But the sleep of the unborn,

Since man looks for a shroud
Either by gun or blade
Or by the atom cloud,
To be rid of the corpse curled
Shrunk small in the ambuscade
Of the soul—our Christ of death
For whom the midwives mourn—
Deaf monster of a world,
A child that has no breath
Not able to be born!

Yet a drunk who goes by night
Towards the Scroggs Hill farm
May see a blaze of light
In a sod hut, and there
A girl with a child on her arm,
The rounded Maori face,
A blue dress loosely worn,
And mercy to swamp despair
At the gorgehead of grace
Where the Christ of fire is born,

From which he would come down
To the bride no worm can touch,
To the gravel roads of the town,
School, store and bowling green,
To the old in their bleak hutch
And the chaingangs of the young

Struck wild by summer's horn,
And praise the living scene
With an unwounded tongue
In the land where I was born.

1964

Letter to Robert Burns

King Robert, on your anvil stone
Above the lumbering Octagon,
To you I raise a brother's horn
Led by the wandering unicorn
Of total insecurity.
Never let your dead eye look
Up from Highland Mary's book
To the fat scrag-end of the Varsity.
Kilmarnock hag and dominie
Watch there the grey Leith water drum
With laughter from a bird's beak
At what their learning has left out.
They tried to make my devil speak
With the iron boot of education
(Psychology, French, Latin)—
But though they drove the wedges in
Till the blood and marrow spouted out,
That spirit was dumb.

Robert, only a heart I bring,
No gold of words to grace a king,
Nor can a stranger lift that flail
That cracked the wall of Calvin's jail
And earned you the lead garland of
A people's moralizing love,
Till any Scotsman with the shakes
Can pile on your head his mistakes
And petrify a boozaroo
Reciting *Tam o' Shanter* through;
And there's an old black frost that freezes
Apollo's balls and the blood of Jesus
In this dry, narrow-gutted town.
Often enough I stumbled down

From Maori Hill to the railway station
(When Aussie gin was half the price)
Making my Easter meditation
In the wilderness of fire and ice
Where a Puritan gets his orientation.

King Robert with the horn of stone!
Perhaps your handcuffs were my own;
Your coffin-cradle was the blank
Medusa conscience of a drunk
That hankers for the purity
Of an imagined infancy,
And after riding seven whores
Approaches God upon all fours,
Crying, 'O thou great Incubus,
Help me or turn me to a walrus!'
And in hangover weeps to see
A playing child or a walnut tree.
If, lying in the pub latrine,
You muttered, 'Take me back to Jean,'
The reason for your mandrake groans
Is wrapped like wire around my bones.

Not too far from the Leith water
My mother saw the mandrake grow
And pulled it. A professor's daughter,
She told me some time after how
She had been frightened by a cow
So that the birth-sac broke too soon
And on the twenty-ninth of June
Prematurely I looked at the walls
And yelled. The Plunket nurse ran in
To scissor off my valued foreskin,
But one thing staggered that grimalkin:
Poets are born with three balls.

Biology, mythology,
Go underground when the bookmen preach,
And I must thank the lass who taught me
My catechism at Tunnel Beach;
For when the hogmagandie ended
And I lay thunder-struck and winded,
The snake-haired Muse came out of the sky
And showed her double axe to me.

Since then I die and do not die.
'Jimmy,' she said, 'you are my ugliest son;
I'll break you like a herring-bone.'

I fill my pipe with black tobacco
And watch a dead man's ember glow.

1963

A Family Photograph 1939

Waves bluster up the bay and through the throat
Of the one-span bridge. My brother shoots
The gap alone
Like Charon sculling in his boat
Above the squids and flounders. With the jawbone
Of a sperm whale he fights the town,
Dances on Fridays to the cello
With black-haired sluts. My father in his gumboots
Is up a ladder plucking down
The mottled autumn-yellow
Dangling torpedo clusters
Of passion fruit for home-made wine.
My mother in the kitchen sunshine
Tightens her dressing gown,
Chops up carrots, onions, leeks,
For thick hot winter soup. No broom or duster
Will shift the English papers piled on chairs
And left for weeks.
I, in my fuggy room at the top of the stairs,
A thirteen-year-old schizophrene,
Write poems, wish to die,
And watch the long neat mason-fly
Malignantly serene
Arrive with spiders dopier than my mind
And build his clay dungeons inside the roller blind.

1961

Only verses 3 and 4 of 'School Days' are reproduced in *The Man on the Horse*; it was first published in full in the *New Zealand Poetry Yearbook*, IX, 1960.

School Days

I touch them with a word, so close they stand
After a thousand hours and days,
Older than Cocteau, in the dream museum
Of corridors and changing rooms:
A palace, jail and maze.

There I imbibed, as at a breast, truth
Beside the simple streams and elms;
England, my wet nurse, with her bitter milk.
So from sugared childhood came
On to the watershed of tears
With those small angular companions,
Handlers of the penis and the pen.

Hard to forgive them even now,
Precursors of the adult nightmare—
Franey, Nero of the dormitory,
Holmes, with the habits of a jaguar
And the sleek animal hide,
Waiting in a bend of the high stone stair.

Plunged early into the abyss of life
Where the tormentors move,
At war with God, the terrible Watcher,
An octopus behind a round glass window
With knives and justice, but no love.

That guilt grew wrongly, driven underground
With the first prickings of raw sense.
Yet there was friendship, comics, dominoes,
A dried newt like a bootsole in a drain,
New conkers like peeled testicles,
Sharing of exile, and the habit, pain.

The village like a mother stayed outside
With wells and horses, till the coat
Of manhood could be stitched and worn—
And the green mandrake Poetry
Born whole and shrieking one bleak night
Under stiff sheets and wincing at the dawn.

1958

Note: Baxter has annotated the manuscript of this version 'Sibford'—a reference to the Quaker school he attended in the English Cotswolds.

A Small Ode on Mixed Flatting (1967)

A Small Ode on Mixed Flatting

Elicited by the decision of the
Otago University authorities to
forbid this practice among students

Dunedin nights are often cold
(I notice it as I grow old);
The south wind scourging from the Pole
Drives every rat to his own hole,
Lashing the drunks who wear thin shirts
And little girls in mini-skirts.
Leander, that Greek lad, was bold
To swim the Hellespont raging cold
To visit Hero in her tower
Just for an amorous half-hour,
And lay his wet brine-tangled head
Upon her pillow—Hush! The dead
Can get good housing—Thomas Bracken,
Smellie, McLeod, McColl, McCracken,
A thousand founding fathers lie
Well roofed against the howling sky
In mixed accommodation—Hush!
It is the living make us blush
Because the young have wicked hearts
And blood to swell their private parts.
To think of corpses pleases me;
They keep such perfect chastity.
O Dr Williams, you were right
To shove the lovers out of sight;
Now they can wander half the night
Through coffee house and street and park
And fidget in the dripping dark,
While we play Mozart and applaud
The angel with the flaming sword!
King Calvin in his grave will smile
To know we know that man is vile;
But Robert Burns, that sad old rip
From whom I got my Fellowship
Will grunt upon his rain-washed stone
Above the empty Octagon,

And say—'O that I had the strength
To slip yon lassie half a length!
Apollo! Venus! Bless my ballocks!
Where are the games, the hugs, the frolics?
Are all you bastards melancholics?
Have you forgotten that your city
Was founded well in bastardry
And half your elders (God be thankit)
Were born the wrong side of the blanket?
You scholars, throw away your books
And learn your songs from lasses' looks
As I did once—' Ah, well; it's grim;
But I will have to censor him.
He liked to call a spade a spade
And toss among the glum and staid
A poem like a hand grenade—
And I remember clearly how
(Truth is the only poet's vow)
When my spare tyre was half this size,
With drumming veins and bloodshot eyes
I blundered through the rain and sleet
To dip my wick in Castle Street,
Not on the footpath—no, in a flat,
With a sofa where I often sat,
Smoked, drank, cursed, in the company
Of a female student who unwisely
Did not mind but would pull the curtain
Over the window—And did a certain
Act occur? It did. It did.
As Byron wrote of Sennacherib—
'The Assyrian came down like a wolf on the fold
And his cohorts were gleaming in purple and gold'—
But now, at nearly forty-two,
An inmate of the social zoo,
Married, baptized, well heeled, well shod,
Almost on speaking terms with God,
I intend to save my moral bacon
By fencing the young from fornication!
Ah, Dr Williams, I agree
We need more walls at the Varsity;
The students who go double-flatting
With their she-catting and tom-catting
Won't ever get a pass in Latin;
The moral mainstay of the nation
Is careful, private masturbation;

A vaseline jar or a candle
Will drive away the stink of scandal!
The Golden Age will come again—
Those tall asthenic bird-like men
With spectacles and lecture notes,
Those girls with wool around their throats
Studying till their eyes are yellow
A new corrupt text of *Othello*,
Vaguely agnostic, rationalist,
A green banana in each fist
To signify the purity
Of educational ecstasy—
And, if they marry, they will live
By the Clinical Imperative:
A car, a fridge, a radiogram,
A clean well-fitted diaphragm,
Two-and-a-half children per
Family; to keep out thunder
Insurance policies for each;
A sad glad fortnight at the beach
Each year, when Mum and Dad will bitch
From some old half-forgotten itch—
Turn on the lights!—or else the gas!
If I kneel down like a stone at Mass
And wake my good wife with bad dreams,
And scribble verse on sordid themes,
At least I know man was not made
On the style of a slot-machine arcade—
Almost, it seems, the other day,
When Francis threw his coat away
And stood under the palace light
Naked in the Bishop's sight
To marry Lady Poverty
In folly and virginity,
The angels laughed—do they then weep
Tears of blood if two should sleep
Together and keep the cradle warm?
Each night of earth, though the wind storm,
Black land behind, white sea in front,
Leander swims the Hellespont;
To Hero's bed he enters cold;
And he will drown; and she grow old—
But what they tell each other there
You'll not find in a book anywhere.

1967

a death song for mr mouldybroke (1968)

a death song for mr mouldybroke

i don't want to die mr mouldybroke
do you call it unpatriotic?
i don't want to die mr mouldybroke
is it you or me that's neurotic?

when the fire bombs fell on dresden
it was all right by the yanks
20,000 ft up they couldn't hear
kids and women howling in the boiling water tanks

it didn't bring back the springtime
it didn't bring back the jews
i'm a funny person mr mouldybroke
the smell of people cooking gives me the blues

when the death bomb fell on nagasaki
some of the people were going to mass
it didn't stop them from having their skins
peeled off like stockings by the big bright flash

i'm a funny man mr mouldybroke
i never learnt to think like a well fed well paid MP
a white baby fried or a yellow baby fried
they both look like fried baby to me

one day at bellamys mr mouldybroke
when you're mopping up a drop of gin
you just might get some napalm in your hair
so that your face runs down all over your chin

if it happens that way mr mouldybroke
don't ever be sad about it
because you tell us jellied petrol is a conventional weapon
and no sane man could be silly enough to doubt it

i'm a funny man mr mouldybroke
i'm tired of hearing all about the reds
it'll be too late mr mouldybroke
when the booze has polished out the inside of your head

i'd like you just to get the point mr mouldybroke
before you & me & malcolm muggeridge are equally dead
frying 50 kids a day to keep the reds away
is a bloody sight worse than being red

1967

from *The Flowering Cross* (1969)

Tangi

(to my wife)

You had tied green leaves around your head;
I laced a green branch in my lapel.
On the concrete path to the meeting house
It was the women who cried out,

Calling and replying, the voice of those
Who have accepted death. And inside the door
(A thing unacceptable to the world we inhabit, in which
No one is allowed to speak of death)

The dead man was conqueror!
I saw him lying in the open boat
Of his own coffin, with shut eyes, winged moustache;
Though his widow was weeping, he was not,

And I knew for the first time the meaning of
The yellow woven tukutuku panels,
The shark's tooth, the flounder, the tears of the albatross,
Understandable only when death is accepted

As the centre of life—The opening of a million doors!
The rush of canoes that carry through breaking waves
The dead and the living!—I was glad to be
Participant. I washed my hands before eating.

1967

from *The Rock Woman: Selected Poems* (1969)

The Rock Woman

Here the south sea washes
Kelpbed and margin of the drumhard sand.
Its grey surf-pillars thundering

Concede no altar, no denial
But an obscure torment
At the mind's edge trembling, about to be.

Continually, as a boy, I came to this
Rock ledge above the sinuous wave
Where dogs and gulls left excrement,
As if the sea-split ground could set at ease
The wish to be no longer man
That wrenched me then, that overstrides me now.

A rock carved like a woman,
Pain's torso, guardian of the place,
Told raining beads. I did not know
What grief her look wrung dry,
In what blind rooms and tombs
I and my fellows would walk heavily.

Magdalen of the rock
Unvirgin pray for us.
In the wave's throb our agonies awake
Rise to your true-all-suffering kiss.
In hewn rock of prayer
You ask for us the death hour's peace.

1955–68

Seven Year Old Poet

(after Rimbaud)

The mother, shutting the schoolbook, walked off blind
And well content, not seeing the hatred of work behind
The child's bumpy forehead, and under the blue eyes
An enemy self not built to fraternize.

Obedient he'd drudge all day; a quite
Intelligent boy; but somehow the sour bite
Of hypocrisy showed in his habits. Passing along
Mildewed passages, he'd stick out his tongue
And clench both fists in his groin, watching the spark
Of tiny specks that floated in the dark
Under his eyelids.
If a door on the evening air

Was open, you'd see him gasp, half up the stair,
Like a drying frog, under the gulf of day
That hung from the roofs. He'd hide himself away
In summer, clubbed flat, torpid, in the dell
Of a latrine, peacefully drinking the smell,
And it was cool there.
                                        Sometimes when winter moonlight
Had washed the bushes, and antiseptic night
Drove out the daytime odours, he'd lie at the foot
Of a wall behind the house, like a cabbage root
Half underground, rubbing his eyes in order
To see visions, and hear each scabbed leaf shudder.
Quite tragic! His companions were those bent
Children whose clothes have a smell of excrement,
Old-fashioned, black-earth-knuckled, sometimes toothless,
Talking together in idiot gentleness.

And if, catching him out in some foul act
Of pity, his worrying Mother grubbed round the fact
For evidence, out of sick love he'd raise
A screen, and she'd believe it—that blue-eyed liar's gaze!

The seven-year-old would make up yarns inside
His own head, of the wastes where Freedom glows like a bride:
Savannahs, great trees, suns and shores—He'd rush
To coloured magazines, and stare and blush
At Spanish and Italian girls.
                                                From time to time a wild
Tomboy, the next-door family's dragged-up child
Brown-eyed and skittish, would jump on his back from behind—
Just eight years old—tossing her plaits; and blind
As a weasel in a burrow, he'd use his teeth
To bite her bare arse from underneath
(She never wore pants)—then, bruised by her heels and her claws,
He'd mooch to his room with the taste of her flesh in his jaws.

Sundays in winter, hair flattened with brilliantine,
At the pedestal table, reading a salad-green-
Edged-Bible—he hated it. In the alcove at night
Millstone dreams would grind him, till day's light
Drying the sweats of terror, pink as a dove,
Came back to the gable.
                                        God he did not love,
But men, men he saw at sunset, dark
From the sun's glare, strolling in smocks to the park

Where the town criers would make the crowd come
To grizzle or laugh at their words, by the thrice-heard roll of a drum.
—He dreamt of the grassy field, where light in waves
Rose up, with a smell like bread, from the groined caves
Waist-high, a place for love!
                                        And more than all else
He liked what is dark: as when, shut from the bells
In the barn of his room—not minding the icy damp
Of the blue walls, he would read of a rebel camp
Among drowned forests, leaden skies, great flowers
Of flesh in starry woods, Andean towers,
Giddiness, flight—while the street chattered below—
Face down, his blue eyes flickering to and fro,
He would live the novel—alone, stretched out on the pale
Coarse linen that caught the wind, a ship in full sail!

1964

On Reading Yevtushenko

When the mine exploded at Kaitangata
Trucks flew out as if from the barrel of a gun,
Trucks and truckers, bodies of men,
Or so my father told me;
                                        and far down
In those dark passages they heard faintly
The waves of the sea hammer
Above their heads.
                              My father's hands are corded
With swollen veins, but my hands are thinner
And my thoughts are cold, Zhenya Yevtushenko;
They are covered with black dust.
                                              Reading you
I remember our own strangled Revolution:
1935. The body of our Adam was dismembered
By statisticians.
                          I would like to meet you
Quietly in a café, where hoboes and freckled girls
Drink, talk; not to pump you; only to revalue in your company
Explosions, waves of the sea.

1962

The Waves

1

Accepted here, here only,
For what one is, not the chalk mask,
Gentility of a robot or a clown,
But the sad mandrake torn
From earth, getting no likely truce on earth,
The brat of sighs, less wise than the afterbirth,
The one who should have not perhaps been born.

The wave ignores, consoles, flowing and ebbing
Without reflection. Sand or oven ash
Trickling from the roots of matted swordgrass
Count thirty-seven years between
The sweet first spout of milk and this dried-up
Poem with no breasts, my concubine.

The wave bangs in channels of gnarled stone.

2

The island like an old cleft skull
With tussock and bone needles on its forehead
Lives in the world before the settlers came
With gun and almanac.
                                        One half-mad
Solitary six-foot fisherman
Blasted a passage out with gelignite
Between the shore and the island templebone
To let his boat come in, changing the drift
Of water from the bay.
                                        There are veins of gold
In the reef below the sand.
                                        I heard
Often, when young, the dialogue
Of wave with wave contending in that gullet
Where now the mussel-pickers go
Safely because the tide is low:
The strangled weight of sex and intellect
Contending and rejected in the cave
Where under weed gates the white octopus
Haunter and waker of the coast
In storms of genesis contains his power.

3

The sound of the sea would enter
That book-lined upper room,
Penetrating the convict dream
Of wordy love, as ropes of semen
Hang useless in the man's groin,
Or the bluebottle husk on the pane
Judged by the spider.

The slow language of the waves
Gave hope of truth to come,
Wideness, a dark meeting
With a woman with a body like the moon,
The mouths of water speaking
Putting aside the barren peace
Of those who are naked only in their graves.

4

At high tide I the burning
Mandrake coffinless stood
And saw the moon stride over
The belly of the flood
Against the tide's turning,
The horned and processional
Goddess of sexual pain
Who kills the mandrake I.
Though every stone and shell
Blazed in the superhuman
Arrows of light that fell
From the double axe and skull,
Lest I should be turned to rock
Or as a serpent glide
Or howl in a wolf's hide,
I called aloud for one
Living and breathing woman
To stand between and cover
My body with her own,
But there was none alive
Between the sea and the rock,
And my own lass who lay
At peace in her deft room,
Being curbed by gentility
Would never rise and run
Down over the black dune

With her grass-green skirt at her knee
To grip the burning ghost,
To lie with the naked man.
That huntress in the sky
Strode on, strode on,
The tide swung back, and I
Under the shade of a green bank stood
With poison crystals whirling in my blood
From the arrow in the breastbone.

5

How to distinguish from the flux of fire,
Salt tides and air, some ruler
Other than octopus, man-killing moon
Or our own twist of thought, breeds pain.
Wings of the albatross whose shadow
Lies on the seas at noon

I take as the type of a spirit bent
By abstract solitude,
Accepting all. The waves do not debase
Or drown what shares their fluid motion,
Yet hard for human blood

Is the habit of relinquishment,
Abandoning of Isaac to the knife
That tortured Abraham. Come now;
Poems are trash, the flesh I love will die,
Desire is bafflement,
But one may say that father Noah kept
Watch while the wild beasts slept,

Not knowing even if land would rise
Out of the barren waves.
That ark I keep, that watch on the edge of sleep,
While the dark water heaves.

1963

The Jerusalem period

By the beginning of 1970 Baxter's Jerusalem commune was well under way. His intention was to form a community structured around key 'spiritual aspects of Maori communal life', to recover values New Zealand's Pakeha urban society had lost. He first recorded aspects of his philosophy of communality in *Jerusalem Sonnets: Poems for Colin Durning* (1970). The thirty-nine sonnets—which may as readily be understood as a long poem in thirty-nine stanzas—were sent, during the first phase of the Jerusalem commune, with letters written to Durning, Baxter's friend and confidant. Appropriately, they form an extended verse epistle. Their loose, unrhymed couplets, reflecting Lawrence Durrell's influence, express friendship, discuss everyday life, and meditate on God. There are hints of a restless quest for meaning in references to journeys, but Baxter also reflects on the ubiquitous 'gap': that place of stillness where the mind is silenced and God is experienced. Behind their deceptive simplicity the poems display a remarkable unity of voice, theme, and setting. With humour and piety, in tones both personal and universal, Baxter's sonnets create that 'tension of belief' that, he once stated, 'gives the poem its edge'.

Jerusalem Daybook (1971) is the first of Baxter's volumes to combine verse with prose. It expresses Baxter's personal perspective on the practice and philosophy of communalism as it relates to the initial phase of his Jerusalem commune. In practice, the commune lacked order: Baxter could not regulate numbers or behaviour; the media sensationalised his activities; and the locals became increasingly uneasy. Problems compounded because he was often away—in Dunedin visiting his dying father; on speaking tours; and on 8 February 1971 protesting with young Maori radicals at Waitangi.

The commune's first phase ended in September 1971, and Baxter returned to Wellington, where he lived for a time in squats and wrote some of his most scathing poetry (see '*Truth* Song', p. 264). But in February 1972 the Jerusalem land-owners permitted him to return with a smaller, more cohesive, group. His last collection, *Autumn Testament* (1972), dates from this period. Published shortly after his death in 1972, it comprises three poetic and two prose sequences. Two short poems bracket the titlepiece. The first of these, 'He Waiata mo te Kare', is Baxter's final verse letter to his wife; the second, 'Te Whiori o te Kuri'—'the tail of the dog/That wags at the end of my book'—is a sequence of seven sonnets. The forty-eight sonnets of the title poem document the life of the Jerusalem community and appear to anticipate Baxter's own end. But his characteristic imagery of death, often a disturbing feature of his poetry, now suggests peace and acceptance.

At around the same time as Baxter was seeing *Autumn Testament* through to publication, he was working on another selection, *Runes*, for Oxford University Press. He may have written, in 1968, 'The book is shut and I have gone/In rags to serve the Virgin's Son' (see p. 244), but Baxter continued to value his earlier writing. *Runes* is therefore a testament of a different sort: in its broad selection from the poetry of the preceding two decades there lies a statement about the value of art.

By August 1972 Baxter was drained, physically and emotionally. He sought refuge in a small commune in Auckland. On 22 October he died of a coronary thrombosis.

A memorable literary and spiritual commemoration ensued. His family escorted his body back to Jerusalem where, in a rare honour for a Pakeha, he received a full Maori tangi and was buried on tribal land. The ceremony and burial were attended by hundreds of people from the many walks of life with which Baxter's intersected. The grave is marked by a boulder inscribed:

HEMI
JAMES KEIR BAXTER
I WHANAU 1926
I MATE 1972

from *Jerusalem Sonnets: Poems for Colin Durning* (1970)

Poem for Colin—1

The small grey cloudy louse that nests in my beard
Is not, as some have called it, 'a pearl of God'—

No, it is a fiery tormentor
Waking me at two a.m.

Or thereabouts, when the lights are still on
In the houses in the pa, to go across thick grass

Wet with rain, feet cold, to kneel
For an hour or two in front of the red flickering

Tabernacle light—what He sees inside
My meandering mind I can only guess—

A madman, a nobody, a raconteur
Whom He can joke with—'Lord,' I ask Him,

'Do You or don't You expect me to put up with lice?'
His silent laugh still shakes the hills at dawn.

Poem for Colin—2

The bees that have been hiving above the church porch
Are some of them killed by the rain—

I see their dark bodies on the step
As I go in—but later on I hear

Plenty of them singing with what seems a virile joy
In the apple tree whose reddish blossoms fall

At the centre of the paddock—there's an old springcart,
Or at least two wheels and the shafts, upended

Below the tree—Elijah's chariot it could be, Colin,
Because my mind takes fire a little there

Thinking of the woman who is like a tree
Whom I need not name—clumsily gripping my beads,

While the bees drum overhead and the bouncing calves look at
A leather-jacketed madman set on fire by the wind.

Poem for Colin—10

Dark night—or rather, only the stars
Somebody called 'those watchfires in the sky'—

Too cold for me the thoughts of God—I crossed
The paddock on another errand,

And the cows were slow to move outside the gate
Where they sleep at night—nevertheless I came

As it were by accident into the church
And knelt again in front of the tabernacle,

His fortress—man, His thoughts are not cold!
I dare not say what fire burned then, burns now

Under my breastbone—but He came back with me
To my own house, and let this madman eat,

And shared my stupid prayer, and carried me up
As the mother eagle lifts her fluttering young with her wings.

Poem for Colin—11

One writes telling me I am her guiding light
And my poems her bible—on this cold morning

After mass I smoke one cigarette
And hear a magpie chatter in the paddock,

The image of Hatana—he bashes at the windows
In idiot spite, shouting—'Pakeha! You can be

'The country's leading poet'—at the church I murmured, 'Tena koe',
To the oldest woman and she replied, 'Tena koe'—

Yet the red book is shut from which I should learn Maori
And these daft English words meander on,

How dark a light! Hatana, you have gripped me
Again by the balls; you sift and riddle my mind

On the rack of the middle world, and from my grave at length
A muddy spring of poems will gush out.

Poem for Colin—14

I had lain down for sleep, man, when He called me
To go across the wet paddock

And burgle the dark church—you see, Colin, the nuns
Bolt the side door and I unbolt it

Like a timid thief—red light, moonlight
Mix together; steps from nowhere

Thud in the porch; a bee wakes up and buzzes;
The whole empty pa and the Maori dead

Are present—there I lie down cruciform
On the cold linoleum, a violator

Of God's decorum—and what has He to tell me?
'More stupid than a stone, what do you know

'Of love? Can you carry the weight of my Passion,
You old crab farmer?' I go back home in peace.

Poem for Colin—15

To give away cigarettes,
That's the hard one, Colin!

To live on rolled oats, raisins,
Potatoes, milk, raw cabbage,

It's even a pleasure—but I confess I need a smoke
More than I need a woman!

It's more like breathing—ever since I broached the guests' tobacco
(Along with the guests) I've been a doomed man!

Perhaps earlier yet—at six years old,
When I kept what I stole from my father in a rusty tin

Under the house, mixed with old rotted
Cabbage tree fibres—was it original virtue

Or original sin? I roll it now, and draw deep
The herb of darkness, preferring Nirvana to Heaven.

Poem for Colin—18

Yesterday I planted garlic,
Today, sunflowers—'the non-essentials first'

Is a good motto—but these I planted in honour of
The Archangel Michael and my earthly friend,

Illingworth, Michael also, who gave me the seeds—
And they will turn their wild pure golden discs

Outside my bedroom, following Te Ra
Who carries fire for us in His terrible wings

(Heresy, man!)—and if He wanted only
For me to live and die in this old cottage,

It would be enough, for the angels who keep
The very stars in place resemble most

These green brides of the sun, hopelessly in love with
Their Master and Maker, drunkards of the sky.

Poem for Colin—19

At the centre of my mind the stone lies
And the bullock bleeds there—be it so,

Be it so, be it so,
Now and—you know, Colin,

What I mean when I say, 'Te Kare'—my life winds out
And winds back to that hard stone,

The rock of unknowing—this old bullock will kick
Once or twice, but offers himself again

To the knife of love—Te Kare, wave of the sea
On which the Dove moved before the world began,

For you I weep, for you I become a child,
Since only children have power to grip the lightning

Unharmed—by doing nothing I will do
What you desire, and bring you one day to the earthly garden.

Poem for Colin—23

First I strip the sods off; then I shake them
To get the earth loose, and carry them

A few yards to make a wall that might
Shelter some beans—Sister Aquinas in her

Dark blue dress hoeing beside the cowshed
Tells me—'The couch grass seems to grow the more,

'The more you cultivate'—I lay the long white roots
Inside a broken tank for the sun to kill

By slow roasting; and begin to spade the earth,
Diagonally of course—this man has to make a game

Even out of digging; my pants and shirt
From Father Te Awhitu; my boots from the Vincent de Paul

Society—when the wind flutters round my chest
It seems to say, 'Now, now, don't be proud that you are poor!'

Poem for Colin—24

The kids here don't shout out, 'Jesus!'
Or, 'Hullo, Moses!' as they did in Auckland

When they saw my hair—these ones are too polite—
They call me Mr Baxter when they bring the milk;

I almost wish they didn't; but Sister has them well trained—
And soon she wants me to give them a talk about drugs;

What should I say?—'Children, your mothers and your fathers
Get stoned on grog; in Auckland they get stoned on pot;

'It does no harm at all, as far as I know
From smoking it; but the big firms are unloading

'Pep pills for slimming, tablets for sleeping,
On the unlucky world—those ones can drive you mad—

'Money and prestige are worse drugs than morphine'—
That way I'd hit the target; but I doubt if the nuns would think it wise.

Poem for Colin—25

The brown river, te taniwha, flows on
Between his banks—he could even be on my side,

I suspect, if there is a side—there are still notches worn
In the cliffs downstream where they used to shove

The big canoes up; and just last week some men
Floated a ridge-pole down from an old pa

For the museum—he can also be
A brutal lover; they say he sucked under

A young girl once, and the place at the river-bend is named
After her tears—I accept that—I wait for

The taniwha in the heart to rise—when will that happen?
Is He dead or alive? A car goes by on the road

With an enormous slogan advertising
Rides for tourists on the jetboat at Pipiriki.

Poem for Colin—27

Three dark buds for the Trinity
On one twig I found in the lining of my coat

Forgotten since I broke them from the tree
That grows opposite the R.S.A. building

At the top of Vulcan Lane—there I would lay down my parka
On the grass and meditate, cross-legged; there was a girl

Who sat beside me there;
She would hold a blue flower at the centre of the bullring

While the twigs on the tree became black
And then slowly green again—she was young—if I had said,

'Have my coat; have my money'—
She would have gone away; but because I gave her nothing

She came again and again to share that nothing
Like a bird that nests in the open hand.

Poem for Colin—29

Our Lady shifted the demons; no need to talk about it;
It is her habit, lucid, warm,

Miraculous—but if you are consulted
One day, Colin, about my epitaph,

I suggest these words—'He was too much troubled
By his own absurdity'—though I'd prefer—'Hemi'—

And nothing else—today my new job
Is to disentangle the roots of the fourteen small

Green cabbage plants Sister Aquinas gave me
Wrapped in damp paper—one good use, man,

For the written word!—and put them in carefully
Where the beautiful loose earth is that crumbles to the blows

Of the grubber, and later give them a little water
When the sun cannot burn their delicate leaves.

Poem for Colin—30

If Ngati-Hiruharama turns out to be no more than
A child's dream in the night—well then,

I have a garden, a bed to lie on,
And various company—some clattering pigeons roost

At my back door, and when I meditate in the paddock
Under the apple tree two healthy dung-smeared pigs

Strike up a conversation, imagining, I think,
I am their benefactor—that should be quite enough

To keep the bowels moving and the mind thankful;
Yet when the sun rises my delusion hears him shout

Above the river fog—'This is the hill fort
Of our God; it is called Hiruharama!

'The goat and the opossum will find a home
Among the rocks, and the river of joy will flow from it!'

Poem for Colin—32

Tormenting myself with a moral inventory
While I cut the sods and lay them straight

To make a wall to shelter beans,
I think of my two illegitimate children

And how they will judge me when they come of age;
Unfit, I grant it—yet what can a man do

Who is trying to make a wall to shelter beans
But cut the sods and lay them straight;

And what can a man do who is saddled with a woman
But love her whatever way he can

Till his guts drop out? 'Now you're a Lutheran,' mutters
The voice at my earhole; but I laugh,

Remembering the women used no rubber plugs or pills
Because they wanted to have my children.

Poem for Colin—34

I read it in the Maori primer,
'Ka timata te pupuhi o te hau'—

The wind began blowing; it blew for a century
Levelling by the musket and the law

Ten thousand meeting houses—there are two of them in the pa,
Neither one used; the mice and the spiders meet there;

And the tapu mound where the heads of chiefs were burned
Will serve perhaps one day for a golf course—yet

Their children fear te taipo,
The bush demon; on that account

They keep the lights burning all night outside their houses—
What can this pakeha fog-eater do?

Nothing; nothing! Tribe of the wind,
You can have my flesh for kai, my blood to drink.

Poem for Colin—35

The trap I am setting to catch a tribe
Is all but furnished—on Friday Father Condon

Will (if he remembers) bring from Ohakune
The crucifix my friend Milton carved

With its garments made of wood shavings
And a faceless face, Maori or pakeha either

As the light catches it; also the workman Buddha
Hoani lent me, and the Hindu image of Mara

Trix handed on so as to be wholly poor—
What else, Colin? They say it is best

To break a rotten egg in the creek
To get eels—I think I am that egg

And Te Ariki must crack me open
If the fish are to be drawn in at all.

Poem for Colin—36

Brother Ass, Brother Ass, you are full of fancies,
You want this and that—a woman, a thistle,

A poem, a coffeebreak, a white bed, no crabs;
And now you complain of the weight of the Rider

Who will set you free to gallop in the light of the sun!
Ah well, kick Him off then, and see how you go

Lame-footed in the brambles; your disconsolate bray
Is ugly in my ears—long ago, long ago,

The battle was fought and the issue decided
As to who would be King—go on, little donkey

Saddled and bridled by the Master of the world,
Be glad you can distinguish not an inch of the track,

That the stones are sharp, that your hide can itch,
That His true weight is heavy on your back.

Poem for Colin—37

Colin, you can tell my words are crippled now;
The bright coat of art He has taken away from me

And like the snail I crushed at the church door
My song is my stupidity;

The words of a homely man I cannot speak,
Home and bed He has taken away from me;

Like an old horse turned to grass I lift my head
Biting at the blossoms of the thorn tree;

Prayer of priest or nun I cannot use,
The songs of His house He has taken away from me;

As blind men meet and touch each other's faces
So He is kind to my infirmity;

As the cross is lifted and the day goes dark
Rule over myself He has taken away from me.

Poem for Colin—38

'I am dying now because I do not die'—
The song of the thief who hangs upon the tree;

'The house where I was born had seven windows
But its door is closed to me;

Whether I robbed or not I have forgotten,
My death has taken hold of me;

There was a woman once who gave me a cup of wine
And her eyes were full of mercy;

There is not even judgement any more
In the place where I have to be;

I cannot turn my head to find out
Who hangs beside me on the other tree;

Let the woman who is standing down below
Say a prayer for him and me.'

Poem for Colin—39

In Auckland it was the twelve days' garland,
Feast with friends and shouting in the streets;

Now it is the apex and the clean flint knife—
Colin, if you meet him, give my love

To Patric Carey, and if you have the time
Once or twice go out to Brighton

To visit my parents—easy to hang
Imperatives on a good friend from a distance,

But I say, 'If'—one thing, how can the image come
At all to the centre where the mind is silent

Without being false? I had hoped for fifty sonnets,
But here are thirty-nine, my gift to you, Colin,

From Hiruharama,
From Hemi te tutua.

1969

from *The Junkies and the Fuzz* (1970)

Ballad of the Junkies and the Fuzz

(for Hoani)

1

Oh star I do not believe in, speak to me!
Star of the harbour night, wave after wave rising and falling
Under the bows of the Devonport ferry that carries a cargo of
people home to their well-lit prisons,
Boys half lushed and girls in jeans or party dresses, older men
looking vacantly at the black waves, women who do not show
their souls in their eyes—
Star I do not believe in, shining also
In the rickety streets of Grafton where many gather

In a single house, sharing the kai, sharing the pain, sharing the
drug perhaps, sharing the paranoia;
Bearded, barefoot or sandalled, coming out crippled from the bin
or the clink.
(The windows painted black; yet the black paint was scraped off
again)—
In order that the junkie rock may crack and flow with water
And the rainbow of aroha shine on each one's face
Because love is in the look, stronger than lush, and truth is in the
mouth, better than kai—
Rain down your light, oh star of paradise!

3

Baron Saturday, baron of the cemeteries, for whom they cut the
black rooster's throat, whose altar is always a grave at
the crossroads,
You have shifted, man, out of thin Haiti. Now you grow fat on the
fears of five thousand junkies in Auckland.

How strange, man, to see those spruce and angry ghosts
Suddenly materialize
In an old house in the middle of the morning
When several are eating soup, one is playing the guitar, two are
talking about nasturtium leaves,
And the others are snoring after an all-night party—
Suddenly you see them in the centre of the room,
The servants of the Zombie King—
Skorbul the football player with his brown moustache,
Krubble, who has a habit of crushing fingers in doors,
Drooble, who is glad to bang girls' heads on walls,
And one or two other clean-cut eager beagles
Young poltergeists squaring their shoulders, imitating the TV hero,
hoping for a punch-up—
The fuzz are in the house.

'Would you like a coffee, Mr Skorbul?'
'Naow.'
'A cup of soup then?'
'Naow. What y' bin doing round here?'

Star I do not believe in, let your tendrils of light grow
And out of them it may be we can make a vine ladder
To climb back to where God is, that high blue room in the sky.

5

It was necessary of course to invent the fuzz
To fence off the area of civilized coma
From the forces of revolt and lamentation
That rise around it, male and female
Ikons weeping tears of blood.

10

Joanna is lying very fast asleep on a mattress in the smallest room,
A blanket over her naked body, one candle at her feet, the other burning down on the toe of an old boot that smoulders close to her face,
Her face freckled and white, her breathing very shallow on account of the ten Turinol her boyfriend gave her to balance the O.D. on starters.
A black filmy scarf flutters at the window, the wall at her head is a funeral black with one gold crucifix.
Tonight she will live or else die, the junkie princess lying on her chosen bed, two weeks out of the bin,
An inch away from death. To call a doctor would be to call the fuzz
To bust the house wide open. Her boyfriend and another woman
Are shooting junk in the front room, looking for a vein on the arm, cleaning the needle, while the music wails on gently from the player—cool, man, cool—
Their untroubled faces look inward to the dark Nirvana. The candle melts on the boot. The wind flutters the black scarf. Her face is white. Her breathing is very shallow. Either she will die or live.

11

The wing of the black angel is lying over
Us. Leaves had fallen when I met Vanessa
By the sportsground at Oakley. Brother Buddha,
I think love is being eaten by tigers
Inside or outside ourselves. That I accept.
It is time now to become *bodhisattva*.
Let us go together and knock on the doors of a million graves,
Walking on thorns and stones, telling the dead men—
Yourself, myself, Skorbul, Krubble,
And even that sad miscarriage Drooble—
That us each are persons and capable of love.

1969

from Jerusalem Daybook (1971)

Editor's note: poem titles given in square brackets do not appear in the original edition.

People warn me that the community is likely to bust up. Nga mokai may use drugs. They may commit thefts. They may let the dogs worry sheep. They may fall out with the local Maori people who have let us have the use of their land and houses. They may be unable to pay the food bills and the electricity bills.

The ones who warn me want me to be anxious. They want me to 'take things in hand', get a set of rules, turf out the least capable or the least co-operative. It is their own anxiety that speaks. They want me to share this anxiety, to be worried along with them.

But where does worry end? When I spent my life worrying, I also spent it drinking grog, to alleviate the anxiety. In the long run all I did was to make a hole in my head.

I live in an uncontrollable universe which is, in a hidden fashion, under the control of God. If he wants the community to survive, then it will survive; if not, then it won't. The canoe takes water on board every day of the week. Each time I think it will fill up or capsize. But it doesn't.

Certainly one has to bail. But it has not sunk yet. So rickety, so full of holes, how does it float at all? I think Te Atua is keeping it afloat. All he requires of me is my availability, my limited human response to whatever happens. He doesn't require my anxiety. And I have noticed that anxiety impairs one's judgment.

The most anxious critics see me as a threat—but not just me or the Jerusalem community, the whole universe is a threat to them, with its earthquakes, storms, death, sickness, failure, evil, its succession of unpredictable, uncontrollable disasters. If I died tomorrow, their anxiety would still remain.

Plucking Geese

The goose they cooked for dinner had a thick black gravy,
The best kai we've had,—Sandy kissed my head

As she went past in the crowd at the kitchen counter,
And there was soup as well. Mrs Poutini's geese

Were plucked by five of us in the middle room this morning,
Packing the feathers into a box

For her to make pillows,—it brought to mind those early
Pictures of Mother Goose flying above the clouds,

Something done well together. I don't expect
Goose more than once a year, or ever to be

A child again, but the kindness of Te Whaea
Shone among us today. My heart was at peace,

An old man nodding his head and laughing
While the goose down stuck like wool to our coats and jerseys.

1971

Before I go inside the broken fence to the graveyard, I speak to those who are inside it—'He manuhiri au, ko taku haere e te haere o aroha.'

It is the salutation of the poor man at the gate of the pa, the one who has no credentials. This is the pa of the dead, and I think they do receive me. I kneel on the wet grass, beside the concrete tomb of the kaumatua, the Maori elder who lived in the house before us, and say prayers, both in Maori and in English, praying that the souls of the Maori dead may have light and peace, and asking them to bear with our stupidity and put the coat of their aroha over us.

'I am a stranger. My coming here is motivated by love.' The people of the pa may permit my body to be buried in this place. Then, when Te Atua raises our bodies from the dead, I will be able to look for a moment at the faces of those who were bone of my bone and soul of my soul, before entering the fire reserved for those whose love is earthly and not heavenly. At any rate, the graveyard is the place where I erect a necessary tentpole of meditation.

'Ko te aroha i Te Ariki'—'Where love is, there the Lord is.' It is so also among the dead. And we cease to fear the death of the body as we slowly recognize that to love is to die the deaths of all men along with them. Yet I am a timid man, and the three burdens he requires our souls to carry—great pain, great cold, great darkness—do quite often make me afraid. But to ask for it to be otherwise would be to ask not to be a member of the human race.

[Winter Monologue]

One has to die here on earth,
My beard has got the stink of the ground already,

The opossum thuds in the roof like a man dropping bricks,
My belly is content enough

With two cups of tea and two bits of cake
Wehe gave me today as I sat on her doorstep,

But the night comes like a hammer cracking on an anvil
And all nga mokai huddle in the big house,

Playing the guitar, lighting up the little stove,
Not finding fault—one has to die

In order to water the roots of the tree with blood,
Guts, nerves, brains—once I was a word-maker,

Now my bones are buried at Hiruharama,
But the bones talk, brother. They say—'Winter burns us like black fire!'

Ah well, soon I will go up the hill
To where the drain and the ditch and the new pipe

Are tangled in the dark—How cold it is!
The plumber has laid on running water

From the spring above the road—water, water,
That has to flow in the furrows of the garden,

That has to wash dishes, pots, old muddy clothes,
That has to be added to porridge or coffee

Before we can eat or drink—water is the sign of God,
Common, indispensable, easy to overlook—

How cold it is! Death will kill the cold
With one last stab, they say, and bring us to the sun-bright fields of Canaan,

But I must stay outside till the last of nga mokai
Straggle in—time then to soak myself in the hot springs of Heaven!

1971

Christ is my peace, my terror, my joy, my sorrow, my life, my death, but not my security. Are lovers 'security' to one another? I think not.

Who is harsher than this God of ours? Who is harder to love or be loved by? The God they imagine, and pray to very often in the churches, is a God of sugar compared to the terrible One who grips our living entrails, who drives both good and evil from our souls, as if both were his enemies, and fills us with anguish and darkness. I would not advise any man to follow him. He comes like the sandstorm out of the desert, or the avalanche on a mountain village, or tons of black water from the depths of the sea.

You think he might take away your health or your happiness or your sanity, but he will always leave you your morality. Don't count on it. Remember he told Abraham to kill his son, and made Jeremiah curse his own countrymen, and made Paul wish to be damned so that the same people might be nourished and cherished. It is possible that he drove Luther against the Church and turned Lenin into a revolutionary. He may shatter your morality as you yourself step on a snail alongside your doorstep. What is our morality to be but God himself?

He turns this man into an old coat and a broken stick. He makes him the nuns' devil and a bad smell in the noses of good churchgoing people. It is not a pleasant vocation.

If we claim to love him we have to love our own death. Blessed be God. No god we can create is like him, not even the image of him we create for our orthodox comfort, out of what he has told us about himself. May he save us from himself. I think he has already done so. He lives our life and dies our death for us and within us.

Christ is the winter sea whitened by whirlwinds. He is also the albatross floating at the centre of endless calm.

Why do I go barefoot? Why do I have long hair and a beard? Why do I wear old clothes till they become unwearable? Every time I meet people in the towns they ask me these things. It is not enough to say that appearances don't matter.

Poverty is the actual answer. All men are required by God to have a spirit of poverty. But God may touch a man here or there—no less a sinner than his fellows—and say to him—

'It is your business to be visibly poor—to do without everything you can do without—shoes, a barber, a house of your own, a fire to sit at, a desk to write at, some varieties of food and occasionally all food, the approval of your neighbours, your own certainty of being in the right but, above all, the sense of comfort. A comfortable servant might begin to serve comfort instead of serving me.'

To be poor is not to become good. Poverty is availability. It is to be that void, that nothing, on which Te Wairua Tapu moved at the beginning of the world, and still does move. I am incapable of being good—my soul is a mass of faults and contradictions—but when I know I am nothing, then through the eye of that needle God can do what he wants to do. It is when I think I am something that my life backfires on me.

The woman who said to me, when she came to Hiruharama to drag her daughter away—'You think you're the Thirteenth Apostle'—may have hit nearer the target than I thought at the time. The actual Thirteenth Apostle is Judas, the one who carried the bag. And I carry dollar notes in my top pocket to pay the community bills for food and waterpipes and electricity and old boards bought at half price from the demolition yard for renovations. It's all justifiable. The money does not belong to me. It belongs to all of us.

That's what Judas said to himself. And one day he went out and hanged himself.

There is also the matter of mental poverty. The man called James K. Baxter, who is like a dead body in the ground, swells up and gives off a stink of words. I suppose he does it for money and kudos.

It is absurd to say I am really a poor man while I keep on putting words together. Words set in order are mental possessions. Well, best for me to write my words, and then forget what I have written. Dead leaves do not clog a stream for ever. The smoke of rubbish burning can be shifted by the wind.

JD, *pp. 12–17*

[The Ikons]

Hard, heavy, slow, dark,
Or so I find them, the hands of Te Whaea

Teaching me to die. Some lightness will come later
When the heart has lost its unjust hope

For special treatment. Today I go with a bucket
Over the paddocks of young grass,

So delicate like fronds of maidenhair,
Looking for mushrooms. I find twelve of them,

Most of them little, and some eaten by maggots,
But they'll do to add to the soup. It's a long time now

Since the great ikons fell down,
God, Mary, home, sex, poetry,

Whatever one uses as a bridge
To cross the river that only has one beach,

And even one's name is a way of saying—
'This gap inside a coat'—the darkness I call God,

The darkness I call Te Whaea, how can they translate
The blue calm evening sky that a plane tunnels through

Like a little wasp, or the bucket in my hand,
Into something else? I go on looking

For mushrooms in the field, and the fist of longing
Punches my heart, until it is too dark to see.

JD, *p. 23*
1971

from *Autumn Testament* (1972)

He Waiata mo Te Kare

1

Up here at the wharepuni
That star at the kitchen window
Mentions your name to me.

Clear and bright like running water
It glitters above the rim of the range,
You in Wellington,
I at Jerusalem,

Woman, it is my wish
Our bodies should be buried in the same grave.

2

To others my love is a plaited kono
Full or empty,
With chunks of riwai,
Meat that stuck to the stones.

To you my love is a pendant
Of inanga greenstone,
Too hard to bite,
Cut from a boulder underground.

You can put it in a box
Or wear it over your heart.

One day it will grow warm,
One day it will tremble like a bed of rushes
And say to you with a man's tongue,
'Taku ngakau ki a koe!'

3

I have seen at evening
Two ducks fly down
To a pond together.

The whirring of their wings
Reminded me of you.

4

At the end of our lives
Te Atua will take pity
On the two whom he divided.

To the tribe he will give
Much talking, te pia and a loaded hangi.

To you and me he will give
A whare by the seashore
Where you can look for crabs and kina
And I can watch the waves
And from time to time see your face
With no sadness,
Te Kare o Nga Wai.

5

No rafter paintings,
No grass-stalk panels,
No Maori mass,

Christ and his Mother
Are lively Italians
Leaning forward to bless,

No taniko band on her head,
No feather cloak on his shoulder,

No stairway to heaven,
No tears of the albatross.

Here at Jerusalem
After ninety years
Of bungled opportunities.
I prefer not to invite you
Into the pakeha church.

6

Waves wash on the beaches.
They leave a mark for only a minute.
Each grey hair in my beard
Is there because of a sin,

The mirror shows me
An old tuatara,
He porangi, he tutua,
Standing in his dusty coat.

I do not think you wanted
Some other man.

I have walked barefoot from the tail of the fish to the nose
To say these words.

7

Hilltop behind hilltop,
A mile of green pungas
In the grey afternoon
Bow their heads to the slanting spears of rain.

In the middle room of the wharepuni
Kat is playing the guitar,—
'Let it be! Let it be!'

Don brings home a goat draped round his shoulders.
Tonight we'll eat roasted liver.

One day, it is possible,
Hoani and Hilary might join me here,
Tired of the merry-go-round.

E hine, the door is open,
There's a space beside me.

8

Those we knew when we were young,
None of them have stayed together,
All their marriages battered down like trees
By the winds of a terrible century.

I was a gloomy drunk.
You were a troubled woman.
Nobody would have given tuppence for our chances,
Yet our love did not turn to hate.

If you could fly this way, my bird,
One day before we both die,
I think you might find a branch to rest on.

I chose to live in a different way.

Today I cut the grass from the paths
With a new sickle,
Working till my hands were blistered.

I never wanted another wife.

9

Now I see you conquer age
As the prow of a canoe beats down
The plumes of Tangaroa.

You, straight-backed, a girl,
Your dark hair on your shoulders,
Lifting up our grandchild,

How you put them to shame,
All the flouncing girls!

Your face wears the marks of age
As a warrior his moko,
Double the beauty,
A soul like the great albatross

Who only nests in mid ocean
Under the eye of Te Ra.

You have broken the back of age.
I tremble to see it.

10

Taraiwa has sent us up a parcel of smoked eels
With skins like fine leather.
We steam them in the colander.
He tells us the heads are not for eating,

So I cut off two heads
And throw them out to Archibald,
The old tomcat. He growls as he eats
Simply because he's timid.

Earlier today I cut thistles
Under the trees in the graveyard,
And washed my hands afterwards,
Sprinkling the sickle with water.

That's the life I lead,
Simple as a stone,
And all that makes it less than good, Te Kare,
Is that you are not beside me.

1972

[Oh early in the morning]

Oh early in the morning
I wake up in Firetrap Castle
Where the rats run free and the grots are smashed
And the leaves grow thick at the window,

And first I light myself a smoke
With a mouth like old leather,
Then I put on my strides and a belt and a coat
To hold myself together,

And I go down to the Courtroom
To watch old Gabguts there
Riding with an iron saddle
On the backs of the poor,

For the fate of a boobhead is
That men do him bind
And plant him in the digger
Till he goes out of his mind,

And if you want to know more about it
Go and ask my friends
At the Duke or the George or the Bistro,
For the story never ends,

And the rich men pay the fuzz
And the fuzz arrest the poor,
And it's nothing new I'm saying to you,
It's all been said before,

And if you come by Firetrap Castle
Pay us a visit there,
But mind your head on the golden chandeliers
And watch out for the loose boards on the stairs.

1971

Note: A boobhead is a man regularly in and out of jail.

Shorts
234 7951

iggo
Modest mouse
The Ship Project.

from *Autumn Testament*

1

As I come down the hill from Toro Poutini's house
My feet are sore, being bare, on the sharp stones

And that is a suitable penance. The dust of the pa road
Is cool, though, and I can see

The axe of the moon shift down behind the trees
Very slowly. The red light from the windows

Of the church has a ghostly look, and in
This place ghosts are real. The bees are humming loudly

In moonlight in their old hive above the church door
Where I go in to kneel, and come out to make my way

Uphill past a startled horse who plunges in the paddock
Above the nunnery. Now there are one or two

Of the tribe back in the big house—What would you have me do,
King Jesus? Your games with me have turned me into a boulder.

2

Wahi Ngaro, the void from which all life comes,
Has given us these woven spider-cages

That tie together the high heads of grass,
A civilisation in each. A stick can rip the white silk,

But that is not what I will do, having learnt
With manhood mercy, if no other good,

Two thousand perhaps in the tribe of nga mokai
Scattered like seeds now in the bins and the jails

Or occupied at their various occasions
Inside the spider-cage of a common dream,

Drugs, work, money. Siân, Kat,
Don and Francie, here with me at home

In the wharepuni—One great white flower
Shakes in the wind, turning a blind head towards our verandah.

4

Wahi Ngaro, the gap from which our prayers
Fall back like the toi-toi arrows

Children shoot upwards—Wahi Ngaro,
The limitless, the silent, the black night sky

From which the church huddles like a woman
On her hillock of ground—into your wide arms

Travelling, I forget the name of God,
Yet I can hear the flies roam through the rooms

Now at midday, feel the wind that flutters
The hippie goddess picture somebody painted

On an old blind and nailed on the wall. I can see
The orange flowers withering in a milk bottle,

Taste my tobacco phlegm, touch, if I like, the great bronze Christ
Theodore put up, on the poles of a cross he cut and bound himself.

5

Wahi Ngaro, now the ego like a sentry
At the gate of the soul closes its eyelids

For a moment, as today when
A crowd of ducks rose flapping at the place

Above the rapids where I go to bathe
Naked, splashing the water on my thighs,

And later I walked barefoot over the smooth boulders,
Thinking, 'There need be no other Heaven

'Than this world'—but rain spat soon
Out of a purple cloud, and I hid under

The willow leaves and bramble, as Adam did
Once from the Father. I brought back for Francie

A sprig of wet wild mint
That should go well tomorrow with the potatoes.

6

The darkness of oneself returns
Now that the house is empty,

A sense of danger in the room half dark,
Half lighted, seen through a squarish doorway,

Sticky rings left by cups on the table,
Darkness, the flutter of a moth,

A table spread in a tomb for the dead to eat at,—
That's it, the Dead!—'Why did you pay

'A visit to Toro at night? Night is the time for the morepork,'
Wehe told me today, as we sat down to

Fried Maori bread, meat and pickle,
We who will certainly each of us one day return

To our mother the grave. The darkness of oneself
Comes from knowing nothing can be possessed.

7

To wake up with a back sore from the hard mattress
In a borrowed sleeping bag

Lent me by Anne—it was her way, I think,
Of giving at the same time a daughter's

And a mother's embrace—friend, daughter, mother—
These kids have heart enough to nourish the dead world

Like David in his bed—to wake up and see
The sun, if not the light from behind the sun,

Glittering on the leaves beside the graveyard
Where some of them cleared the bramble and placed on the bare
  slab

A jam jar full of flowers—to wake is to lift up
Again on one's shoulder this curious world

Whose secret cannot be known by any of us
Until we enter Te Whiro's kingdom.

11

At times when I walk beside the budding figtree
Or on the round stones by the river,

I meet the face of my dead father
With one or two white bristles on his chin

The safety razor missed. When he was younger
He'd hold the cut-throat with the ivory handle

And bring it with one deft stroke down his jowl,
Leaving the smooth blue skin. 'Old man,' I say,

'Long loved by me, still loved by many,
Is there a chance your son will ever join you

'In the kingdom of the summer stars?' He leaves me
Without a word, but like a touch behind him,

Greener the bulge of fruit among the figleaves,
Hotter the bright eye of the noonday sun.

12

The wish to climb a ladder to the loft
Of God dies hard in us. The angels Jacob saw

Were not himself. Bramble is what grows best
Out of this man-scarred earth, and I don't chop it back

Till the fruit have ripened. Yesterday I picked one
And it was bitter in my mouth,

And all the ladder-climbing game is rubbish
Like semen tugged away for no good purpose

Between the blanket and the bed. I heard once
A priest rehearse the cause of his vocation,

'To love God, to serve man.' The ladder-rungs did not lessen
An ounce of his damnation by loneliness,

And Satan whistles to me, 'You! You again,
Old dog! Have you come to drop more dung at Jerusalem?'

14

Soon I will go South to my nephew's wedding
To the quiet land I came from,

Where all the ancestors are underground
And my father now among them. On my mother's wall

The picture Theo Schoon once painted
Shows him as the Iron Duke

With lines around his chin and mouth
Carved by the ploughshare. So he did look

In the time when a Labour Government planted my brother
On the Hautu prison farm for five years

For walking in my father's footprint
And refusing to carry a gun. Now in my mother's house

The picture is an icon. Father, is it easier to fight
The military machine, or the maggots of one's own heart?

15

The creek has to run muddy before it can run clear!
Here in this very room I have seen it happen,

The lads and the girls in chairs, some kneeling, some standing,
Some wearing headbands, one strumming the guitar,

And Father Theodore setting down an old
Packing case covered with a blanket

For the altar of his Mass. There was no wind
To burst the house door in, no tongues of fire,

But new skin under wounds, the Church becoming human,
As if religion were not the cemetery of hope

But a flowering branch—ah well, it was some time ago,
Sly is in jail under a two-year sentence,

Manu has gone back to the ward at Porirua,
And the Church can count her losses in Pharisaic peace.

18

Father Lenin, you understood the moment
When the soul is split clean, as a man with an axe

Will split four posts from one log of dry timber,
But then your muzhiks still had souls

That smelt the holy bread upon the altar
And knew their mother's name. The mask of money

Hides too well the wound we cannot touch,
And guns are no use to a boy with a needle

Whose world is a shrinking dome of glass
A drug from Hong Kong will splinter open

With a charging elephant on a yellow packet
For riding home to deep sleep. The dollar is the point of it,

Old Father Lenin, and your bones in the Red Square
Are clothed in roubles till the Resurrection.

20

Somebody in my dream was shaking a blanket
Sending a gust of wind with dust and fleas

Over my body—and when I woke,
In the dark room I saw a wavering shape

Like a vampire in a castle in the stories
I used to read as a boy. Whether or not it came

From the graveyard forty feet away
From the house corner, fear increases the strength

Of any kehua—so I crossed over and switched on the light,
Smoked a cigarette, chewed over a few pages

Of Peter Marin, and began to write this poem,
Since a man who'll die some day should hardly fear the dead,

And the tribe need a father who is afraid only
Of ceasing to love them well.

22

To pray for an easy heart is no prayer at all
Because the heart itself is the creaking bridge

On which we cross these Himalayan gorges
From bluff to bluff. To sweat out the soul's blood

Midnight after midnight is the ministry of Jacob,
And Jacob will be healed. This body that shivers

In the foggy cold, tasting the sour fat,
Was made to hang like a sack on its thief's cross,

Counting it better than bread to say the words of Christ,
'*Eli! Eli!*' The Church will be shaken like a

Blanket in the wind, and we are the fleas that fall
To the ground for the dirt to cover. Brother thief,

You who are lodged in my ribcage, do not rail at
The only gate we have to paradise.

23

The heat moves into my bones again
Here on the edge of the veranda

Father Te Awhitu mended hour by hour
With new boards where the rain had rotted them

Pouring down from a roof that has no spouting,
And when I asked him why, replied, 'Mahi mo Te Atua'—

'Work done for God'—the day the house was ready
I lit the stove in the front room,

That cost me twenty dollars secondhand in Wanganui
And had a broken lid—wood, stove, matches,

The first flame rising—so the house became
Inhabited with the flame of non-possession

That burns now and always in the heart of the tribe,
Too simple a thing for the world to understand.

27

When I stayed those three months at Macdonald Crescent
In the house of Lazarus, three tribes were living

In each of the storeys—on the ground floor, the drunks
Who came there when the White Lodge burnt down;

Above them, the boobheads; and scattered between the first
And second storey, the students who hoped to crack

The rock of education. The drunks are my own tribe.
One Sunday, the pubs being shut, they held a parliament

In the big front room—Lofty with his walking stick,
Phil the weeper, Taffy who never spoke much,

And one or two others—in conclave they sat, like granite columns
Their necks, like Tritons their faces,

Like tree-roots their bodies. Sober as Rhadamanthus
They judged the town and found it had already been judged.

28

Both the girls are sick. I find it a drag
To cook kai for the two of them,

Ferry cups of tea, read some verse to Francie,
Or carry a blanket for Siân—that's honest enough!

I do it. It has its moments.
I meant to go and rave down at Otaki

Among the Catholic laymen, but this is more to the point
With Kat and Don away. Francie becomes active,

Sleeps in draughts, wanders through the house,
Siân lies quiet in a Buddhist cloud

Of 'flu bugs and vegetarian torpor,
A girl from the Welsh hills. The mood of family

Soon takes over, and they become my daughters,
I their Granpop. We get to know each other well.

29

I think the Lord on his axe-chopped cross
Is laughing as usual at my poems,

My solemn metaphors, my ladder-climbing dreams,
For he himself is incurably domestic,

A family man who never lifted a sword,
An only son with a difficult mother,

If you understand my thought. He has saddled me again
With the cares of a household, and no doubt

Has kept me away from Otaki
Because I'd spout nonsense, and wear my poverty

As a coat of vanity. Down at the Mass
Today, as Francie told me to, I took Communion

For her (and Siân as well) cursing gently
The Joker who won't let me shuffle my own pack.

32

Life can be a hassle. Are you free of it, Monsignor,
While you dispute the changes of the liturgy

Or polish up your golf style? At one p.m.
Either in your house or my house

The soul may plunge into pain like a child who slides
Through the grass at the lip of a mine-shaft,

Therefore don't ask me, 'What do you mean by that statement
You made to the *Weekly News*?'—or—'What precisely is

'Your relation to Sally X—?' A man is a bubble
Sticking to the edge of a mighty big drainpipe!

Let us be content to play one game of chess,
Share a coffee and biscuit, let Christ work out the deficit,—

There were eight souls, they say, with Father Noah;
Neither you nor I might have made it to the gangplank.

33

'Mother, your statue by the convent path
Has chips of plaster scattered round it

'Where rain or frost have stripped you of your mantle—'
'It doesn't matter.' 'As you know, in winter

'I often kneel there under the knife-edged moon
Praying for—' 'I hear those prayers.'

'Mother, your blue gown seems like stone,
Too rigid—' 'What they make of me

'Is never what I am.' 'Our Church looks to the young
Like a Medusa; they want to be—'

'Free, yes; Christ is the only Master.'
'They are taught to judge themselves.' 'Suffer it.'

'But sin—' 'I see no sin. My secret is
I hold the Child I was given to hold.'

36

This fine windy morning I think about
The leper lying beside the fruitstalls in Calcutta

Under the shade of the great bridge. The oil-stained bandages
Around his limbs, the flies moving slowly

In and out of his nostrils, over his eyelids;
That lion face of dark mahogany

Turned up its brow to the overlying cloud
Behind which Rahm might live, from which a few spots

Of rain aspersed the pavement. I threw some coins
Into his tin dish. The policeman, built like a Maori,

Guarding the fruitstalls in his khaki shorts,
Said, 'They're no use to him.' But the man was not quite dead.

When he was younger he should have had a gun.
There or in Karori, the sickness is, not to be wanted.

38

Last night a grey nimbus round the moon,
Today the rain comes from the west;

The leaves on all the trees look greener,
Rangimotu is burning piles of dry grass in his garden,

The flames go up to the low heaven,
And Wehe shouts to him from the door of her kitchen,

'You, come in out of the rain!' He only smiles
And goes on raking. I carry up the hill

A milk bottle full of sauce, bread and a parcel of sausages;
I plug the jug in and wait for it to boil

While the girls lie in bed. 'I like the rain.'
'I like it too. Aren't you afraid, Hemi,

'Of catching the 'flu?' 'Not exactly.
It's only that—' The rain comes down in a dense white curtain.

42

The rata blooms explode, the bow-legged tomcat
Follows me up the track, nipping at my ankle,

The clematis spreads her trumpet, the grassheads rattle
Ripely, drily, and all this

In fidelity to death. Today when Father Te Awhitu
Put on the black gown with the silver cross,

It was the same story. The hard rind of the ego
Won't ever crack except to the teeth of Te Whiro,

That thin man who'll eat the stars. I can't say
It pleases me. In the corner I can hear now

The high whining of a mason fly
Who carries the spiders home to his house

As refrigerated meat. 'You bugger off,' he tells me,
'Your Christianity won't put an end to death.'

44

This testament, a thing of rags and patches,
Will end soon. I cannot say, like Villon,

'Pray for me and for yourselves,'
For this is another century. That poor man ate his lunch

With the corpses of streetboys hanging overhead
And was part owner of some kind of brothel,

But the harps and lutes of paradise on the church wall
Were just as real as the bogs of fire,

The burghers sweated in their high fur gowns,
The slaves lay down to sleep on a straw mattress,

And most of it made sense. As if God had opened
A crack in the rock of the world to let some daylight in,

Saying, 'Be poor like Me.' Our life is the one
We make in darkness for ourselves.

45

Tomorrow I'll go down to Wellington,
Hitching, if I'm lucky, a ride down the river road

Past the karaka trees and the town houses
That turn the river into the Wanganui ditch

With shit that floats upstream below the bridges
When the tide pushes home. I'll go then

Southward among the sad green farms
Where the sheep get more freedom than their masters,

Past beaches with the plumes of toi-toi blowing
In a wind that only Maori kids on horses

Can bargain with, down, down the straight coast road
To the dream city, the old fat sow

Who smothers her children. I'll wear no diving suit
And sit cross-legged in a pub doorway.

46

After writing for an hour in the presbytery
I visit the church, that dark loft of God,

And make my way uphill. The grass is soaking my trousers,
The night dark, the rain falling out of the night,

And the old fears walk side by side with me,
Either the heavy thump of an apple

Hitting the ground, or the creaking of the trees,
Or the presence of two graveyards,

The new one at the house, the old one on the hill
That I have never entered. Heaven is light

And Hell is darkness, so the Christmen say,
But this dark is the belly of the whale

In which I, Jonah, have to make my journey
Till the fear has gone. Fear is the only enemy.

47

On the scrim of the walls the tribe have written up—
'You're all freaks'—'Men only'—

'Humpers Unite'—'Blessed are the peacemakers'—
'The slowest beasts are strongest and live the longest'—

'This is the tumour on Jo's brain'—
'Fuck War'—'The Mighty Merkin'—

'Love is like nothing else but love'—
'A simple, goodly person called Mumma lived here'—

The chorus of their chaos becomes a possible Christ
When the light behind the face begins to shine,

Who wear no shoes in the street because
Rain was invented to kiss the feet of the poor.

I go south tomorrow with the river
And leave no lock on my door.

48

The spider crouching on the ledge above the sink
Resembles the tantric goddess,

At least as the Stone Age people saw her
And carved her on their dolmens. Therefore I don't kill her,

Though indeed there is a simpler reason,
Because she is small. Kehua, vampire, eight-eyed watcher

At the gate of the dead, little Arachne, I love you,
Though you hang your cobwebs up like dirty silk in the hall

And scuttle under the mattress. Remember I spared your children
In their cage of white cloth you made as an aerial castle,

And you yourself, today, on the window ledge.
Fear is the only enemy. Therefore when I die,

And you wait for my soul, you hefty as a king crab
At the door of the underworld, let me pass in peace.

1972

from *Te Whiori o te Kuri*

1

Two trucks pass me in a cloud of dust
As I come up the road from the river,

So I put the bathing towel over my mouth
And breathe damp cloth. Taraiwa on the old bridge

Is cutting the iron struts with a blow torch,
But he tells me—'Kua mutu'—'The oxygen is finished.'

I climb the long track to the wharepuni,
Meditating on the words of Thomas Merton—

'At the end of life God presses down a seal
On the wax of the soul. If the wax is warm

'It receives the mark; if not, it is crushed to powder'—
So be it. My own heart may yet be my coffin.

Up here they give me a cup of crushed apple pulp
To drink. In autumn the kai falls from the trees.

2

The dark light shines from the graves of the saints,
By which I mean the humble ones

Buried beside our house and under the bramble
That hides the fallen pas where sheep are grazing

And leave their clots of wool. The dark light shines
At the heart of the tangi where a tent has been put up

To hold the coffin, and a widow with a
Three-day-sleepless face is waiting for the

Resurrection. I remember
When the church was shut at Ngaruawahia,

Kneeling instead in front of the stone statue
Of Te Whaea, darkened by rain, eroded by moss,

Under an apple tree. The dark light shines
Wherever the humble have opened a door for it.

6

'Te whiori o te kuri'—this is the tail of the dog
That wags at the end of my book;

After a dispute with one dear Maori friend
I walk all night on the road to Raetihi,

Thinking, 'Twenty-four miles will pulp the pads of my feet
Till the soles of them swell up like balloons;

'Pain in my feet; pain of my hara.' This morning
I saw the sun rise molten and red

Over the hill at Herewini's house
At Raetihi. But staggering on the stones

Last night, I had to stop, and looked up at the stars
And saw those ribs of white fire

Hung there like the underside of punga leaves
Planted for our human shelter.

7

To go forward like a man in the dark
Is the meaning of this dark vocation;

So simple, tree, star, the bare cup of the hills,
The lifelong grave of waiting

As indeed it has to be. To ask for Jacob's ladder
Would be to mistake oneself and the dark Master,

Yet at times the road comes down to a place
Where water runs and horses gallop

Behind a hedge. There it is possible to sit,
Light a cigarette, and rub

Your bruised heels on the cold grass. Always because
A man's body is a meeting house,

Ribs, arms, for the tribe to gather under,
And the heart must be their spring of water.

1972

from *Letter to Peter Olds* (1972)

4

The revolution doesn't need guns;
It happens whenever a man arrested for being

Out of work, and booted into the meat wagon,
Begins to laugh instead of squaring his fists;

It happens whenever a screw in Paremoremo
Walks out of his job instead of standing and watching

Twenty men bumming a boy. It happens
When the owner of the restaurant sits down with a moneyless customer

To pass the time of day. It happened for me
Lately at Taumarunui, when I stood on the grass of the marae

Beside one kuia, and said to her,
'When I am beside you I know that the earth below

'My feet is our mother. It gives me a sense of peace.'
The revolution happens when the eyes begin to open at last.

from *Ode to Auckland and Other Poems* (1972)

A Birthday Poem to Myself

To undo the inside trouser button
And sit on a wooden lavatory
Watching birds—an ethical occupation
Though once it was not so,

The belt undone, the man in his hot skin
Entering what he should not enter,
A woman, a door, a gap in the high stone wall
That constitutes life—let us suppose,

In charity, too drunk to remember it,
Among tangled creepers at the party's end!
Now let God be glad, or sad, who made the creature
And gave him that great sack of guts,

For he is decorous now, concentrating
On cold draughts, bills, wet feet, his bowel motion,
Or anything safe—this old wattled Adam
Back in the garden; behind the safe stone gate.

1967

In Baxter's notebook (Hocken MS 704/27) the above poem is titled 'Safety'. Weir prefers the MS title for the *Collected Poems*.

Ode to Auckland

Auckland, you great arsehole,
Some things I like about you
Some things I cannot like.

I came to the Art School, carrying the paintings
Of an eighteen-year-old chick.
On the door of one room somebody had written 'Life'
But there was death inside it.

A skeleton hung there by a hook in its skull
Its ribs brown with earth, age, or varnish.
The statue of a Greek god lay on the floor
With his prick and balls knocked off by a chisel.
'Alison,' I said, 'they've buggered the god of death,
They've cut the balls off the god of love.
How can their art survive?'

'Roimata ua, roimata tangata—'
The tears of rain are falling,
Tears of rain, tears of men.

I went to Mass at Newman Hall,
Then visited the Varsity Cafeteria
With six Catholic acquaintances.
One wanted to show me the poems he had written,
One talked about the alternate society,
One wanted to convert the world,

One girl in glasses gave me the glad eye,
Another praised the pentecostal movement,
Another hoed into his plate of cheese and camel turds.

I said, 'Excuse me a minute, there's a Maori friend of mine,
If he doesn't get a place to crash tonight
The cops will pick him up for the four crimes
They dislike most in Auckland,
Not having a job,
Wearing old clothes,
Having long hair,
Above all, for being Maori.
When they shift him to the cells in the meat wagon
The last crime might earn him five punches in the gut.
Could any one of you give him a night's lodging?'

They were extremely sorry.
The bourgeois Christ began to blush on the Cross.
The Holy Spirit squawked and laid an egg.
One had landlord trouble,
One had to swot for exams,
One was already overcrowded,
One didn't know exactly,
One still wanted to show me the poems he had written,
And the last one still silently consumed his plate of camel turds.

I took the Maori lad to Keir Volkerling's place.
He slept on a mattress in the bathroom.
Keir was not a Christian, or a student.
He worked ten hours a day
Digging drains or mixing concrete
To support an average of twenty-five people
Who would otherwise have been in jail
For being out of work,
For wearing an old coat,
For having their hair down to their shoulders,
And above all, for the crime of being Maori.

Christianity has weakened my brain cells, brother,
I haven't got the fortitude of Keir Volkerling.
The Auckland Varsity gives me a pain in the rectum.
I am waiting for the day
When its wedding cake tower goes down in a pile of rubble
From a bomb planted by an intelligent boobhead
Or a not-so-intelligent Varsity radical.

The Auckland Art School gives me a pain in both my testicles.
They don't know the best of Illingworth.
They admire the worst of McCahon.
Why not burn the Art School down
And get some old houses and do a bit of painting
Either with a brush on the ceiling
Or with a brush on a bit of canvas?

I paid a visit to an old friend
Who used to write some good poems.
The door of his office was painted black and yellow,
The colour of the plague flag.

'Peter,' I asked him, 'could you spare me a dollar?'
He looked unhappy.
He was putting on some ceremonial robes
For a meeting of the University Council.
'I'm sorry, man,' I said,
'I didn't mean to interrupt you.'

Outside his office the wind rustled
Dead leaves on the concrete pavement.
I shook hands with an old moss-grown statue
And went barefoot down the road.

Auckland, even when I am well stoned
On a tab of LSD or on Indian grass
You still look to me like an elephant's arsehole
Surrounded with blue-black haemorrhoids.

The sound of the opening and shutting of bankbooks,
The thudding of refrigerator doors,
The ripsaw voices of Glen Eden mothers yelling at their children,
The chugging noise of masturbation from the bedrooms of the bourgeoisie,
The voices of dead teachers droning in dead classrooms,
The TV voice of Mr Muldoon,
The farting noise of the trucks that grind their way down Queen Street
Has drowned forever the song of Tangaroa on a thousand beaches,
The sound of the wind among the green volcanoes,
And the whisper of the human heart.

Boredom is the essence of your death,
I would take a trip to another town
Except that the other towns resemble you exactly.

How can I live in a country where the towns are made like coffins
And the rich are eating the flesh of the poor
Without even knowing it?

O Father Lenin, help us in our great need!
The people seem to enjoy building the pyramids.
Moses would get a mighty cold reception.
They'd kiss the arse of Pharaoh any day of the week

For a pat on the head and a dollar note.
At another time in another place
Among the Ngati-Whatua
When they brought the dead child into the meeting house

She opened her eyes and smiled.

18 October 1972

from *Runes* (1973)

from *Words to Lay a Strong Ghost*

(After Catullus)

1 The Party

A kind of cave—still on the brandy,
And coming in from outside,
I didn't like it—the room like a tunnel
And everybody gassing in chairs—

Or count on finding you there, smiling
Like a stone Diana at
Egnatius' horse-laugh—not my business exactly
That he cleans his teeth with AJAX,

But he's the ugliest South Island con man
Who ever beat up a cripple . . .
Maleesh—the booze rolls back, madam;
I'm stuck here in the void

Looking at my journey's end—
Two breasts like towers—the same face
That brought Troy crashing
Down like a chicken coop—black wood and flames!

1966

12 The Rock

Arms of Promethean rock
Thrust out on either
Side of a bare white strip
Of wave-ridged sand—long before

I ever met you, Pyrrha,
The free world held me in its heart,
And half my grief is only
The grief of a child torn from the breast

Who remembers—who cannot forget
The shielding arms of a father,
Maybe Poseidon—out there
Where the waves never cease to break

In the calmest weather, there's a hump-backed
Jut of reef—we called it Lion Rock—
Growling with its wild white mane
As if it told us even then

Death is the one door out of the labyrinth!
Not your fault—to love, hate, die,
Is natural—as under quick sand-grains
The broken bladders lie.

1966

13 The Flower

They've bricked up the arch, Pyrrha,
That used to lead into
Your flat on Castle Street—Lord, how
I'd pound the kerb for hours,

Turning this way and that
Outside it, like a hooked fish
Wanting the bait but not the barb—
Or else a magnetized needle!

Well; they've bricked it up—fair
Enough! You've sunk your roots in Australia,
And I'm free to write verses,
Grow old, be married, watch my children clutter

Their lives up . . . It was always a tomb,
That place of yours! I didn't know
Then how short life is—how few
The ones who really touch us

Right at the quick—I'm a successful
Man of letters, Pyrrha—
Utterly stupid!—a forty-year-old baby
Crying out for a lost nurse

Who never cared much. The principle
That should have made me tick went early
Half underground, as at the paddock's edge
You'll see in autumn some flower

(Let's say a dandelion)
Go under the farmer's boots
Like a faded sun
Cut with a spade.

1966

Daughter

Daughter, when you were five
I was your Monster;
Leaving the pub, less than half-alive,
Hurtling in a taxi to the Play Centre—

You'd ride like a jockey up Messines Road,
Thumbs in my eyes, your bulky legs
On each side of my booze-filled head—
A red-suited penguin!

I'd spoon you out dollops of mushroom soup,
Peel off the penguin skin, and tuck you down,
Uncap a bottle of White Horse, dredge up
My hangman cobbers from the town . . .

Five years later I'd wake at 2 a.m.
And see an upright ghost in a nightie
Standing beside my bed, mumbling
About a bad dream it had had—

You'd settle in with me like a bear cub
And wrap your arms halfway round my chest—
An atomic blast set off in the Sahara
Of my schizoid, never-quiet mind!

Incest? The quacks don't know their job.
I was your father,
I treated you like bone china,
Sent you sleepwalking back to your cot.

At seventeen your face is powder-white,
Your hair is a black dyed fountain,
Mooching round the house you slam doors
And wait to be rung up.

Why won't you work? That boil on your heel
Comes from going barefoot
In the wet streets. Last night
I dreamt I burnt a fish-skin coat

To turn you back into a human shape—
Wouldn't you yell! Yet I was glad
When you hoisted your private flag
Against the bourgeois gastanks—You're *my* daughter!

When I go in to wake you up
On a morning of ice and boredom,
You sleep with your mouth open
Like a soldier struck down in battle,

And I'm Narcissus bending over
The water face! From the edge of the pillow,
Red-veined, grape-black,
My own eye looks back.

1966

Mother and Son

1

Blowflies dive-bomb the sitting-room
Table, this dry spring morning,

In my mother's house. As I did in my 'teens,
I listen again to the Roman-lettered clock

Chiming beside the statue of Gandhi
Striding towards God without any shadow

Along the mantelpiece. Time is a spokeless wheel.
Fantails have built a nest on the warm house wall

Among the passion vines. The male one lurks.
The female spreads her fan. Out in the rock garden

White-headed my mother weeds red polyanthus,
Anemone, Andean crocus,

And the gold and pearl trumpets called angels' tears.
Mother, I can't ever wholly belong

In your world. What if the dancing fantail
Should hatch tomorrow a dragon's egg?

Mother, in all our truces of the heart
I hear the pearl-white angels musically weeping.

2

There's more to it. Those wood-framed photographs
Also beside the clock, contain your doubtful angels,

My brother with hair diagonally brushed
Over his forehead, with a hot dark eye,

And myself, the baby blondish drowsing child
So very slow to move away from the womb!

Saddled and ridden to Iceland and back by the night-hag
He learnt early that prayers don't work, or work

After the need has gone. Mother, your son
Had gained a pass degree in Demonology

Before he was twelve—how else can you make a poet?—
Yet we're at one in the Catholic Church.

I go out to meet you. Someone is burning weeds
Next door. The mother fantail flutters

Chirping with white eyebrows and white throat
On a branch of lawsoniana, and the darting

Father bird comes close when I whisper to him
With a susurrus of the tongue.

1966

At the Fox Glacier Hotel

One kind of love, a Tourist Bureau print
Of the Alps reflected in Lake Matheson

(Turned upside down it would look the same)
Smiles in the dining room, a lovely mirror

For any middle-aged Narcissus to drown in—
I'm peculiar; I don't want to fall upwards

Into the sky! Now, as the red-eyed tough
West Coast beer-drinkers climb into their trucks

And roar off between colonnades
Of mossed rimu, I sit for a while in the lounge

In front of a fire of end planks
And wait for bedtime with my wife and son,

Thinking about the huge ice torrent moving
Over bluffs and bowls of rock (some other

Kind of love) at the top of the valley—
How it might crack our public looking-glass

If it came down to us, jumping
A century in twenty minutes,

So that we saw, out of the same window
Upstairs where my underpants are hanging to dry,

Suddenly—no, not ourselves
Reflected, or a yellow petrol hoarding,

But the other love, yearning over our roofs
Black pinnacles and fangs of toppling ice.

1966

At Kuri Bush

A few days back I climbed the mound
Where the farmhouse had stood,

As green as any that the Maoris made
Along that coast. The fog was blowing

Through gates and up gullies
Hiding even the stems of cocksfoot grass

That had sprung up in place of
The sitting-room table and the small brass

Kerosene lamp my mother lighted
Every night, whose white wick would burn

Without changing colour. Somebody must have
Used the old brushwood fence for kindling

Twenty years ago. Outside it
My father stood when I was three or less,

Holding me up to look at
The gigantic rotating wheel of the stars

Whose time isn't ours. The mound yielded
No bones, no coins, but only

A chip of the fallen chimney
I put in the pocket of a damp coat

Before I bumbled back down to the road
With soaking trousers. That splinter of slate

Rubbed by keys and cloth like an amulet
Would hold me back if I tried to leave this island

For the streets of London or New York.
I hope one day they'll plant me in

The kind of hole they dig for horses
Under a hilltop cabbage tree

Not too far from the river that goes
Southwards to the always talking sea.

1966

Winter River

Nothing is colder than this water in winter
when winds crack the lopped pines
on the Domain bank and send cones
rolling down to the water . . .

Thick bare brown roots tangled
below the sod wall. The boys
and their girls would sit on Saturdays
in a fog of awkwardness and watch

the river run out to the bay.
Ah well—it's easy
to come back, more or less alive
inside one's own unbreakable

glass dome, a dying Martian,
and think about youth.
I never liked it much.
I did not venture

to touch the thick blonde matted curls
of those man-swallowing dolls, our big sisters.
I had no sister.
Their giggles made me tremble

and coast away to the bathing shed latrine
in itchy summer torpor,
furiously inventing a unicorn
who hated the metal of Venus.

Yet they weren't metal. Now
they sag on porches, in back rooms,
flabby as I am, and the river
carries a freight of floating pine cones.

1966

Iron Scythe Song

An appearance of control
Is what the waves could drown;
Seawater like the soul
Is ownable by no one
Though safe enough to watch,
And as I barge through each

White haggard tumbling top
The cold surf bangs my head,
And quickly I go up

To change in the bathing shed,
Leaving my wife and son
To plunge alone,

Then fat and fortyish
With a king-sized ice cream
Snug in its cone, I splash
Through the warm creek and come
Up the road's stony edge
To my father's hawthorn hedge . . .

'The scarlet hawthorn flowers
Flaring and fragrant stand,
Land bird and sea bird bears
Hope of new sea and land'—
If the words are callow
I made them long ago,

But while the wind moves
Behind his hat today
The green glittering leaves,
My father lifts and shows me,
Still usable, though rusted,
The scythe his father lifted,

And like the iron scythe
That hangs out of the rain,
By sharpener and by wrath
Worn down to its backbone,
My life has the shape
That it will keep.

1967

Summer 1967

Summer brings out the girls in their green dresses
Whom the foolish might compare to daffodils,
Not seeing how a dead grandmother in each one governs her limbs,
Darkening the bright corolla, using her lips to speak through,
Or that a silver torque was woven out of
The roots of wet speargrass.
 The young are mastered by the Dead,

Lacking cunning. But on the beaches, under the clean wind
That blows this way from the mountains of Peru,
Drunk with the wind and the silence, not moving an inch
As the surf-swimmers mount on yoked waves,
One can begin to shake with laughter,
Becorming oneself a metal Neptune.
                                        To want nothing is
The only possible freedom. But I prefer to think of
An afternoon spent drinking rum and cloves
In a little bar, just after the rain had started, in another time
Before we began to die—the taste of boredom on the tongue
Easily dissolving, and the lights coming on—
With what company? I forget.
                                        Where can we find the right
Herbs, drinks, bandages to cover
These lifelong intolerable wounds—
Herbs of oblivion, they lost their power to help us
The day that Aphrodite touched her mouth to ours.

1967

Letter from the Mountains

There was a message. I have forgotten it.
There was a journey to make. It did not come to anything.
But these nights, my friend, under the iron roof
Of this old rabbiters' hut where the traps
Are still hanging up on nails,
Lying in a dry bunk, I feel strangely at ease.
The true dreams, those longed-for strangers,
Begin to come to me through the gates of horn.

I will not explain them. But the city, all that other life
In which we crept sadly like animals
Through thickets of dark thorns, haunted by the moisture of women
And the rock of barren friendship, has now another shape.
Yes, I thank you. I saw you rise like a Triton,
A great reddish gourd of flesh,
From the sofa at that last party, while your mistress smiled
That perfect smile, and shout as if drowning—
'You are always—'
                        Despair is the only gift;

When it is shared, it becomes a different thing; like rock, like water;
And so you also can share this emptiness with me.

Tears from faces of stone. They are our own tears.
Even if I had forgotten them
The mountain that has taken my being to itself
Would still hang over this hut, with the dead and the living
Twined in its crevasses. My door has forgotten how to shut.

1968

Part 2

Part 2 moves away from the careful structuring of the first section to present a range of posthumously published, published but uncollected, and unpublished poems ordered chronologically by date of composition. As the pool of unpublished and uncollected poems runs into the thousands, this section can only gesture towards the type of things Baxter was writing that inhabit the margins of what has become the Baxter canon. It can be seen from 'The British Bull-dog' (p. 170) that the attitudes expressed in Baxter's later political poems were fully formed by his teens; that at 18, when the popular view was that his verse was largely tortuous romanticism, he could write the moving 'Unwritten Elegy' (p. 173) to his imprisoned brother in imitation of e.e. cummings; and that he could also write something as ephemeral as 'The Iron Cradle' (p. 209), as harrowing as 'The Dying Nazi Guard' (p. 205), and as biographically significant as 'The book is shut' (p. 244), while also paying a delightfully backhanded compliment to many of his fellow writers in 'The Boathouse by the Sea' (p. 195). The value of his early, imitative verse is revealed in the way his first attempts at a sestina in 'What Shall be Heard?' (p. 171, modelled on Auden's 'Paysage moralisé') would be powerfully repaid in some of his very last poetry (see the selection of sestinas beginning on p. 274).

In the late 1930s Baxter lived for two years in England and Europe with his family, returning to their home town of Brighton towards the end of 1938. In 1939 he spent an unrewarding year as a boarder at the Quaker-run Friends' School in Wanganui (see McKay, ch. 2), the setting of the following poem.

At School I Have No Time to Dream

At School I have no time to dream
As sailing on Life's steady stream
The bustling hours go by;
But when at night my Muse awakes,
Then soaring wings my Fancy takes
Far to the land of Poesy.

When I awake I am bereft,
For nothing but the leaves are left
Of all my faëry gold:
Once more the busy day begins,
'Mong darkening clouds my vision thins
And lesson-times unfold.

Hocken MS704/1
1939, aged 13

The British Bull-dog

The brainless British bull-dog stands alone,
Especial object for facetious mirth
Among the other nations of the earth,
A pseudo-democratic to the bone—
Supremely contemplative of his own
But quite unconscious of the others' worth
Majestic in deportment, mien, and girth
(And sure that Winston's right in all that's done!)

But if the old conservatives were shot,
If Eire 'gets sore' and India should rebel
While Church and congregation go to hell—
With Stock Exchange and 'precedent' forgot:
He would, when quite recovered from the shock,
Call his valet and drown himself in hock!

Hocken, MS704/4
1941, aged 15

What Shall be Heard?

(sestina)

What shall be heard of us in the far places
When peaceful wells flow glittering, flow more swiftly
What shall be heard of us, the salt, the leaven?
Shall they who pass us by arise and hearken
Smearing our names with words we never uttered,
Twisting with long illogic our fiery phrases?

We are the leaders, we by scarce-spoken phrases
May sway the multitudes of many places:
Take heed of all that we in secret uttered—
They shall be catch-words shouted skyward, swiftly.
Raise up your heads, O rulers, now and hearken:
The moulded dough may froth from the rising leaven!

Ye would bake bread without the needed leaven
Moving but few with oft-repeated phrases.
And is it to the war-lords men will hearken?
Behold a flame within the desolate places,
Behold the loathèd canker spreading swiftly
And power undreamt of, slogans now not uttered:

What shall be done when our cries in the city are uttered?
What cause for agitation and fear-leaven
When bloodless barraging shall batter swiftly,
Bid battle cease despite the war-like phrases
And idols crash in hidden sanctuary places—
Such is the meed for all who will not hearken.

With small rejoicing shall the minions hearken:
Expected ultimatum is unuttered,
Peace is proved possible in warring places
Where trust is surely the essential leaven:
We who approach dead foes with friendly phrases
See brothers, loosed from corpses greet us swiftly!

Move on our pathways, change all action swiftly—
Dullards shall be wise though last to hearken.
When we have ended there shall be no phrases,
Cause will have passed for lamentation uttered:
Though seeming anarchy, such is the leaven
That shall be known as gospel in all places!

We from uncharted places come right swiftly,
We who were long the leaven—all shall hearken:
We have the wisdom uttered in true phrases.

Hocken MS704/5, 1942

Baxter's friend, imprisoned pacifist Noel Ginn, submitted 'Now While the Bugles Blare' to The Link: Organ of the New Zealand Methodist Bible Class Movements. *The poem was published in XVI.9, 5 July 1943: 3; making this the earliest known publication of one of Baxter's poems.*

Now While the Bugles Blare

Now while the bugles blare
Their arrogant fanfare,
Now is the time for prayer.

Pray for the banners straining
The soldier new to training
The wild west wind complaining.

Pray for the combatant too:
As strong a man as you
Grunts, with his face smashed through.

Pray to the Lord—ah, list!
Descends the Eucharist
To armies in the mist.

Pray to ye know not what.
O sorrowful, wonder not!
For the Lord Christ is shot.

He as a child is mangled
(The Christmas bells have jingled)
He as a man is strangled.

Hocken MS704/9, 1943

Unwritten Elegy

o i
had thought of writing an elegy
but decided not to

because an elegy
is bound to be
unreal

for one doesnt know the poor b
whos got bumped off
so cannot expand on

his sensations
my brother who was a welder
has been 2 years in a conchie camp

peeling potatoes
and cutting scrub
for scrub to grow

my brother is a good sort
sensitive and strong
so ends the song

Hocken MS704/12, February 1944

Not all of Baxter's verse found its way into his poetry notebooks or was published under his own name. This example, 'Horatian Ode: On the Banishment of Beer', appeared in the Otago University Student Magazine Critic *on 22 June 1944. Baxter kept the page among his papers and deposited it in the Hocken Library (MS 975/182), having signed his initials next to the pseudonym.*

HORATIAN ODE
On the Banishment of Beer

Of late I saw (it pierced my soul)
Upon a wall this bitter scroll:
    Warning (it said): No beer
    Or drunks permitted here.

Just then, from out the doorway thrown,
And landing on his collarbone
A friend whom I revered
Unheralded appeared.

'The b's,' he said, 'they chucked me out
For trundling a small keg of stout
(Which they will answer for)
Upon the dancing floor.'

'Courage my son'—sadly I spoke—
'Such would be taken as a joke
Or nothing, as one learns,
In the home town of Burns—

'Of whom a statue may be seen,
His back to the cathedral green,
And pensive eyes turned—well,
Towards the O Hotel.

'And learned Greek authorities
Contended that Euripides
When most inspired paid toll
To the Muse of Alcohol.

'But in this philistinian age
Stooges of moderation rage—
Blue-ribboned hounds, alack,
Are baying on our track.

'Envying our ecstatic trance
And that supreme self-confidence
They even seek to bar
The innocent motor-car—

'Whose chaste accoutrements will wail
The banished beer, the bygone ale,
What time the festive horde
Were wont to cram aboard.

'Hearken,' I said, 'I fear 'twere best
That we be sober with the rest
And abnegate the brew,
Or get them shikkered, too.'

Envoi:
He listened; but I fear that I
Had slight effect: for by and by

He drew from his hip-pocket
A flask and tilted it.
And as he wandered on his way
I heard him sing this curious lay:
'Keep your champagne, keep your sherry,
Give me beer when I feel bad—
Just enough to make me merry
Not enough to make me mad.'

—*I. MARVEL.*

The following three poems are from Cold Spring *(Oxford University Press, 1996), which would have been Baxter's second published collection had the Caxton Press agreed to proceed with it. Early in 1945, before his first book had even left the binders, the 18-year-old Baxter had this second collection ready in manuscript form. He thought it 'rather better' than* Beyond the Palisade *(1944) and spent months unsuccessfully attempting to persuade Caxton's editor to publish it. Baxter's use of dense classical allusions to express a private symbolism makes many of the poems difficult to penetrate. But occasional glimpses of a lighter touch—as in 'I Have Cut from My Heart' and 'Clarity'—suggest later love lyrics and sonnets, and 'Under the Dank Leaves' is his first articulation in a poem of a conscious decision to become a 'New Zealand' poet.*

I Have Cut from My Heart

I have cut from my heart
her green-sickness;
it is better to be a tall and lonely man
than stand and cry for the moon.

The moon is older than the sun.
Why should a man set his soul
in the house of a girl?
To be alive is to be alone.

It is better to look and turn away.
She is beautiful where she walks;
she is beautiful where she stands;
as any flowering tree.

October 1944

Under the Dank Leaves

Under the dank leaves of a Cotswold autumn
Loveless my eyes wander. I told you, darling,
That one loves first the feeding breast and after
Landscape to sate a cold and flourishing eye:
And last women, when the pressed cider of Eden
Makes the upright man. In fear of falling
I stand: you dead in me: return so softer
To mothering leaves.

But O below the sky
There is no recompense for your long death.
I will turn from the rooks of an imagined England
(Unrest alone she lent me); turn to the strange
And snarling abyss of this lank land of my birth
That her hourly whims may oust your needle second:
Drown me in glaciers stiller than stonehenge
And the immense seas of change.

November 1944

Clarity

I have recaptured clearness: while the light
Falls long to southward. Winds are motionless;
Where midges spin, and each to each birds chirrup
Harshly. The ranking waves incessant wear
On wounded rock. Clouds ragged float
Red-orange-veined. And the cool sea caress
Murmurs below these gaudy roofs asleep.
I have regained my sight but forfeit nature.

World upon world the midges mate and die:
I envy them their long oblivious moment.
The scene were full without me: nor does bramble
Grow her wild rose and greener filigree
For my brief tenderness. Cloud over ageless headland
No crag, no cloud, but paranoiac symbol.

November 1944

from *Cressida*

9 Her Second Song

The books grow clear upon the shelf,
Locke, Berkeley, Hume.
The wind loves no one but itself
That sings outside a rented room
And rustles in the lilac tree—
O my dear and only.

I had a love who pleased me well
(Locke, Berkeley, Hume)
He left me single for a spell.
Brief and brisk it seemed to him
But a long dry road it was to me—
Yes, my dear and only.

Once work and fancy were enough
(Locke, Berkeley, Hume)
Few to speak to, none to love,
Easy go, easy come—
Till you and I touched knee to knee,
Yes, my dear and only.

Three white angels at my head,
Locke, Berkeley, Hume
One stands at the foot of the bed:
Black Abaddon is his name,
He is stronger than the other three,
O my dear and only.

1951

10 Bar Room Conversation

A lorry made the windows shake
And noon light on the sour spilt beer
Quivered. 'A widow's an easy make'

He said, 'you pedal and let her steer;
Or the next best is a girl inclined
To play, but her man's away for a year

'And she's too shy or he's too blind.
None of your nattering flirts—they're hard—
But one of the Sunday School teacher kind

'Ripe and ready behind her guard.'
Gently the other sipped his drink;
The barman wrote on a doubles card.

He said, 'I saw her first at the Rink,
Danced and yarned and took it slow.
She's come to trust me now, I think.

'Ten weeks of bringing her home by moonglow
With a kiss and cuddle at the gate—
No more. Tonight we'll go to a show

'At Dan's—I bet you a dollar, mate,
With a drink or two she'll turn it up.'
In the yard a lorry unloaded a crate;
The barman polished a football cup.

1951

11 Her Decision

Show me the face, cold mirror, that the world
Can see and prize: myself you'll never show.
Eyes wide apart, forehead a trifle low,
Rose-ruddy cheeks, the ripe mouth cupid-curled.
Blonde hair, they say, is fickle: I'm a blonde.
Then I'll stay home and read a book tonight;
Let him tire waiting, walk the lawn in spite.
They say, Fidelity's a standing pond
(But I'll not listen). How the mean thoughts swarm
Like flies in sunlight, sparks behind a grate!
It was not so: too much alone of late
I grow unsure. The waste wind blowing warm
Can ruffle the deep well of happiness
But never dry it. Oh the moon controls
Our sex, the subtle mercury our souls!
—The amber necklace then, and the grey dress.

1951

Song of Tinbum Kelly

The eagles in the middle air
        Have built their strident nest,
But Old Jack Kelly's heart nowhere
        Has found a moment's rest.

The fecund knowledge of the night
Dies again in day's light.

My first wife was a harlot,
        We loved but could not agree.
My second wife is a Protestant,
        We live in *felo de se*.

Between the sheets all flesh is news,
A goose's neck is a barnacle goose.

These hands have helped many a mare
        To drop her long-legged foal;
Flanagan's too, before he died
        Like a ferret in a hole.

It is my job to understand
The bar room clock that has no hands.

But holy love and hell's disgrace
        Blaze from the bent sky
A man's face and woman's face
        In the twinkling of an eye.

All the wisdom I have gained
I had more when I was weaned.

The mercy of God is a dum-dum bullet
With Old Jack Kelly's name upon it.

1954

The Parson's Rock

Under the Parson's Rock
Where weeds of love loop every tide
My three dead uncles walk,
The gutted greenbone in their sack
Spilling on scaled stone a sea bright blood.

On beaches to the moon's bell
From a wave's steeple swung,
Old ghosts, the last grief over, tell
How sweetly at the quick of the gilled soul
God's deepsea mercy moves, how praise from stones is wrung.

But I, thin on the moon stranded
Low lovers' dune, alive must grieve
For the true flesh time wounded,
The prodigal Lent of a fisherman's harvest ended
By the dry handed grave.

Only the bald rock
Preaching to fishes, the lupin sheeted
Bed of the swaybacked sinners, these will speak
For the dead fishermen, and the moon awake
On waters by the fingered night braided.

Hocken MS704/17, 1954–55
NZ Listener, *18 February 1955*

It is difficult to date Baxter's poems for children with any degree of certainty, as they cover a period from 1953 to 1966, and most did not find their way into his poetry notebooks. However, as the bulk of the poems were written as teaching aids during the period in which he was assistant master at Epuni School (February 1954–April 1956) a selection of five poems is inserted here.

The Tree House

John and Judith
And Billy and me,
We have our own house
In a willow tree.

It's built of boards
And battens and tin
From the packing case
That the tractor came in.

Up the slippery trunk
Of the tree we climb
With a rope to help us,
One at a time;

But once we're up
And safe inside
Only the wind knows
Where we hide.

Down in the paddock
The brown horse neighs
And in stormy weather
The whole house sways

Like a ship at sea
While the branches roar
And birds fly past
At the open door.

If I were King of Sweden

If I were King of Sweden
I would never wear a crown,
But I'd ride in a golden carriage
With the window down.

I would wake up very early
In my palace by the sea;
I would breakfast on marshmallow
And have the same for tea.

Each day would be my birthday,
I'd buy fizzy drink in kegs;
Once a month there'd be an Easter
With enormous Easter eggs.

If I saw a man or woman
Who looked hungry in the street,
I'd invite them in to dinner
And give them pies to eat.

If I were King of Sweden
I'd go walking to and fro,
And every person that I met
Would stop and say, 'Hullo!'

Swing, Swing, Swing

Swing, swing, swing,
Swinging wide and high—
If you swing high enough
Your feet will touch the sky.

If your foot should touch it
Then the sky will break.
It'll make no difference when you say
You did it by mistake.

The sun will growl and grumble,
The stars will tumble down,
And the weather Man come running
In a long, black gown.

The rivers will run backwards,
The sums will add up wrong;
You'll come to school on Saturday
And play the whole night long.

It will take a ton of thistledown,
A ladder brought from Spain,
And a new magician's hammer
To patch it up again.

The Big Black Whale

I wish I were a big, black whale
Out in the deep green sea.
He blows like a hose
Through the top of his nose,
As happy as a whale can be,
And the sailors look pale
When they hear his tail
Go smack, smack, smack,
On a big wave's back
Out in the deep green sea.

Hokitika Bill

Hokitika Bill,
Hokitika Bill,
He worked for a day
At the threshing-mill.

He worked for a day
Where the sacks were filling
For a penny and a pound
And a silver shilling.

Then Hokitika Bill
He called for his pay,
Climbed on his saddle-hack
And rode away.

Hokitika Bill,
Hokitika Bill,
Rode on his saddle-hack
Over the hill.

With a billy full of sugar
And some flour in a bag,
All wrapped up
In a blanket swag.

In 1956, the year Baxter graduated BA from Victoria University College, Wellington, he recalled for the VUC student magazine Salient *his first failed attempts as a student some twenty years earlier in the poem 'Reflections on a Varsity Career'.*

Reflections on a Varsity Career

Friend or enemy, draw near;
Wellingtonians, lend an ear;
I too had a Varsity career
In the early, early days.

I'll tell you nothing but the truth.
In the Queen City of the South
Our drinking habits were uncouth
In the early, early days.

My thoughts were neo-pagan then.
I didn't belong to the S.C.M.
They didn't like me and I didn't like them
In the early, early days.

I never held it was a sin
To sink a quart of orange gin.
On Thursday my weekend would begin
In the early, early days.

Peculiar things were done and seen
In the Robert Burns and the Bowling Green.
God did not choose to intervene
In the early, early days.

I liked to look at the birds and trees;
My textbooks gathered mould in peace;
I regarded swotting as a loathsome disease
In the early, early days.

For recreation I played Slippery Sam
With a sailor on an oilboat from Abadan.
The johns caught up with him, poor man,
In the early, early days.

My girlfriend had a flat of her own
With japanese tea-cups and fingerbones.
In a fortnight I lost half a stone
In the early, early days.

Together we studied jet propulsion.
I never drank my Lane's Emulsion;
I avoided Psych. Prac. with revulsion
In the early, early days.

Life went faster in '44.
I didn't have time to find it a bore
Between her place and the bottle store
In the early, early days.

The lecturer's head was bald, of granite;
I admired the flies that skated upon it
And watched the clock shift minute by minute
In the early, early days.

My cobber lived in Prince's Street.
The things we discussed I won't repeat.
There was lots to drink and little to eat
In the early, early days.

Formal attire was seldom worn;
The parties kept on going till dawn
And saveloy skins were left on the lawn
In the early, early days.

My relatives told me I'd wake with a bump
When I ended up on the rubbish dump;
But I lived like a camel off my hump
In the early, early days.

Till the little green canary was eaten by the cat,
Till an octopus climbed from the brewer's vat,
Till the vulture squawked on the front door mat
In the early, early days.

Ashes to ashes, dust to dust:
If the grog doesn't kill you, hard yacker must.
I think my physique was more robust
In the early, early days.

Now my song must have an ending;
But you all must agree who have heard me sing
That a Varsity career is an excellent thing
As it was for me in the early days,
In the early, early days.

Hocken MS975/26, 1956
Salient *XX.6 (22 June 1956): 6.*

The Private Conference of Harry Fat

Said Harry Fat to Holyoake,
'With fools outside the door,
Wise men within, I'll tell you straight
I hate the sulky boor
Who flaunts his dirty fingernails
And never owned a store.'

'Oh, yes indeed,' said Holyoake,
'We've met their kind before.'

Said Harry Fat, 'I've read about
A doll who liked to sing,
And when you tapped his wooden head
His little bell would ring.
I like the kind of country where
The little man is king.'

'I quite agree,' said Holyoake,
'It is a splendid thing.'

Said Harry Fat, 'I've heard it said
    The Civil Service needs
Protection from the Communists
    Who sow rebellious seeds.
The right man in the right place
    Will pluck them out like weeds.'

'We must keep watch,' said Holyoake,
'On any man who reads.'

Said Harry Fat, 'If you will take
    A business man's advice—
Tell me a voter's income
    And I'll tell you his price;
Although it's wiser not to come
    With the same promise twice.'

'Upon my word,' said Holyoake,
'The point is very nice.'

Said Harry Fat, 'I call the man
    Who digs my garden, "Bert".
He has his place and I have mine,
    His job's to shovel dirt.
But I'll have no truck with a Chinese ape
    Who wears a peasant shirt.'

'Except with guns,' said Holyoake—
'The message then is curt.'

Said Harry Fat to Holyoake,
    'To falter would be sin;
But oh I had a fearful dream
    When the small hours begin;
I dreamt I was a mouse inside
    A mangy lion skin.'

'We are the truth,' said Holyoake,
'The truth will always win.'

1956

Harry Fat and Uncle Sam

Said Uncle Sam to Harry Fat,
    'Your folks are fine to know
And it's great the way your island

Keeps afloat there Down Below,
But you need the global attitude
To produce a first-class show.'

'Just give me time,' said Harry Fat,
'And the tourist trade will grow.'

'It's not my place,' said Uncle Sam,
'To give advice to you,
But you don't know how to break a strike
Of monkeys in a zoo.
Our Company policemen could
Teach yours a thing or two.'

'I'll change the Law,' said Harry Fat,
'It's an easy thing to do.'

'The dollar talks,' said Uncle Sam,
'And you've a lot to learn.
How come you let your Varsity Reds
Play possum in the fern
With no interrogations?
Turn on the heat: they'll burn.'

'We'll start today,' said Harry Fat,
'And fry them each in turn.'

'Your folks don't know,' said Uncle Sam,
'What entertainment means
For a trigger-happy tourist
With a dollar in his jeans.
No whorehouse on the corner
Was a grief to our Marines.'

'Try Mazengarb,' wrote Harry Fat,
'For some talent in the teens.'

'To tell you straight,' said Uncle Sam,
'Your hotel service stinks.
Each dame should get an orchid
At her table with the drinks;
And we're used to a Negro bellhop
Who'll say sorry when he blinks.'

'Try Corbett next,' wrote Harry Fat,
'And find out what he thinks.'

'With a few things done,' said Uncle Sam,
'I guess your country soon
Will make the grade—Jeepers! I'd like

To hear a crooner croon
With an off-white broad beside me
Under a Pig Island moon.'

'Bring dollars in,' said Harry Fat,
'And you can call the tune.'

1956

Note: Dr Mazengarb had explained in an article in the Evening Post *that Maori, by having too many children, were endangering the purity of New Zealand morals.*

By the Dry Cardrona

I can tell where cherries grow
By the dry Cardrona,
Where I plucked them long ago
On a day when I was sober.

My father wore a parson's coat
By the dry Cardrona;
He kept a tally of the sheep and the goats,
And I was never sober.

My mother sewed her Sunday skirt
By the dry Cardrona,
They said she died of a broken heart
For I was never sober.

O lay my bones till the judgement crack
By the wild Cardrona!
The blanket swag upon my back
Will pillow me drunk or sober.

I loved a girl and only one
By the dry Cardrona:
She up and married the banker's son
For I was never sober.

I courted a widow of forty-nine
By the dry Cardrona,
She owned a stable and a scheelite mine
But I was never sober.

All rivers run to the rimless grave,
Even the wild Cardrona,
But the black cherry bent my way
One day when I was sober.

1956

Note: 'By the Dry Cardrona' is from Baxter's play Jack Winter's Dream. *It does not appear in any of his poem notebooks.*

Resolutions at Thirty

'What will you do now, old man,
When you look in the mirror and the mirror doesn't lie,
When the girls grin like hags and the barrel's dry
And ghosts walk at noon and there's blood in the sky,
When you've lost the wish to live and still want to die,
What will you do, old man, old man?

'Will you join the civil service? Will you cut your neighbour's throat?
Will you sit on a committee and give your friends a vote?
Will you be a square-jawed parson and wear a blackbird's coat?
Will you give advice on morals? Will you emulate the stoat?
Will you be a Grand Old Man?

'Will you rave about Ouspensky? Will you snore in the last ditch?
Will you praise the dullest poets? Will you drink to drown the itch?
Will you prod a hangdog mistress and complain she is a bitch?
Will you sidle up to schoolboys with a nervous twitch?
Will you be a drooly old man?

No, for I can put my fist through your cardboard cage:
Each day a different sun is born, each night love comes of age.
No bigger than a hazel nut, that ripens in a season
The world rests on its Maker's hand, and love is its sole reason.

So I can mock the devil that hammers at my door,
Though he may make me sweat again as I have done before;
The swagger and the Magi on the same journey start,
He knows his mathematics, but not the human heart.

I'll light the gas and take my love a cup of tea in bed;
I'll talk at length in coffee-shops of books I haven't read;
I'll say a prayer for the roaring-boys who are six feet under;
I'll praise the Holy Trinity and fart against the thunder.

MS704/18, 1956
Here and Now, *March 1957*

An Horatian Ode

to Frank Sargeson

Benignest friend, immortal Sarge,
Lay down the steely blade and targe
With which you front your foes
In deft, satiric prose.

Soften that strict, impartial eye
With the mild dew of charity;
And to your chaste abode
Admit this shambling ode.

No longer Johannine I come
To strike the Jordan waters dumb,
Hurling forked lightning loud
From the Sinaic cloud.

I'll write a song, if you so want,
Less lewd than my *Ballade of Cunt*
For that horrific dream
Where Kendall lets off steam.

But surely Kendall never slept;
God and his angry gonads kept
The poor old man awake
With an alternate ache

As they have kept me many a time,
Until the Catholic Faith sublime
Gave me this counsel deep:
To pull, and pray, and sleep.

I finished just the other day
A thirty-minute radio play
Booze, blood and sex, its theme;
The name—*Jack Winter's Dream*.

The medium, part verse, part prose;
Rhetorical; perhaps too close
        To Dylan Thomas' method
        To please the local synod—

Who will say, 'Clever; but of course
Another Baxter *tour de force*;
        Bad Thomas by the mile;
        Pastiche; a borrowed style . . .'

Not seeing that the theme's my own,
The style forged on the anvil bone
        And therefore bound to hack
        The same Welsh jungle track.

The hero is a drunken swagger;
The landlord whets a rusty dagger;
The only sober one's his daughter
Who wisely mixes her's with water;
She gets done over in her bunk
When all the boys are snoring drunk . . .

A charming idyll; but I guess
Too broad for the NZBS
        Who carefully castrate
        What men or God create.

These little verses never will
Alas with coy italics fill
        An honourable page
        In the bible of our age,

Where Holcroft like a hoodie crow
Shits to the open mouths below
        Of our tame bourgeoisie
        Under the upas tree.

Gladly would I with axe and saw
Lay waste that bower, and brave his caw,
        But canniness forbids
        Loss of potential quids.

Some day I will come north to share
Your food, and breathe the milder air
        Maternal Auckland spreads
        Above her pumpkin beds.

There dark imaginations brood
Above the racetrack multitude;
    There quakes the carnal earth
    With Babylonian mirth;

Or so at least it seems to one
Who wakes to a civil servant sun
    And grey conformity
    Draped over Lambton Quay.

Accept this empty ode in lieu
Of a more real tribute due;
    And pray that you and I
    May keep our powder dry.

November 1956

Be Happy in Bed

One landscape, many women:
Ambition of that savage empty boy
Haunting the bathing sheds and diamond bay,
Composing verses in an upstairs room.
Now the long windings of a broken sense
In humorous elegiacs write his doom.

Boathouses on the edge of Nowhere
Recur to trouble after-dinner sleep,
White legs among the cords and rowlocks—
'There is a spirit in the moving water
Forgives and understands us
Though God has gone inside and slammed the door.'
Where the boats ride endlessly
Grip and hold the sea king's daughter.

Sex taught him sadness: like St Lawrence
Roasting on the grid of conscience:
'One side is brown; now try the other.'
The self so persecuted by enigmas
Prefers a mountain to a nagging mother.

Put off the past: you have endured it,
Enjoyed, or else confessed it.
This luxury like cut veins in a bath
Stains too much the moving water.

No meaning now in that direction
Though skeletons toward the salt pans creep.
The age of sex, the age of centaurs
Returns to punish after-dinner sleep.

1958–59

Mr Baxter's Evening Liturgy

Coals crack. Frost glazes the back step.
Long rains and heavy push down stones
To the scouring creek. Ah well,
It's good to be back
From India. My wife in slacks
And tree-brown jersey bends her bones
Incredibly to read—NO ONE IN HELL,
PARSON'S STATEMENT: BISHOP DISAGREES.
The coal fumes make me sneeze.
Beggars, tombs and banyan trees
Stand up in Delhi. Soon we'll both retire
From the red, clinkered fire
And dream of porcupines. Till day.
Timor mortis non conturbat me.

1959

Spring Song of a Civil Servant

In corridor and cubicle
The vine is pulling bricks apart
Underneath my fishbone armour
Beats a wild Othello's heart
And between the cup and saucer

Many a savage dream is born
Of Desdemona's eyeballs popping
Fantasy ah fantasy
Above my dome the flies hedge hopping
Come to a perfect three point landing

Nevertheless notwithstanding
Eighteen hundred memoranda
A girl with sand inside her socks
Would find me ready to philander
But my Sunday spouse awaits

Car key door key vacuum cleaner
And the Lions cannot win
Caged up in Athletic Park
Tonight I'll have a double gin
The outlook for the id is dark.

1959

Winter

Winter unbundles a sack of storms
Above the flat scrub country.

Far at sea a trawling captain
Watches a double rainbow arching,
Noah's good sign, along the black horizon,
Hopes for groper, fat cod, terakihi.

A bureaucrat lights the gas fire
That warms his raw-edged afternoon,
Plucks a folder from a grey steel file,
Coughs, and eyes the telephone.

A housewife sees her washing, three-days-wet,
Hang draggled in the tugging wind,
Measures the old chair for new covers,
An ache of winter in the mind.

A child dawdling home from school
Builds little twig dams in the gutter,
Sings to himself although his shoes
Are damp, and bullies lurk at Butcher's Corner.

Winter unwraps a parcel of stones
For old and sick and sad, and homeless walkers.

1960

To Jacquie

(a dedication)

Statesman, prophet, dancer,
On their high tightrope walk.
A few fire-hardened verses
Shaped by a tomahawk
May help in an hour of storm
To hold the great tent firm.

And if it should blow over
As it has done before,
Let us go and plant together
A hedge of sycamore.
That windy scent will rise and grow
Beyond the fire, beyond the snow.

1960

The Boathouse by the Sea

I was drunk, boys, drunk, when the message came to me
That a party had been started in the boathouse by the sea,
So I buttoned up my braces and I ran to join the spree
With a fol de rol de rolly O.

They were turning up in dozens; there were taxis by the score;
And old Uncle Schroder was sitting at the door
A-clipping of the tickets, till they rolled him on the floor
With a fol de rol de rolly O.

Upon the wall was written 'No Journalists Allowed'
But Holcoft and Bertram were mixing in the crowd
Talking with Patrick Lawlor about the Holy Shroud
With a fol de rol de rolly O.

And there was Uncle Charlie with a pair of pruning shears
Waiting for a masterpiece, as he has done for years,
To chop its private member off and scrub its dirty ears
With a fol de rol de rolly O.

Old Uncle Sarge was a-sitting on the dyke
Singing to himself 'I like what I like'
Making noises like a bodgie on a broken motor bike
With a fol de rol de rolly O.

And there was Uncle Allen, trying hard to jive,
With a bowler-hatted penguin, very slow to arrive,
More insects in his cranium than any man alive
With a fol de rol de rolly O.

There was Uncle Jason Glover with a bucket full of gin,
Too shallow for a bath but deep enough to paddle in,
Eating all the saveloys and blowing up the skin
With a fol de rol de rolly O.

There was music sweet and solemn from a Bureaucratic Band
With the roar of printing presses tape-recorded from the stand,
There was singing in the boathouse, there was dancing on the sand
With a fol de rol de rolly O.

Oh the Women Writers' Group were on the grass outside
With lemonade and biscuits smeared with treacle thick and wide,
Holding an endless seance with the ghost of Robyn Hyde
With a fol de rol de rolly O.

And there was Cousin Marilyn a-gadding round the room
With matchbox and spectroscope against the Day of Doom,
And there was Cousin Sylvia all trembling at the womb
Till Monte slipped her half a length and took away her gloom
With a fol de rol de rolly O.

And there was Cousin Morrie upon a crying jag
With a big Bulgarian sausage and a Chinese workers' flag,
And there was Cousin Ian with the country in his bag,
Ready and grim with his eye on quim, lighting up a fag
With a fol de rol de rolly O.

And there was Cousin Louis with a ball of bindertwine,
Doing it by numbers, waiting for a sign,
With a vegetable marrow a-dangling from its vine:
When Uncle Charlie tripped on it he rammed him up the spine
With a fol de rol de rolly O.

And there was Cousin Erik with a Mormon archetype,
And there was Cousin Peter with a Hong Kong belly-gripe
Squeezing the ladies' coconuts to see if they were ripe,
And there was Cousin William a-sucking at his pipe
With a fol de rol de rolly O.

There were half a hundred others, but I couldn't stand the strain,
So I clambered out the window and I staggered home again
And I fell asleep a-listening to the rattle of the rain
Not caring that our writers have water on the brain
Or whether we've a culture to fiddle down the drain
With a fol de rol de rolly O.

Hocken MS704/21, 1960

Brighton

Glass-fronted baches stand and look
On the brown hurdling waves

That die at a brackish river mouth
Choked by the sand at every tide.

A township full of ears! They used to send
A springcart round the sandhills to bring in

The drunken elders. Toi-toi, marram grass,
Teach nothing to the narrow church of tin.

Beyond the high-banked green domain
Where boy and girl lying in lupin mazes

Pluck the dragon's apple, older now,
I go on beaches when the tide is low

And fish for poems where my four dead uncles,
Jack, Billy, Mark and Sandy,

Let down their lines from laps of broken stone
For the fat red cod and small-mouthed greenbone.

1955–61

Christmas 1943

Mud-crabs were talkative on Sundays
Along the flats below the farm;
Swinging a pitchfork in the barn
I put on muscle and grew sideways.

Charlie, the bee-keeping brother,
Coddled his rheumatic heart
And spoke of Christ; the young one, Walter,
Taught me how to split dry logs with a mallet

And work the hillside plough.
Uneasy, celibate,
Dropping asleep I often heard
The grass in the orchard grow,

The rain throbbing in the creekbed,
And dreamt of a girl I bought
A ticket for on a tram in Castle Street,
[Loaded] with sorrow like an unhatched egg.

1961

At Raspberry Hut

Ice cold and clear
The water from the mitred mountain.
The black mare of rock
Neighs to the sky stallion.

1961

The Rubber Monkey

Very late at night my son's red monkey
Crouches on the bookshelf, ready
To beat a tom-tom automatically

If you squeeze the bulb. It is
A relevant emblem. Operation Phoebus
Equally rubs out stupidities

And honourable speeches. There will come
From radio dials a speechless hum,
The rubber monkey whacks his drum

And mushrooms grow above the cities
Cruelly dissolving in their furnace
The powers of youth and age, the flask of pities.

1961

A Prayer to St Joseph at the Time of the New Bomb Tests

Joseph, the moon is bible-black tonight
Behind a cloth of cloud. Dust hides her. Look!
Your Child has gripped the nails; His fingers bleed;
The strings of spittle on His beard are white.
Once in a picturebook
My father's mother's father's father's father's
Uncle, a giant in a frock-coat, ran
With a smoking gun (I hadn't learnt to read)
From the Red Fox whom he had shot, a horseman
With balls of lead under his spine. Dust gathers,

Joseph, on the enormous book of Cain
That never shuts. The jet-planes engined by
The fear of Cain search for the shrivelled moon
Hiding in the high void her woman's pain,
A Mary of the sky.
It is her Child and yours the soldiers kill
With blood upon their riflebutts. I dreamt
A tree of cloud, its trunk carved with a rune
Of fire, had cracked the crystal firmament
Above Otaki. White on Hangman's Hill,

Joseph, our faces sweat and cannot see
The crust of blood on His anklebones. Bring down,
Old carpenter, the body of your Child
Who writhes upon the crossbeam of the tree,
So that the black moon's black gown
May open and her eyes give endless light
To the red soldiers in their wine-doped sleep
Who dream of love without a cross. The tiled
Roofs of the town yawn. Joseph, they weep
For bread, not fire. The moon is black tonight.

Hocken MS704/22, 1961

An English Officer in a Berlin Whorehouse Remembers Belsen

This fraulein has no tits; her skull mask grins—
Is death venereal? My blood rehearses
The barracks where those dung-black skeletons

Were washed and laundered by the German nurses.
The sheets are dirty here. To die or drink
Foul water from the mains our bombs had burst
At Hamburg—where's the choice? I vomited
When genitals they cut from corpses fed
Them better than our soup. Lord God, I thirst
For earth, air, light. In this war none escaped
The bite of typhus fleas, the cannibal stink;
Least of us all, this kid the Russians raped
In a tenement cellar, as navvies drill flat stones.
The streets, the streets are paved with living bones.

Hocken MS704/22, 1961

The Tree

Nothing was evil then. The editing came later.
Thirty years back, down time's rock shaft, I see,
Too early for the heart-and-arrow sign,
A tree of vulvas oozing golden resin
Where I and my wire-muscled cousin
Climbed endlessly. Its bird-shit-spattered branches
Invoked the gross maternal mystery
That fed his life and mine.

Smoking my father's tobacco in a sly
Tree house, or edging up a shaking mast
To a cradle open to the sky,
Riding those giant fronded arms,
I seemed to be included by
The wind in its long conversation
About some secret known to birds or men;
Perhaps what made my uncle die;

Something too hard for words. My cousin,
Climbing the ladder after me,
Would call me barmy, slither down the tree
Like an opossum, wrestle with
Scissors and headlock, order me to try on
His boxing gloves. And fighting him
I quite forgot I carried in my pocket
Green macrocarpa nuts, the seeds of time.

1962

The Rains

The monsoon wind had spread its purple
Cobra's hood. Like cruel nurses
Vultures on the banyan
Branches watched them as they came
Down. Chain lightning leapt
From the Himalayas to the jungle's womb.
That boulder-muscled, lion-bearded man
Said, '*Adonai!* I am
Your servant.' But the gaunt
Woman behind him tightened her sari, and wept
Hard sobs, as if in her own body slept
The cold seed of the serpent.

1961–62

Us

When you catch my eye through the clouded air
Of the coffee house, patting your hair
As if you were made only for men to look on,
I remember another body also human,
That leper wound in filthy bandages
Dying beside a fruit stall in Calcutta
With a few coins in a metal dish,
His lion's face of black mahogany
Turned upwards to the sky:
He, you, I.

So I love, but not as you would wish.

Hocken MS704/22, 1962

The Boys

I cannot go
Where the boys go, up creek in wet canoes
In summer, past the cattle ground,
Till at the rock bend
Their flailing paddles bruise

A black wide looking-glass where ngaios gaze
And spread their thighs,
A hole going down to the world's centre,

Waiting to swallow the sun. I think I am
The invisible drowned man floating there
Above a mud couch, nuzzled
By eel and trout, too tightly held
By the weed's arms to rise
Again to the dazzle of day, the shouting boys,
The boats, the gorse-pods blown across the water.

1962

The Pain of God

Lord, to go like a blind beast is hard
To that Jerusalem we have not seen,
Were it not for the fiery goad that You have planted
In the soul's cloven rock. The scourge of sin
Is biting Your children. We dream of the slaughter-yard.
Unknowable God, You who have charge of the dead
In the fields of fair sight, consider, remember us
In our confessing darkness. You have sown
The sparks of Your pain in Adam's flesh and bone
And faith itself is hard. Do not render
Consolation, if that pain is nearer
The springs of light than any joy could be.
Grant that I may hang on the right hand tree
And hear at last the words You spoke to Dismas.

Lord, the Roman athletes and Greek ladies
Are dust of dust. Beauty is hideous
Compared to Golgotha, where we stand
Without excuse and gaze on the murderous
Meaning of the world. The meaning of
Our night is seen in Your dismembered love,
And we will thirst till morning is at hand
Now that the pain of God belongs to us.
Unknowable God, our fatal toys
Of intellect and art are the soldier's whip,
The scars of Cain, the rage of hydrogen.

A dead man's message in Your mother's eyes,
Mercy beyond hope I recognize.
The nails of mercy, Lord, go deep.

Master, I sleep. Under the cavernous
Night of truce that You have given us
I and my elder brothers dream of love
Without a cross. The rain will rust our harness.
Shall we wake strangling in the pain of Judas?
I do not know. The night, the dream,
Are cloths that bind Your body in the grave.
And all things, even sin, must bear Your sign.
Unknowable God, O break truce and come
To give us that bright shirt of flame
You promised us. Instead
You lie alone in Your dark shirt of blood,
Man born between two beasts and dead
Between two thieves. Lighting our darkness.

Easter 1961–Easter 1962

The Bureaucrats

Like salamanders we don't realize
The element we live in—Us

Bureaucrats I mean. A tight
Cramp like the impulse to masturbate

Squeezes me as I tilt back on the chair
Of bent tubes and sponge rubber

Between the loaded desk and the door shut
By a forgotten choice. It is not

New: this nausea, a flicker of
Cold fire. My wife's photograph

With canoes in her eyes, and a steel crucifix
Pinned on the wall, shatter the reflex

That yielded for an instant to the invisible flame
Of nothingness. Caesar is not. I am.

1962

At Serrières

Blue water of the Rhône in its rock bed
Stalling, circling in pools behind
The island lousy with snakes: down I sank
With stones inside my bathing dress
To the mud bottom, to walk like a crab,

All that green summer drank
Air, knowledge. Bitter tough-skinned grapes
In a wild hilltop vineyard,
And the days, the days, like long loaves
Broken in half, as I fished with a cord

And a pierced stone for Yvette, the manager's daughter,
Killing hens in the hotel courtyard.
That castle where my brother broke his arm,
Yes: convolvulus vines, starved ghosts in dungeons . . .
But the family album does not include

The new guitar of sex I kept on twanging
Inside the iron virgin
Of the little smelly dyke, or that Easter Sunday,
Through a chink in the bedclothes, watching my mother dressing:
The heavy thighs, the black bush of hair.

Those wild red grapes were bitter
Though you could not tell them, by just looking, from the table kind.

1962

The Home-Made Raft

When we made that flax-stick raft and floated
Down the Oreti creek, we found
Holes in the shingle bottom
We had to step around
Or else ride over. The swirl of the river
Was indeed a thousand-headed
Serpent for those who could not swim;
Yet buoyancy, lightness, is what I remember,
Brown waves below high banks of manuka
Sprawling; and though we straddled it round the clock
The black wet bundle did not sink or break.

1962

The Dying Nazi Guard

Mother, your hands are red,
Speckled like salami . . . The little black hen died;
We fed her gobbets of bread
In the carved coop where you painted
Gottes gute gabe, under the sycamore
Whose whirling seeds are planes shot
Down in the Fuhrer's War . . . The Fuhrer lied
When he promised us the Rhingold, hot,
Burning our fingers. At Buchenwald
I hoisted the young Jew
Up by the thumbs till the swine sweated blue
With a pine cone in his arse . . . The door
Won't shut against the unburied ones who stink
All day. At Buchenwald
The Christ-Child walks the barracks, blue and thin,
With bread for someone else's sin,
And I am Buchenwald. These foul sheets smother;
They are hoisting me up, Mother!
Your schnapps is Jewish blood; I cannot drink.

Hocken MS704/23, 1962

The Pit

It has been forgotten, I think,
The pit, the cell they lowered you into,
Somewhere between the taking and the scourging.
          Your nose
Broken by blows,
And the torture still to come. They gave you
Nothing to eat or drink,
And the dark hole with its coiled stink
Of human dung, under, under all
The city, the barracks, the judgement hall,
Is where I look for you. My King, my King, you lean
Enclosed in the womb of the last trinity
Of man (Monotony, Atrocity, Anarchy)
As my heart is now. Was this the dream
Of the governor's wife? This deep
Bomb-shelter—the ridges of rock

Are new to my touch. Sleep,
My Dear, and I will keep
Watch . . .

Hocken MS704/23, 1962

The Town under the Sea

The town was usual enough: it had
A creek, a bridge, a beach, a sky
Over it, and even a small tin church
I never went to. My brother, my cousins and I
Did what boys do—dozed in the hot

Schoolroom, made bows and arrows, dodged the mad
Boatbuilder, crept like rabbits through the black
Under-runner with a weak torch,
Burnt dry rushes, wrestled or swam,
Doing nothing important. The difference, looking back,

Was that we did not see our own
Death in an oil-fouled seagull's death,
And the copulation of dogs did not
Remind us of ourselves. At puberty,
Or the first deadly sin, the sea rose up in one

Pounding night and swallowed the land. Shark
And octopus triumph in the dark
Doors of the human breath,
And the spider-crab is strong. Kelp-bladders, tangled, thrown
Up by the cannibal sea

Glitter immense. My father's gun,
My mother's gold ring,
And that toy lamb I lost and wept for, lie inaccessible, deep
Among the bivalves. Nor do any
Bells ring, on a windy day, from those wide

Guts of the coffin-making tide.
It is a natural sleep.
Yet some have said (not fools, not ruled by money)
Beyond this dying world and the prison house
Of Purgatory, a land lies

Lovely for human eyes, where smashed love, broken vows,
Are healed again. Water must
Exist (they say) to answer thirst;
Our thirst is great. That second Paradise
We measure by the first.

1962

The Glass Lamp

I remember mainly how
The river bent like a bright sabre
Out of the farther gorge. My mother
Led me past the hissing gander, over
The paddock to another house
Where somebody lit a kerosene lamp, a plaited white
Wick of cotton in a glass
Chimney, shoving back the dark,
A rose of flame in a room in a house by the rivermouth.
I remember it quite clearly now.

1962

Home Thoughts

I hate this boneyard peace
Of ceremonious dying, where
My mother, squat, strong-minded, with white hair,
Watches thc iceland poppies catch the breeze
Delicately. I hate and love
The tree of time, the dusty wattle grove,
And the blind devil on the stair
Who guarded and still guards the spidered room
That I wrote poems in. It seemed more safe to drown
In the fat pubs of the harbour town
And rummage in the ash-pit
Of God, for some live coal to light the gloom;

Indeed no child of Adam wished
Only for peace. The thought of it
Is death. I see the rainbow stand above
Those troubled waters where I fished too long,
Too late, and caught
Leviathan. I hate and love
That garden where my father taught
Me early, yes, too early how
The cut worm must forgive the spade, the plough,
Or grafted apple twigs on stumps of hawthorn.
Wrong, right; right, wrong;
In contradiction, lady, I was born.

1962

Martyrdom

Balancing on two boards up under
The spouting I fiddle with a brush.
My wife tells me I'm slow;
I just wonder
Will Our Lady grab me if I dive
Thirty feet
Down like a bull seal to the concrete?
I doubt it.
In the kitchen she sings, 'Ko tenei te po,'
Like an Opunake thrush.
My rigours make her thrive;
I'm gaining merit.
My daughter grizzles down below
About some bad word someone said, or that
Fat plaster-eating mouse
Who camps under my bed.
She thinks I'm an acrobat
In a travelling show. This night my son
Brings me a spider in a bottle—red
Like old burnt clay its hypodermic head—
Look, Daddy, look! The house
Of Atreus glitters in the midday sun.

1961–62

The Iron Cradle

(from Baudelaire)

Get well fonged. The whole world's there outside your skin;
it's the one thing that matters. In order not to feel the terrible
swag of time cracking your shoulder-blades, and pushing
you down to the earth like a loaded branch—get well fonged.
Don't give yourself a break.
Don't worry about the label on the bottle. There's grog, poetry,
even virtue. Take your pick; as long as you get fonged on it.
And if for a minute, or a minute-and-a-half, on the steps of
the Post Office, or in the long grass beside the cable car,
or worst of all, in your own flat, you start to wake up
and the fong begins to shift—Ask the wind, the waves of
the harbour, birds, clocks, the stars in the sky, whatever
rolls, speaks, cries out, murmurs, runs away; ask
them what time it is, and they'll all answer—
'Time to get well fonged! There's no other way out of the
iron cradle. Grog or poetry, or even virtue—whatever
you like, go and get well fonged on it.'

Hocken MS704/23, 1962
Argot, 1.3 (1962), 4.

The Buried Stream

Tonight our cat, Tahi, who lately lost
One eyebrow, yowls in the bush with another cat;

Our glass Tibetan ghost-trap has caught no ghost
Yet, but jangles suspended in the alcove that

We varnished and enlarged. Unwisely I have read
Sartre on Imagination—very dry, very French,

An old hound with noises in his head
Who dreams the hunt is on, yet fears the stench

Of action—he teaches us that human choice
Is rarely true or kind. My children are asleep.

Something clatters in the kitchen. I hear the voice
Of the buried stream that flows deep, deep,

Through caves I cannot enter, whose watery rope
Tugs my divining rod with the habit some call hope.

1962

Father to Son

Childish in me to appreciate
So much your approval, when you let
Me squeeze into your 'fort'

In the abandoned railway house
With smashed windows where you
Uncovered the necessary secret space
Just by lifting a board—

I should not care. Better for you
If I take no shelter with you
(There is not room for two

In one life) and I, being elder,
Must be myself a bomb shelter
To wife, child, friend, not digging for
Payment of approval. No.

How terrible if you should see my need
In the space inside where the dying 'I' bleeds,
And be disconcerted,

Saying, 'Aren't you happy?' Not long
After you were born (O star of beginning
In the black sliding pit) I would swing
Clumsily out of bed

To give you your bottle. Half-boozed
I had the sweet joy of being used
By one who did not ask

Where I had been, whether my hands were clean,
But was glad to be held and fed.
Such joy must be dissembled, my dear son,
By holding its light in a husk

Of indifference, a dark lantern,
Lest it should too brightly burn.
To be a father

Needs most of all, I think, an easy touch:
Better by far to clown too much,
Loudly break wind, visit your fort when requested,
Than to usurp the sighs of a mother.

Hocken MS704/23, 1962

Wellington

Otherwise than I had supposed it—'A grey town', they said;
But I found instead a grid of coffee bars
On which the young, my friends, bake bread
Out of invisible stones. The hills too are young,
Bush triangles in their groins. But the old notice a black noose hung
Between monotonous pavements and the inexplicable stars.

1962

To Any Young Man who Hears my Verses Read in a Lecture Room

When some cheese-headed ladder-climber reads
    A poem of mine from the rostrum,
Don't listen. That girl in her jersey and beads,
    Second row from the front, has the original nostrum

I blundered through nine hundred parties and ninety-eight pubs
    In search of. The words are a totem
Erected long after for scholars and yobs
    Who'd make, if they could, a bicycle-seat of my scrotum.

1963

An Ode to the Reigning Monarch on the Occasion of Her Majesty's Visit to Pig Island

Madam, I beg to quarrel with
Your trip across the water—
Pig Island needs no English myth
To keep its guts in order,
Though our half-witted housewives yearn
At your image on the TV screen.

Forgive me that I cannot praise
The Civil Service State
Whose blueprints falsify the maze

It labours to create,
And plants above that sticky mess
Yourself in an icing sugar dress.

The dead who drink at Bellamys
Are glad when school kids clap
A Fairy Queen who justifies
The nabob and the bureaucrat,
In a land where a wharfie's daughter can
Marry some day the squatter's son.

While the stuffed monkey, dog and sow,
Play ludo in the void,
The Auckland pavements carry now
Six hundred unemployed,
And the bought clerks who sneer at them
Will crowd to kiss your diadem.

The girls in Arohata jail
Are very rarely dressed in silk—
Let us take a Glasgow cocktail
Bubbling coal gas into milk,
Drink up to Mary, Kate and Lou,
No better and no worse than you.

Before my birth your soldiers made
A football of my skull
At Mud Farm when they crucified
My father on a pole
Because he would not take a gun
And kill another working man.

I give you now to end our talk
A toast you will not like:
MacSweeney the Lord Mayor of Cork
Who died on hunger strike.
It took him eighty days to drown
In the blood and shit that floats the Crown.

While Big Ben bangs out stroke on stroke
And the circus wheel spins round,
The Maori looks at Holyoake
And Holyoake looks at the ground,
And there will be more things to say
When the Royal yacht has sailed away.

1963

Ballad of the Three Monkeys

Down to the Wharf Commission I went
(A bag of nails and a union card)
For a regular job on the waterfront
(And the cash would have come in handy).

And a big Samoan he said to me
(A bag of nails and a union card)
'They put you through like bloody sheep'
(And the cash would have come in handy).

Two grown men and three young codgers
(A bag of nails and a union card)
Sat on the bench and none of us bludgers
(And the cash would have come in handy).

The first man in he got nowhere
(A bag of nails and a union card)
He hadn't got that servile manner
(Though the cash would have come in handy).

The second man was the big Samoan
(A bag of nails and a union card)
His mother had the wrong colour of skin
(And the cash would have come in handy).

The third man in was crook with the drink
(A bag of nails and a union card)
The fourth had done a spell in clink
(But the cash would have come in handy).

They opened the door and I was the next
(A bag of nails and a union card)
I saw three monkeys behind a desk
(And the cash would have come in handy).

'Can you read or write?' The first one said
(A bag of nails and a union card)
'We don't want a man with brains in his head'
(And the cash would have come in handy).

Said the second monkey, 'You must be a slob'
(A bag of nails and a union card)
'To want to get out of a Government job'
(And the cash would have come in handy).

'The point is, sir,' I said—'Shut up,'
(A bag of nails and a union card)
'There is no point,' said the third grey ape
(And the cash would have come in handy).

Those three grey apes will sit in the sun
(A bag of nails and a union card)
And scratch for fleas and drop their dung
(And the cash would have come in handy).

And while those monkeys rule the land
(A bag of nails and a union card)
There's no luck here for a working man
(And the cash would have come in handy).

1963

The Axe-Blade

Watching my father sharpen a notched axe-blade
On the lurching grindstone

Worked by a treadle, I liked the whirr that it made
And the way the steel shone

Star-bright when gouts of water played
On the grit, not guessing from the edge's groan

How year by year the lurching world would abrade
Nerve, heart, mind, flesh, bone.

1963

Shingle Beach Poem

There is (conveniently) a hollow space
Between the upper and the lower jaws

Of the world serpent. There, as if all days
Were one, the children whack

Their seaweed balls, brag, tussle, comb the shores
For little crabs. There's no road back

To the dream time, and I endure instead
This hunger to be nothing. I supplicate

Dark heaven for the peace of that woman they
Lifted out of the breakers yesterday,

With blue deaf ears, whom Poseidon banged on the kelp-beds
Though she was a good swimmer, her body oatmeal-white

Spotted with shingle. To and fro
She was rolled by the undertow.

This I understand. Sister, remember
Us who wrestle yet in the coil of life's hunger.

1963

To My Wife Going to Patea to Raise the Rental of the Maori Lands in Which She is a Part-Owner

Voices not muskets will
Contend for the holy land,
The fish of Maui hacked and eaten
By legislators. Go then,
Speak quietly of the rent due for a skull,
Unconquerable one. Your body is
My whare, my strong fort, my battle-ground.

Hocken MS 704/24, 1963

High Wind at Hokio

That day the gale blew hard, if
I remember rightly—so
we left the car by the bridge
and trod the rough grooved beach, deaf
with the air's army that blew
snakes of sand from the dune's edge

to fill our shoes. A low plain
of toi-tois opened her knees
on the tumbling brown-white flood
of waves like the chaos when
Earth was born . . . But what bound us
together and apart did

not slacken—mother, father,
daughter, son—held by the yoke
that rubs us raw yet teaches
a kind of truth: that nowhere
can the heart finally speak
or cease burning, as air touches

the dry sand and makes it flow,
or as that Maori girl rode out
on a sideways cantering
horse, from the bridge where a boy
chucked hollow reeds on the mute
creek, against the gale blowing.

1964–65

House Painting

An afternoon of spitting
rain, teaching nothing—the grey
under-coat got wet when I
painted below the spouting

where spiders load black cotton
in corners. The south wind shoves
against our ladders and lives
just this—the sense of an un-

inhabitable chaos
outside our skins, in whose tight
grip the will grows numb. I put
new white paint round the windows

of the washhouse, thinking of
the Roman scourge, nailed wristbones,
rough timber cut for the Son's
necessary death—but grief

grew from primitive knowledge
that the place of a skull is
where we crouch, in vacant peace,
unable to crack the cage

from the inside. Belief kills
the root it sprang from. There's room
left in God's grave for each dream
of God we bring to it—else

we would not share that foul cave
which is the void. Before night
half the job was done, and it
looked right enough then to leave.

1962–65

To a Print of Queen Victoria

I advise rest; the farmhouse
we dug you up in has been
modernized, and the people
who hung you as their ikon
against the long passage wall
are underground—Incubus

and excellent woman, we
inherit the bone acre
of your cages and laws. This
dull green land suckled at your
blood's *frigor Anglicanus*,
crowning with a housewife's tally

the void of Empire, does not
remember you—and certain
bloody bandaged ghosts rising
from holes of Armageddon
at Gallipoli or Sling
Camp, would like to fire a shot

through the gilt frame. I advise
rest, Madam; and yet the tomb
holds much that we must travel
barely without. Your print—'from
an original pencil
drawing by the Marchioness

'of Granby, March, eighteen nine-
ty seven . . .' Little mouth, strong
nose and hooded eye—they speak
of half-truths my type have slung
out of the window, and lack
and feel the lack too late. Queen,

you stand most for the time of
early light, clay roads, great trees
unfelled, and the smoke from huts
where girls in sack dresses
stole butter . . . The small rain spits
today. You smile in your grave.

1951–65

Ballad of Nine Jobs

At Purakanui I buried my shadow
Under the edge of a hillside plough.

At Wanaka I rode a stumble-
Footed pony without a saddle.

At the Burnside works I still stank
Of dead sheep, sober or drunk.

At Green Island I watched the iron
Burst from the rolls like a red-hot dragon.

On Cashmere Hills in the TB wards
I smuggled booze and scrubbed the morgue.

At Epuni with a buttoned fly
I taught the children how to lie.

In Wellington I did it hard
Carving stones in Caesar's graveyard.

Now I carry a postman's bag
In Wadestown through the grit and fog.

All the time inside my scone
I peel away the onion skin
Till the earth talks through the man.

1965

The Strike

I saw the bright bones of Lenin
Glitter in the air above
The house we wintered in, ten or twelve
People like lovers, and the rising sun

On the harbour waves; Lenin's bright bones
In the air assembled, instructed
Us—'Sharpen your axes
Against the tree of the State. I am necessity

'Alive in the liberal grave'—We won the strike,
And fell back to our squabbles,
Counting shillings, drugs, cosmetics.

Lenin did not come back
To us. He slept again
In man's heart, the holy mountain.

1965

The Anniversary

(to Bob Lowry)

Time breeds a distance like the space between
A drunk and sober man at the same bar.
It is the drunk who tries to make a scene
And follows up a street his lurching star

As if betrayed. The dry man keeps his place
And queries the wall mirror where a world
Looks back at him, but not the cadaver's face
Of one whom the avalanche has killed.

After a year in the black Auckland ground
Your body will have swollen like a sack
And shrunk again, while you yourself have found
What I have need of, yet prefer to lack,

The last, undrugged condition. It is I
Who stagger in the street, and you who stay
At the Queen's Ferry bar, a twelvemonth dry,
Watching in the square glass our monstrous day.

1965

At Wanaka

In the broken stone houses
Patched with pebbles, the miners lay

Down at night in their own coffins
But rose up in fine cold air to fossick

For the treasure buried under schist.
They went. I trudge on the lakeshore with

My son, my wife, my two nieces,
Our feet scuffing the yellow poplar leaves,

And all the tribes have died of thirst inside us.
The great launch roars out like a bus.

I remember how I walked to Luggate once
To get drunk, and waded lost

All night beside Mount Iron, through
The wrong fords under a mottled moon.

Getting pine cones for the black stove in the hut
I grant time lost, time gained, but nothing happens yet

Between the bought cribs and the lake outlet
To ease in us what lives, groans, yet turns to rock.

1966

The Maori Jesus

I saw the Maori Jesus
Walking on Wellington Harbour.
He wore blue dungarees.
His beard and hair were long.
His breath smelt of mussels and paraoa.
When he smiled it looked like the dawn.
When he broke wind the little fishes trembled.
When he frowned the ground shook.
When he laughed everybody got drunk.

The Maori Jesus came on shore
And picked out his twelve disciples.
One cleaned toilets in the Railway Station;

His hands were scrubbed red to get the shit out of
  the pores.
One was a call-girl who turned it up for nothing.
One was a housewife who'd forgotten the Pill
And stuck her TV set in the rubbish can.
One was a little office clerk
Who'd tried to set fire to the Government Buildings.
Yes, and there were several others;
One was an old sad quean;
One was an alcoholic priest
Going slowly mad in a respectable parish.

The Maori Jesus said, 'Man,
From now on the sun will shine.'

He did no miracles;
He played the guitar sitting on the ground.

The first day he was arrested
For having no lawful means of support.
The second day he was beaten up by the cops
For telling a dee his house was not in order.
The third day he was charged with being a Maori
And given a month in Mount Crawford.
The fourth day he was sent to Porirua
For telling a screw the sun would stop rising.
The fifth day lasted seven years
While he worked in the asylum laundry
Never out of the steam.
The sixth day he told the head doctor,
'I am the Light in the Void;
I am who I am.'
The seventh day he was lobotomized;
The brain of God was cut in half.

On the eighth day the sun did not rise.
It didn't rise the day after.
God was neither alive nor dead.
The darkness of the Void,
Mountainous, mile-deep, civilized darkness
Sat on the earth from then till now.

1966

The River

Nothing as broad as
the river can be seen
these days: it was dark
brown and deep
at corners where cattle graze,

and ran silently
by Mackenzie's cottage
where he made his boats
at its edge
choosing the thwarts cunningly

from bent manuka,
and we'd paddle upstream
past the ducks' island
in a dome
of daylong silence never

to be broken—I
break it now! The river
is foul weed and sludge
narrower
than I had supposed, fed by

a thousand drains: thus
the heart is twisted free
by thought's knife: the creek
runs to sea
finding its way without us.

1966

Travelling to Dunedin

We ride south on a Wednesday
Into the clearer weather,

Gently packed like foetuses in the dead
Belly of the thunderbird,

Down to the city of our youth
(My wife and I)—it's a quiet place;

But the pattern shifts a little. Those houses on Lookout Point
(Skull-grey as something painted by Utrillo)

Ambiguously glitter. We notice now
That a quarry like a cancer

Has cut away half of the smaller breast
Of Saddle Hill. And I remember

How in these parts the dead sleep
Under rough clay, who will rise up

In rage and hope at the Judgement Day,
Denying the quiet town, the quiet clouds,

Their hard, sod-cutting hands, so like our own,
Bent in the cramp of lifelong separate pain.

1966

At Queenstown

If you go up on a clear dry morning
You may find a few dog tracks in the frozen slush

Of the steep road, and round the next bend
The fir trees with their pollen-bearing candles,

Then at the top of the long hill
A chalet, not a monastery,

From which one looks down at the view:
The boats like water beetles,

Wooden motels and pine tree islands . . .
And later a full moon will take

Her own photograph of the Remarkables,
Black rock veined with August snow!

Now as the blind eye
In your brain struggles to open,

Admit: It's nice, but not quite human,
A dipsomaniac's limbo,

To sit like a sack of shit in a smart bar,
Never out of the death trance, looking at

The faceless terraced hills, the enormous blue
Vacant eyeball of the lake

That won't notice whether you go or stay
But only whether you have the money.

1966

At Brighton Bay

Two concrete pillars whittled by the tide
Regard the meeting of the bay and river,

Useless as some authority
Whose function is evaded by the water

That flows in wandering channels. I'd go down
In winter, when rain spattered on the wide

Corrugated levels, my body not
My own, but gutted by

The opposites of sex and pain,
Like new-cut banks the river had gouged out

For me to kick down ritually—
That grotesque adolescent fury

We never grow beyond! Today I hoisted myself
Up the rock stair that's called Jacob's Ladder

This end of the bay, shoving through gorse, and stood
On the smooth edge of the flax-covered cliff

That tempted me to suicide
In those times. No squid-armed Venus rose

Out of the surf, but through the smashed gate
Of many winters, from the hurdling water

Came to my heart the invisible spirit
These words have given shape to.

1966

The Bridge

Far up the creek I
often rode in
a rented canoe, my
paddles barely touching
the water's pollen dusted skin

where gorse-pods floated,
and slid under
the Black Bridge's rusted
bolts and tarry roof: there
one could make sherbet from water

with a matchbox full
of fizzing fine
powder. It tasted well,
nipping the tongue, in high
summer, when crickets chirred at noon

on each bush—lately
I went that way
not thinking, and saw the
bridge under fifty bull-
dozed yards of gravel and dry clay.

1966

Home Pleasures

What can disturb us? The rent is paid.
The doctor certifies I am not insane;

Pulse as usual . . . Why does the demon come
Disguised as an angel of light? This evening,

Sitting late at a wood fire dusted with white
Thick funeral ash—yawning, talking, thinking,

I feel, like the boy's hand squeezing the giant's heart,
This wandering, useless, imageless pain

Connected hardly at all with the black wings
Unloading napalm on jungle villages . . .

Ten years ago I would have killed it quickly
With a teacupful of Bols gin,

But now I don't even say, 'Bugger!'
When clods and roots of trees break through the walls,

Recognizing the grave will enter the house
Whether the door is shut or open.

1966

Grandfather

Old and
bald-headed as a turtle,
I remember you,
grandfather, at the trembling kitchen range—

(all your hopes drawn in
to a pond where the light
flickered and gripped you from above,
your dead wife's love)—

so hot with the damper out
a match would flare
at a touch of its explosive tip
on the black glossy surface!

Ah yes—you'd take
the white bone chanter
down from its rack, finger it and play it
so sweetly, lightly, the wristbone of a man

hollow at each end, or so
I think of it, life measured
into a tube wound round
with bands of silver.

You'd caught the notes, you'd stolen them
long ago, sitting like a young
ferret in a flaxbush while your father
tried to teach the elder son.

He taught you then. A champion piper
you could never read a note,
you *were* the tune! It didn't
help you much

when the bailiffs were in,
and the butcher of God's Word
dragged you in half, much later,
so that you gave up smoking and whisky,

fell, rose, fell, rose, fell,
always a worry to your wife—
my looking-glass twin,
when the fumes were boiling in your head

on a black morning, the horses stamping
unfed, the manuka dripping
in gullies mortgaged to the hilt,
did you say '*I* am Hell'?

I salute whatever
burns, our brother Lucifer
raging! This I understand.
Never the unhurt quiet end.

1967

The Grand Tour

(a conversation between Keith Holyoake and Marshall Ky)

Said Holyoake to Marshall Ky,
  'I'd rather you didn't come here;
We've got some trouble on our hands
  In the Election Year,
And if the price of wool goes down
  Up goes the price of beer.'

Said Marshall Ky to Holyoake,
  'You pedal, and I'll steer.'

'You understand,' said Holyoake,
  'I'm a simple democrat,
And though I much admire the way
  Your landlords have grown fat
By feeding off the peasants,
  We can't quite live like that.'

'All you need,' said Marshall Ky,
  'Is a baseball player's bat.'

'We're both of us,' said Holyoake,
'Good friends of the USA;
We need their dollars, you need their troops
And dollars, just to stay
In the saddle—but tell me, what do *you* do
When the unions get in your way?'

'A firing squad,' said Marshall Ky,
'Will stop strikes any day.'

'I must admit,' said Holyoake,
'Sometimes it worries me
To see the way the Viet Cong
Are fighting endlessly—
Why is it, Marshall, you can't teach
Them your democracy?'

'When we've smoked out the villagers
They'll know who's boss,' growled Ky.

'That napalm now,' said Holyoake,
'Must make a frightful stench—
When they burn like wetas in a log
Does it put you off your lunch?
Of course you dropped a pile of it
When you flew for the French?'

'The French or the Yanks,' smiled Marshall Ky
'Are a well-paying bunch.'

'I'm glad of that,' said Holyoake—
'And what about our boys?
Are they well fed and fighting hard
Among the jungle trees?
It's nice to know that in this war
The Kiwi has a place.'

'To tell the truth, man,' grunted Ky,
'They count no more than flies—

'But Washington has made it clear
New Zealand must be in
To give them another paper dart
To throw at Ho Chi Minh,
And Washington's told me to make this tour
Or else they'll have my skin.'

'We're both in the cart,' sighed Holyoake—
'Here, have another gin.'

1967

The River

My brother started the boat engine
Tugging on a cord, and I steered

Upriver with the tide behind us
Close to the outlet of the gorge:

No problem, except when somebody's
Plastic leggings, floating under water,

Twisted round the propeller. That same afternoon,
Lying down flat after lunch, I heard

The river water slapping, and thought about
Three buried selves: child, adolescent,

The young unhappy married man
Who would have hated this place—ah well,

Space is what I love! The three selves dance
In the great eddy below the Taieri bridge,

And I am glad to leave them, sprinkling water
Over the embers that heated the Thermette,

Having at last interpreted the speech
Of the river—'Does it matter? Does it matter?'—

And carrying like salt and fresh inside me
The opposing currents of my life and death.

1967

At Naseby

'Mountains are mothers'—I wrote
those three words in an MS.
book, beside a new poem,
long ago with a pen cut
from a rooster feather, when
the earth and I were much less

compatible—living then
in a lean-to at the side
of a sun-dried-brick cottage
a yard or two up the road
where they've put a FOR SALE sign—
no bigger than a garage,

but it's the place that counts—I
must have been mad! There are no
mountains here; just the poplars
raining down orange leaves to
rot in ditches, and a spry
shop that sells bread, potatoes,

chutney, magazines—far off
on the skyline a small spoor
of hills, but nearer at hand
nothing apart from the moth-
bright family baches and
sod houses worn by weather

shapeless as graves, among which
water-courses ramble like
veins of memory. I'm not
haunted much, climbing the track
to the swimming-dam, by that
grim boy step by step at watch,

my judge below the larches,
his mind like a coiled spring wound
tight by dread and hope, a quill
tucked in his pocket—because
I have forgotten his wound,
and trudging towards nightfall

I find that whatever is
other than self sleeps now like
a wife at my elbow, with
rough breasts of stone, from whose kiss
I turn, so as not to break
the hymen of Sister Death.

1967

Reflections at Lowburn Ferry

They take trucks on board for the river crossing.
Not always safe. It has been known to happen
That the ferry tipped and the truck slid back
Slowly into the Clutha with ten men cursing
And three men praying that the stuck
Cab door would shift. But the willows are green

Low down on the water. I've often thought that when
I finally flake, or a minute after, the gate will open
On this damned ferry. Very likely they won't have heard
Of Good Pope John. They will ask me why
I have no obol under my tongue,
Or a cent, or a penny—unless the price has risen—
And I will float in the mud like an old sad turd,
Never to live, never to die,
Wishing to Christ that Christ would come along,
Even the Protestant Christ, like Oscar Wilde when young,
To shake a tambourine with the souls in prison.

1967

Air Flight North

I do not like this chariot. It gives me
Faustian dreams. Undoing the seat belt

And lighting up a smoke, I am able to gaze at
Cattle like maggots on

Green porcelain paddocks, till the loops of the Taieri
Give way to a Christmas tree land

Of firs gripping the brown animal fell
Of hills (like what Nils Holgerssen flew over

On the back of a barnyard goose)—and somewhere
To the right down there, close to the tidal mudflats

(May they keep the peace) my wife and my two children
Do this and that in Cumberland Street.

Now the steel hawk is turning towards
That pale blue monster, the undrinkable ocean.

My mother Gea below me is undressed
Showing her stretchmarks got by long childbearing.

One should not look. Above clouds like ice floes
We drift on. I meditate the doom

Of Icarus, while the hostess brings
Coffee in trim red mugs. A calm flight.

1967

Winter Poem to My Wife

Because the fog is a curtain over the town
Because the lights are rare and few like virgins
Because the fire spits little sparks and weeps white resin,
Because I am a wooden husband,

You go away from me down to the roots of water
To find the spiny sea-egg
Whose yolk breaks molten in the mouth,
You go down to the sea gate
And gather the black pods of iron flax!

Because the trees are fur on an old hairy cat
Because the cars travel with windmills in their bellies
Because the houses are shaking their crumbling fists of mildew,
Because I am a warty husband,

You go away from me into the Maori church
To find an old bone flute
Playing by itself in the darkest corner
And the shark's tooth and the flounder
And the tears of the albatross!

I accept these journeys.

Because the wind has lost its powder keg
Because the frost has started to scythe the street
Because the moon is a blind wet crystal,
Because I am a silent husband,

You go away from me to the middle of the bush
To find a coat of stones and staples
Or the lifted hair of the hurricane
That tries to spin the sun in a new direction.
That's not a bad idea.

I accept my fate.

1967

To Mate With

To mate with the air is difficult—
That sinuous invisible creature
Blows hot, blows cold, rubbing her grit of pollen
On the bodies of ploughmen and mountaineers

Who itch and curse! To mate with a river
Or a filled-up miner's quarry, that pleases me;
My cold kind mother, Sister Water,
Has no comment, accepts whatever I am,

Yet one may think of tentacles
Reaching, searching from under the darkest ledge,
And not want to be married. To mate with rock
Is obvious, fatal, and what man was made for,

Whose heart of rock trembles like a magnet
For deserts, graves, any hole in the ground
Where he may hide from Zeus. To mate with fire
Is what the young want most, like salamanders

Weeping in solitary flame, embracing
Red-hot stoves, walking the lava crust
An inch away from fire. Then, my old gravedigger,
To mate with a woman is the choice

Containing all other kinds of death—
Fire, water, rock, and the airy succubus,
Without parable, without consolation
Except that each is the other's boulder and victim.

1967

The Flame

My son sleeps above—my wife is sleeping also—
My son's room smells of the incense that he burns
Before the Buddha—as good a way as any
Of yoking the demons that rise at puberty,

Not demons, other selves. At 4 a.m. I still sit
Awake at the kitchen table
Like a Martian in a space suit
Drinking coffee and writing. In forty years

I haven't found a cure
For being human. I can't get drunk
Now as I used to, dowsing the flame with whisky;
I have to live and burn

Thinking of Christ—Christ, who is all men
Yet has to be discovered
By each on his own—not this morning
His blood only, but his resurrection,

Like the voice of the wind blowing on troubled waves,
Like hard buds of japonica,
Christ who is ointment, and for whom I carry
The incurable wound of life, and stand in the black flame.

1967

The Fear of Change

If you and I were woken suddenly
By the drums of Revolution in the street—
Or suppose the door shot open, and there stood
Upright and singing a young bullfighter

With a skin of rough wine, offering to each of us
Death, sex, hope—or even just an
Earthquake, making the trees thrash, the roofs tumble,
Calling us loudly to consider God—

Let us admit, with no shame whatever,
We are not that kind of people;
We have learnt to weigh each word like an ounce of butter;
Our talent is for anger and monotony—

Therefore we will survive the singers,
The fighters, the so-called lovers—we will bury them
Regretfully, and spend a whole wet Sunday
Arguing whether the corpses were dressed in black or red.

1967

Spring

Girls like red-hot peonies (how nakedly they dress!);
Invisible fingers tugging at my fly;
The sense of being in a bent glass funnel—
Is it the devil? No;

It is the Lord's female lieutenant,
Venus, for once without her brother Death,
Who makes the hard twigs burst—who makes me notice
My own woman's dark mane of hair.

1967

The Fiery Shirt

In the garden by the river, walking
With one woman—clear night, a touch of fog—
The fiery shirt rose up from the turf we trod on
To wind around my ribs.
                                        We lay down
Without speaking. A writhing of worms
Under the sack dress,
And the moon's great ruined face
Gazing up at me from the roots of the grass.

I am tired of what is called life,
This torture room. The chains and hooks and ropes
Are always hung up, ready for use.
Kisses scald, words crush. But the river
Flowed on, in a bell of calm, to whom I said,
'Pray for us, Mother. We are not yet
Able to die—'

1967

The Paddock

I came with my father to a gully above the sea
And left the car parked among the gorse bushes
That nibbled at its paint.
                                        'Here,' he said,
'Was Old Willy's hut. Here on this bank.
There should be a broom bush that grows thorns;
Yes—' He pulled a sprig of it from the hedge
With eighty-year-old fingers. And in the paddock
Beside a dip in the ground, he discovered the place
In which he walked and wept and saw the light—
'There was an orchard. My brother all but hung me
With a wheel and a rope from that branch'—
The branch being invisible. Not a stone of the house standing.

Too many books, too many faces,
Exhaustion—the soul has to become
A stone hidden in the ground

Under a tree that has already been cut down
And sawn up carefully to make timber
For a bridge or a cattle yard.

I inhabit the empty ground.

1967

The Caryatids

Between night and morning but belonging to neither,
The hour when stars lean down to the earth with black flames
That the wise might use as a time for praying or writing letters;
We are not wise.
                    In a bedroom with a steel basin
And a suitcase, being insomniac,
One of us will finally beckon out of the wall
The mad boathouse-keeper with his box of photographs
Whom poets have called Eros.
                              Thinking about women—
And lighting one cigarette from another, while the white globe
Burns as it were on the roof of a cabin in a ship that carries us towards death
With no Brendan's isle to visit—we are driven to acknowledge
The ones that we loved best were the ones who broke us
Limb by limb—those natures uncorrupted by compassion
Except for a sparrow or a cat—they handled words like ploughshares—
As one lifted her face from a stunted field of rocks and grass,
Shouting—'I will not!'—to her God; not to any man—
And one round-faced girl offered herself to be kissed, then wiped her
  mouth and said—
'You are—*nothing!*' And one, a drunk voice on the telephone, muttering—
'The man I love has two phalluses!'
These are the deaf caryatids,
These and their companions, each with the same limbs
And a different soul, who taught us that the flesh is human
And superhuman, lifting up on bruised shoulders
Ton by ton, the pediment of night and day.

1967

The Doctrine

It was hope taught us to tell these lies on paper.
Scratch a poet and you will find
A small boy looking at his own face in water
Or an adolescent gripping imaginary lovers.
And the hope became real, not in action but in words,
Since words are more than nine-tenths of life.
We did not believe ourselves. Others believed us
Because they could not bear to live without some looking-glass.

'Are they real?' you ask—'Did these things happen?'
My friend, I think of the soul as an amputee,
Sitting in a wheel-chair, perhaps in a sun-room
Reading letters, or in front of an open coal-range
Remembering a shearing gang—the bouts, the fights—
What we remember is never the truth;
And as for the body, what did it ever give us
But pain and limit? Freedom belongs to the mind.

That boy who went out and gazed at his face in the river
Was changed, they say, into a marvellous flower
Perpetually renewed in each Greek summer
Long after his tough companions had become old bones.
To act is to die. We ward off our death
With a murmuring of words.

1967

October Water Poem

The wind that cuts the flax like a new pocket knife
The wind that gives the fishermen a rough time
In their boats far out beyond the reef
The wind that rubs the scalp of the hill with salt
A gruff wind not shown on any compass card,
Call it the wind of middle age.

All the canoes in the boatshed where we played when we were young
Are floating like little ducks as the tide comes in
Octopus-white snot-green and sharkish under the bridge,
So strong a gust that the black timbers tremble.

We will not go to the beach in the evening
We will sit by a fire and talk about books
We will yawn and go to bed and have bad dreams
In which the sea has taken charge of the land.

No one can tell us how to get on good terms
With the great sea-devil or the wind of middle age
That smells of the dead year, though not yet our own death.

1968

The Black Star

I do not know when exactly we saw the black star rise
Above the mountains and fields and the places where we
Were accustomed to gather. The colour of the earth was changed
As if by mildew. It was a calm day,
If I remember rightly, with a dry wind blowing over
The fruit-bearing plateau. Blossoms were falling that day
Onto our heads, into the wine
We had set out on tables. Then a child shouted,
'Look at the black star!'
                                        We looked up and saw it,
A spot, a disc, a kind of hole through which
The blue water of the sky was being drained out;
Yet the sun was still there, the wind kept blowing,
The wine held its savour.
                                        There were a few among us
Who wept, pierced themselves with thorns, and cried,
'Deliver us, Christ, from our sin!'
                                                    What sin?
Sins are bred in the marrow of the bones of men,
Painful no doubt, but the wisest learn to live with them.
I forgot to say some of us began to scatter paper money
On the greying earth. No one would stoop to pick it up.
The old people now keep close to their houses,
And the young have grown ungovernable—they run wild wearing masks
Of hair and stick and bone. The middle-aged are finding it
Tolerable; at least I do.
                                        As for the black star,
It whirls, it stands, it governs the day and the night,

And though we prefer not to speak about it,
We regard it in a sense as a new god—god or machine—we call it
The Equalizer.

1968

Grass and Night Wind

No age at all your body has,
For you are the bending toi-toi, or that other grass
The spirits tied in knots for us

To follow by as they
Went north towards Te Reinga and the whirling
Gulf of air and water. I perhaps

Am the wind who comes at night to shake those blades
Chafing them into
Music of a kind. I do not know

What age your body is, because
I did not wonder—'Is she old or young?'—
Or any such condition on the day

We met in that strange garden at
The centre of the world; only that
Without grief, each through each,

We are all that the lost have been.

1968

The Bargain

The rows of pea-plants in my neighbour's garden
Glisten with the dew. Paths of wet asphalt

Climb the near-by hill, under some kind of tree
Whose leaves topple in green waterfalls,

Leading very likely to a car-park or a junk-yard
But able to be thought of as the wandering track

That goes to a place where Brother Ass can bray
Without burdens. I can smoke, type letters, wind

The cuckoo clock, drink lukewarm coffee
In my scrubbed house—I have accepted God's bribe,

To be content with not being dead,
His singing eunuch—and my son who clatters

His hippie bells from room to room, my wife
Who makes pies out of buttered bread at the white range,

Even the grey cat blinking and curling its claws
In the armchair, are certain the bargain's a right one—

Yet if the prisoner ceased one day to sweat and rage
In his cell of jumping nerves and layered muscle,

Dreaming of wild women and guerrilla battles,
Bridges blown up, farewells in African hovels,

I would not be I, and the bargain useless,
For He would be cheated of the aroma of bitter blood

Spilt on the cross-tree, and I would have become
Simply the dead man hanging, the abdicated Jesus.

1968

The Serpent

The snake of lights in the North-East Valley
Curves uphill into a darkness where

Monument and TV tower will wait
The coming of either a nuclear deluge

Or the slow winding down of all our clocks.
I do not worry much. If in Biafra

They bury children under mounds of red dust
My dollars will arrive too late to change

The manner of their dying. Rather I
Must remember the phone call I promised to make

Yesterday—what was it about?
Did the number begin with five or seven

Or was it neither? My friend, perhaps the serpent
Has already eaten us.

1968

To Patric Carey

From beaches grey with ambergris
The pressure of invention came,
Like waves that penetrate through combs of sand,
That single, first, unknowable proposition
Published in theatres of stone
By actors roaring through great hollow masks
Not thunder, no, but the life of Aeschylus
Decaying to a hard wave-polished bone.

And still the mouths of actors vend
With Beckett, Brecht and Behan, what
The audiences know as well
As blood and semen, but forget,
That we are gaps in banks of broken sand:
Lucky the playwright then who keeps
After the public stoning and the praise,
Silence and one producer as a friend.

23 December 1968

Letter to Sam Hunt

Dear Sam, I thank you for your letter
And for the poem too, much better
To look at than the dreary words
I day by day excrete like turds
To help the Catholic bourgeoisie
To bear their own insanity;
And if in Paremata you
Should find a weta in your shoe,

Ugly, hard-shelled, with snapping jaws
A Hitler who has lost his cause,
Don't hit it with a shovel—No,
Christen it JIM and let it go.

Though it may serve no good, in rhyme,
To look back on the fucking-time,
I do recall one evening, drunk
In Devonport on Dally plonk,
Endangering my balls and marriage
With someone's darling in a garage,
Upright and groaning, breaking eggs
Until the yolk ran down her legs—
One of the best of Venus' nuns,
A girl with tits like ack-ack guns
Who sighed and screwed and screwed and sighed
While her grim husband sat inside
The house and meditated death
For her and me with every breath,
Journalist, tombstone-maker, or
Some other kind of social whore.
Last year we met again and she
Not screwing sighed and looked at me,
A swaddled deathshead old and dry,
But there was life in that blue eye.

'Honey,' I said, 'You're thinking of
Another time when love was love.'
'You've struck it, brother,' she replied,
'But now I find the gap inside
Is cold and dark and hard to carry
And Buddha is the man I marry;
He teaches me that love is love
Only when it's past thinking of.'

Dear Sam, if you are twenty-two,
Why should I foist my gall on you?
The answer is that poets live
By a refusal to forgive
The mighty Bog of social shit
That has no use for sex or wit
Or art or hope, but simply is
Internally its own abyss;
At twenty-two or forty-one
You need your gumboots and a gun.

Sam Hunt, Sam Hunt, Sam Hunt, Sam Hunt,
The housewife with her oyster cunt
Has pissed upon what might have been
Lively, original and green,
The old pohutukawa tree
With hairy ballocks on its knee.
The Pill, the Rags, the Summer Sale,
Put Venus and her tribes in jail
Till every fuck's a coffin-nail;
Her husband, that sad pudding-head,
Will pull himself each night in bed
Softly, for fear he'll wake the Dead,
And teach his children how to lick
The Boss's arse and not be sick,—
Not that I blame the poor blind bitch
Who hoped that she would strike it rich
But saw her pretty flowers wilt,
Her cunt turn into a patchwork quilt,
Her handsome Prince become a Frog,
And drowned herself in the Social Bog.

But I must go my own way still
Across Death Brig and up Skull Hill
To learn the science of our grief
Conversing with the Impenitent Thief,
The one unique left-handed saint
Who knows why we must write and paint.
He teaches me that Sophocles
Heard in the thunder of Greek seas
On beaches grey with ambergris,
On the recoiling serpent hiss
A voice proclaiming to the land
That men are banks of broken sand,
And various other things that I
May put in plays before I die.

Dear Sam, this day as I came down
The steps that take me into town,
Rehearsing in my head these rhymes
That hold a mirror to the times,
A perfect omen crossed my track,
A garbage-eater, wild and black,
Pugnacious, paranoid and sly,
A tomcat with a boxer's eye

Dripping a gum of yellow pus,
I thought that he resembled us
Who may write poems well, with luck,
About the dolls we do not fuck,
And hear the dark creek water flow
From a rock gate we do not know.
Till we ourselves become that breach
And silence is our only speech.

1968

Valediction

The death-blue sluggish river in the South
Like veins on a dead man's arm . . . O you hills
Where I was born, the people at times were able
To light fires, to keep lamps burning
For their children to look at.
                                        There is more than one
Schoolhouse looking at itself in a lagoon
Where paradise ducks come down; but I must
Describe also a sadness like flint
Embedded in the eyes of brown-haired children.

It doesn't matter. The country is dragging
Chains of words, chains of money,
Decorated with a necklace of petrol bowsers
And waiting to be blessed by a good
Psychiatrist. My dreams do not go South.
Parents, grandparents, the fire you lighted
Under my arse will keep me moving
For another day at least. I will go North
Tomorrow like a slanting rainstorm.

1968

[The book is shut]

The book is shut and I have gone
In rags to serve the Virgin's Son
James K. Baxter he is dead;
Plant a boulder at his head

And write on it—'Goodbye, good luck,
The words are somewhere in the book;
This bloke inside a broken heart
Carried the spike of time and art,
But now he does another thing
With silence for a wedding ring—
Christ and Mary, greet your guest;
Memine, nihil satis est. Amen.'

Hocken MS975/16, 1968

Ballad of Dives and Lazarus

Two men lived in the same street
But they were poles apart
For Lazarus had crippled bones
But Dives a crippled heart
That made him stare both night and day
At a production chart.

The springtime came, the springtime went,
The tide flowed up the sand;
Lazarus murmured to himself,
'It is a pleasant land;
The sun that shines upon my coat
Is the comfort of God's Hand.'

But Dives in anger cried aloud,
'I spend too much on you!
A blind man cannot watch the dials
That help my engines go;
A deaf man cannot hear the whistle
To tell the end of smoko;

'A lame man cannot fetch and carry
The cheques that I must write—
The graph of my production chart
Is lovely in my sight
As Jacob's ladder was to him
Upon a starry night.

'And you will live, since live you must,
But at a cheaper rate;
A cripple cannot ask the World

To carry his dead weight—
My engines run too slowly
Because of the Welfare State.'

God spoke to Dives upon the hour
(Since God and God alone
Knows what can turn a human heart
Into a heart of stone)—
'My poor blind crippled son,' He said,
'Sit here beneath My Throne,

'Why force My Hand? I did not make
Man for the gap of Hell;
I gave the wild sea and the wind
And limbs that serve him well,
And a heart that is My dwelling place
Where none may buy or sell.

'Go back and learn from Lazarus
To walk on My highway
Until your crippled soul can stand
And bear the light of day,
And you and Lazarus are one
In holy poverty.'

1968

For Hone

Tuakana, I am a hard stone
Thrown from a heavy sling

Breaking through walls and padlocked doors
That time has rusted fast

'Ko wai koe? Ko wai koe?
Te tangi o te manu.'

Tuakana, now I wear your coat
I am a stone man walking

And in the cold night of the town
The gravestones are all shaped like women.

The coat will keep me warm when I lie down.
The cigarette burn on the left side of it

Is better than a pocket full of money.

13 March 1969

Inscription for the Wall of a Power Station

Matiu Jackson fell from the face of the dam,
18 years old and lately out of borstal.
They buried him without a tangi.
John Ball died here, drunk, yelling,
Pinned under the blade of a bulldozer.
Thomas Macfarlane, killed when the tunnel caved in . . .

Ko te Kawana rite ki a Parao.
A thousand nomad workers
Built this power station, tomb and pyramid,
Where even the water is owned by Pharaoh.

The grass bends when the wind blows over it,
But their lives were less to King Cheops than grass,
So many pay packets, so many marks on a sheet,
Today so many statistics of unemployment.

When you plug the cord in for the electric toaster
Remember the blood of men is flowing through it.

1969

Tangi

They have taken the piupiu from the body of the land
Baring those wild timid limbs and thighs

Not in love, but in order
To see her as a thing. The crooked tree

On the cliff face is an old woman mourning
At the tangi of her daughter. Nevertheless

Day and night the waves move
On the broken dunes, caressing and reshaping

What will outlast the asphalt and the towns.

1969

Letter to Max Harris

Brother Max—it did me good
(If any human message could)
To know my verses struck your eye
And touched your heart—thus, in reply,
I offer you this sprig of jasmine
Across the cold waves of the Tasman
Who writes upon a beach of scars
That man is greater than his wars
Because he curses underneath
A fat bed-roll of love and grief.

Ah yes, in Auckland I met Hope,
And nominate him as our Pope
Because he thinks in the Roman way,
An honest swordsman, tough and grey,
Who carves his poems with his prick
In plain Augustan rhetoric,
And stayed with sorrow in his bones
To spread his swag on college stones
And hears the ghostly water sigh
Now that the riverbed is dry.
And then, McAuley—yes, one night
We shook hands (if I have it right)
Under the shade of Mother Church
Who still conducts her ill-starred search
Among the intellectual fringe
For a new Hopkins, yet will whinge
If any hobo takes the pen
To bust the walls of her thieves' den
Where the ice can clink but never melt
And all thought starts above the belt.
McAuley (did he?) seeing the drop
In front of him, became a cop
For our dull Mother, and must prove
To demi-virgins on the hoof

That the only love is married love;
But I may have mistaken him
Because the signs are growing dim.

Shit, man! Christ and Captain Quiros
Are out of town; let the devil steer us,
The dualistic one whom we
Depend on for our poetry!
By which I mean, Max—as I have said
To young Sam Hunt—a man well mounted
On board a girl is somewhere near
The threshold that our bought men fear
And stumble at. The Hindu lass
Who sits cross-legged on her arse
Below my cottage crucifix
Was given me by my friend Trix,
A Buddhist with an open hand
And the best drummer in the land,
A king in his Pig Island bog
Though hunted from here like a dog
By the cops and the clerks and the bourgeoisie
Who have not yet dismembered me!—
As I was saying, that sweet bint
Contains ten Korans in her cunt,
Ezekiel, Pope Paul, Bondi Beach,
Mount Desolation, Kelly's Creek,
The strength to call a spade a spade
And all the verse I ever made;
Though Cardinal McOgg says 'No'
And twelve professors in a row,
Where this man goes she too must go,—
With her, the god of Robert Burns
Who frightened girls at milking churns,
The demon with the double prick
(One for the front, one for the back)
The god of nature born to die
Who is no more than you or I.
But Catholic poets mainly keep
Their distance from these two, and weep
To see the pagans take the field
Using their ballocks as a shield
And write the poems and the plays
And piddle on the crown of bays
Reserved by colleges for such
As spend their lives translating Dutch;

But I'll not waste my tears of phlegm—
They wear their wooden diadem;
I think you had the best of them
In old Ern Malley's deathbed song,
And you were right and they were wrong.
Australia I have found too flat
And that enormous welcome mat
Of dried-up scrub surrounding Sydney
Killed Lawson and might well kill me.
Thus, driven by the butcher's goad,
I turn and take the other road,
Not out but in, and find myself
Stuck like an old maid on the shelf
Here in a cottage, planting beans
With no thin hippie girl in jeans
To roll me pot and share my bed,
And my dear God may be contented
But I am not.
                    Dear Max, my friend,
This letter is the sprig I send,
So wear it in your button hole
And give it some day to a girl.

1969

Song

My love came through the city
And they did not know him
With his beard and his eyes and his gentle hands
For he was a working man.

My love stood on the lakeshore
And spoke to the people there
And the fish in the water forgot to swim
And the birds were quiet in the air.

'Truth'—he said, and—'Love'—he said,
But his purest word was—'Mercy'—
And the fishermen left their boats and came
To share his poverty.

My love was taken before the judge
And they nailed him on a tree
With his strong face and his long brown hair
And the whiteness of his body.

'Truth'—he said, and—'Love'—he said,
But his purest word was—'Mercy'—
And the blood ran down and the sun grew dark
For the lack of his company.

My love was only a working man
And now he is God on high;
I have left my books and my bed and my house,
To follow him till I die.

'Truth'—he said, and—'Love'—he said,
But his purest word was—'Mercy'—
Flowers and candles I bring to him
And no man is kinder than he.

1969

[Letters to Frank McKay]

1

Keeping this heavy-headed
vigil, Frank, I cut my bread,
cheese and garlic on the new
crumb-loaded newspaper spread
as a good tablecloth now
in this cottage kitchen made

for the Sisters; Father O'
Sullivan writes that I
might follow Saint Dominic
by reading Scripture—ah, no,
this old skull carries manic
tendencies, and when Judy

Todd called to stay for a night
it left me excitable,
tugging against the collar

God makes for a donkey—well,
my Scripture is the colour
of beans growing near the gate

where the cows sleep, where I go
with trouser-cuffs tucked in my
heavy boots under cloudy
or star-toothed skies to follow
our dark Lord, lying on the
cold floor in front of the high

sanctuary rail—yet, Frank,
the same bull tosses his horns
here or in Grafton, horns of
absolute love—with gored loins
and breast, seeking, yes, the grave,
we in the desert get drunk

on promises, believing
He will do our will—rather
one should beware the child one
already is, go singing
up like a muddy ploughman
to the gate of the Father.

2

Late at night I sit up, Frank,
with my feet cold in the wet
flopping sandals; they were made
in Auckland; I don't forget
easily the human good
of arms, eyes—yes, I could think

I was a king there, in that
disorderly house beside
the trees of the high Domain,
because I was loved. It is hard
to put off the flowering crown
plaited by hands I cannot

hold again; but it was so
for the man the Aztecs made
their god for a day, and gave
wine, kisses, the rumbling gourd,
proud sleep in a bed of love,
because then he had to go

up steps of the hill of skulls
quite alone, to meet the One
whose emblem was a flint knife,
and lie on the altar stone
to bear also the tribe's grief
to the Master of all souls,

Te Ra—I joke a little,
Frank, but that is how it was
in Grafton. Maybe the myth
belongs to all men. Doubtless
our true commodious Faith
includes both sweet carnival

and ashes on the forehead
after it; but our Lover
troubles me most when He comes
quietly to the back door
and leads me out of all dreams
to share His own solitude.

3

When I take off my thin belt
and hit myself with the brass rings
on the end of it, as I
get ready for sleep—man, my
Scottish peasant back was built
to take a couple of bangs

now and then! But the demons
don't like it—'Hey! Go to sleep!'
they yell—'Unfair! Out of date!
Before and after midnight
belongs to us! You've no sins,
you old masochistic ape,

'only maladjustments! I'll
tell the bishop!'—the last comes
from a clerical-looking
demon who keeps on swinging
an opossum by the tail
to take my mind off dark themes

such as the Scourging; and you
know well enough, Frank, how mad
our friends would count me. Yet what

would they offer this grey goat
as a means to the virtue
of continence? Which one said—

'Man, you're mad'—when I would climb
in or out of bed with a
hippie bird? They were silent;
and God makes me continent
by cracking my lifelong dream
with the thud of brass—I may

add, the old Curé of Ars
looks down from my wall sweetly
with an enigmatic smile
as if to murmur—'Ah well,
child, the science of the cross
cannot be learnt tidily . . .'

1969

Haere Ra

Farewell to Hiruharama—
The green hills and the river fog
Cradling the convent and the Maori houses—

The peach tree at my door is broken, sister,
It carried too much fruit,
It hangs now by a bent strip of bark—

But better that way than the grey moss
Cloaking the branch like an old man's beard;
We are broken by the Love of the Many

And then we are at peace
Like the fog, like the river, like a roofless house
That lets the sun stream in because it cannot help it.

1969

The Labyrinth

(for John Weir)

So many corridors,—so many lurches
On the uneven filthy floor
Daedalus made and then forgot,—'What *right*
Have you to be here?' the demons thick as roaches
Whispering . . .
                    Mind fixed on the Minotaur
I plugged onward like a camel that first night,
Thinking—'Not long, brother, not long now!'—
But now so many nights have passed
The problem is to think of him at all
And not of, say, the fact that I am lost
Or the spark of light that fell upon my brow
From some high vault,—I sit down like a little girl
To play with my dolls,—sword, wallet and the god's great amulet

My father gave me.
                    In the bullfights it was easy
(Though heroic no doubt) because their eyes, their eyes held me
To the agile task. Now I am a child
Frightened by falling water, by each nerve-pricking memory
Of things ill done,—but I do not forget
One thing, the thread, the invisible silk I hold
And shall hold till I die.
                    I tell you, brother,
When I throw my arms around the Minotaur
Our silence will be pure as gold.

1970

Procession

The white skull faces of Vietnam
Are carried on our flags along the street,

Quietly, quietly walking—and the faces of my friends
Are transformed by the ritual of speaking for the dead,

No longer caught in the web of an unloved education
Or the cold bog of a Varsity party—

Our childen of the void, for whom I die each moment
As for the young calf tumbled by the cold river

Until it drowns and dies—but the faces of my friends
Have found their equipoise, they are themselves

At last, the children we kill with poisoned money,
Bribes, drugs, and a thousand lying fables,

Have found their equipoise in pity for the dead,
And the zeros in the eyes of the cold skulls

Reflect the coldness of a city
Where the soul and the body are treated as a thing;

To be bought and sold—Oh you many watchers,
Feast your eyes on your children walking upright at last!

1970

Meditation on my Father's Death

Where my father walked and found
the rock where Abraham took
a knife to offer Isaac,
a new tree catches the wind
from the nut a bird dropped down
in a crevice of the rock,

and it sprouted and grows tall,
leaning above the demon—
hearted breakers and the worn
elbows of seastone.
                              Angel
of our dark searching, tell us
why the dead blaze like the sun

between our thoughts! My father
has wood and earth on his face,
yet hardly a flake of loss
blows to me from the bonfire
of his great joy; and I stand
barefoot under the gallows

of my forty-fourth year, gripped
by the rope of mercy, stoned
on the blood of God.

The wind
has blown the tree, swept and shaped
its arms to fit the earth's hard
jail where all limbs have to bend.

1970

Song for Sakyamuni

1

Loose as the washed pants and blouses that flap
On the thin wire they've tied round the corner post of the veranda,

My words are no longer the words of Apollo
But the river in its high gorges, life and death together,

Or the river in its shallows, mud and broken timber—
The body is a wound, Sakyamuni said,

Covered with damp skin, oozing out foul juice
From seven orifices, the wound we must bandage each day

In order to act and live in the light of the *Dharma*,
And my wound is half my trouble—the other half

Is the folly of believing I am I
In spite of contradiction—How hard to stop imitating

That waterlogged bee I saw on a clover head this morning,
Clinging to its red petals while the winter rain crashed down!

2

A thread can hold the bird back from rising
Just as well as a domed wire cage;

My loves, I grant, are all self-love,
Except for the love I cannot call my own,

The wind that moves in the branches of the tree
Without premeditation—Can the stomach never vomit up

Those broken bits of mushroom, the poisoned food of Yama?—
'I am, I am, I am,

'A poet, a Catholic, a dry alcoholic,
A man of forty-four'—you, Jesus, you, Sakyamuni,

Help me out of the pit! No ladder is necessary;
Ladders are part of the pit—my brothers, when the minute comes,

You will not see me; I will have gone out through the crack in the rock
Like an old lizard—No more, no more, no more Becoming!

3

There was a man who lived at Jerusalem,
He had an old coat, he wore his toenails long,

The newspapers made up stories about him
To entertain the housewives—why couldn't he live

In the Kingdom of Anxiety like any other man
And go into his house like a rabbit to its burrow?

God was his problem; God and the universe;
He had, let us say, a problem of identity—

Now, if you go to the valley of Jerusalem,
You'll find that the silence is like any other silence,

You'll find that the river is like any other river,
You'll find that the rain is like any other rain,

But the old man has gone out of the picture,
Leaving an empty picture frame.

1971

from *He Waiata mo taku Tangi*

(for Eugene)

1

At the beginning of March,
nineteen-seventy-one,
I'll open, if you like,
my guts for the world to see,
having nothing to lose,
not even hat or shoes,—
wife, home, reputation,
that too is gone,—

and if just after light
I go by the riverside
to eat the dusty fruit
from a bush of blackberry,
or wash my cut feet,
or kneel and meditate,
don't suppose it comes
from a cloudburst of sanctity!

My days go past like smoke,
my soul has long since grown
blind as an old opossum
in the roof of a Maori church,—
I think of the Cistercians
I met at Kopua,
God-loving Irishmen
with faces like children,—

Yes, they're my brothers, man,
because God makes me poor
and drives me out to walk
on the road to Wanganui
with an old coat and bare feet
and convent beads at my belt,
but I'm a madman
and the monks are sane men!

My father has followed his plough
into the darkest paddock,—
my mother is growing old
with Christ for company,
she won't last for ever,—
friend after friend has gone
into Te Whiro's hut
whose doors are made of stone,—

and like a man who rakes
for the live ones in a plague pit,
I do what I can,—
politeness, chastity,
or even a clean shirt,
are a great luxury
for one who throws his heart
for the mad to feed on,—

and I don't count how many
have climbed in the sack with me,
girls out of the bin
or those whose bodies stink
of lush or amphetamine,
to hide a muddled head
underneath my beard,—
may Christ have mercy

on us when we die!—
the tribe of nga mokai
who can do nothing well,—
may he keep us out of Hell
and bring us to the place
where the Maori corn grows green,
not for what we have done
but because we wanted peace!

Men out of the clink
come here and share their kai
at Hiruharama
in the coil of the taniwha,—
when mouths are peeled by thirst
they have to get water,
it is good to see them come,
the burnt and the lame,—

but my own soul one day
will lie in the dust
like a dead cicada,—
God makes a man,
we give him a name,
he goes back into the womb
of the earth and is lost,
unless God lifts the stone!

One tooth is left only
at the back of my bottom jaw,
there's kapok in my beard,
my guts are shrunk with fasting
among the Tama Toa,
I don't get sleep,—
this body falls to bits
like a mattress that gapes open,—

it would be nothing, man,
if the soul burned softly,
like a candle that's lit
in a windowless whare
to give us good dreams,—
but if I come to God
it will be by a road
where there's not even starlight,—

only the voice of rivers,
Rakaia, Rangitata,
Ohau, Clutha,
and now the Wanganui
who washes my body
before its burial,
will say nga karakia
mo Hemi te tutua,

the one who has become
a gap in a wall,—
like holy mothers
who speak for the child
who has lost his breath and voice
under the waterfall,—
and if they hold a tangi
at the wharepuni,

a river stone will do
well enough to hide
what lacks identity,
the kumara they throw
across the fence to rot
in the middle of the brambles
when the clean red ones are gathered
to cook in the hangi,—

and my wife Te Kare
is the one I give
stone, seed, breath, blood,
because Te Atua
joined us together,—
may she be the bird
on a branch by the river
who sings in joy for ever.

Kumara Poem

(for Sam Hunt)

Too many and too much,
the people and the happenings
left standing like dry bramble
when the fire eats inside it;
if there is a testament
it will never now be written
by this gun-shy ex-poet,

nevertheless, Fog-Arse,
I love you, man. The nun's cows
flap their slack udders out
there in the wet grass; Zema
with her shirt outside her jeans
is cooking rolled oats in a little
pot, and humming her own tune;

and this is Hiruharama . . .
To be a bad Dad, Sam,
with a house of wild friends,
so gentle the day, so quiet
the rain beginning to fall
and the smoke beginning to rise
from the cigarettes in the rooms,

that the slipped disc in my spine
hardly ticks; and I forget
the song of Heremaia
raving among the mildewed
smashed houses where the kehua
stands at noon—'Aue, aue
kua mate Te Atua!'—

All of the students who get here
in family Jaguars or
with swollen feet, say—'Man,
it's bad! I've blown my mind;
I need . . .' They don't know what,
and I don't either; except maybe
the same notes in a different tune;

but up at the old house
nobody is slamming cards
on the table at 4 a.m.

and shouting—'Holy fuck!'—
there I can be poor at last
and even sleep for two hours
in a Maori cloud. You know, Sam,

my feet are nailed here to the ground,
the house of words has fallen down,
and this old kumara will rot
while the young red ones grow slowly
out of his gut . . . What is it
to lose the I, the instrument
we made our own sod hutch with?

'Kua mate Te Atua'—
the great ghost has gone
with his brandy and canticles;
down here, down low, it is to
eat the bread a girl
baked for herself and us
with sixty scars on her arms.

1971

Ballad of the Third Boobhead

In a rackrent house not far from Aro Street
    One dark morning
Four men sat with a bottle of wine at their feet,
    And the rain was falling.

The first man said, 'The Government's not my mother,
    I worked on the boats for twenty years
And all I've got to show for hard skippers and bad weather
    Is the price of five beers.'

The second man said, 'The screws and the magistrates
    Are wearing me down,
I've been in too many boobs and too many fights
    In too many towns.'

Then the third man said, 'I've not seen Jesus Christ,
    But if he came
To earth he should either have had a gun in his fist
    Or stopped the whole game.'

The fourth man reached for the bottle and said nothing
    But the light from the window
Showed like a graveyard lamp that his hands were shaking
    And his skin was like calico.

And the third man said, 'It will take more than talk
    To make this a country
Where the men who were treated like slaves will be able to work
    For other things than money.'

Then the four boobheads caught on the horns of the beast
    Saw on that dark morning
Above the town like lightning in the east
    The bones of Lenin shining.

1971

from *Ballad of Firetrap Castle*

2 Truth *Song*

Macdonald Crescent is my home,
J. K. Baxter is my name,
Francie and Esther live with me,
Two Richards and two Waynes,

Peter, Tony, John and Vince,
And many another one,
But since the fuzz cracked down on us
Most have split to Hamilton.

Now the old sick vulture of the Press
Has dropped a great fat turd on me,
They reckon our accommodation
Is hardly sanitary,—

As if a scabbed bitch who'd been fucked
By every prick in town
Should snarl at a lively friendly chick
For wearing an old gown,—

Truth, Truth, Truth, Truth,
You call yourself a paper,
Like an old moll who can hardly sell
Her bread-box for a dollar,

You'll do to wrap the greasy chips,
You'll do to wipe my arse,
You'll do to light the fire at night,
But I read you for a laugh,—

To hear an old moll moralize
About the state of man
Will make me laugh and shit myself
While sitting on the can,—

Truth, Truth, Truth, Truth,
When did I ever see
More lies set down on a single page
Than what you say about me?

And so I think it's hardly safe
To rub your ink on my bottom,
The poison might creep up and make
My haemorrhoids go rotten,—

You old shit-rag, I think you have
A beautiful vocation
Poisoning for forty years
The arsehole of the nation.

Old octopus that lives in drains,
Does it make you feel secure
To suck the ballocks of the rich
And trample on the poor?

Truth, Truth, Truth, Truth,
Sell your twat while you are able,
The horse for honest men to ride
Will come from another stable.

5 Sad Father Song

Old Father Caulfield gave us the runaround
When they turfed us out of Jerusalem,
He reckoned I must be running a brothel,—
He never donated an ounce of cum.

With due respect to the Catholic priesthood
I wish at least he had visited the place,—
The farmers lost one or two sheep in a hangi
But they didn't have the nerve to meet us face to face.

Oh late in September I came down to Wellington
Wearing my bare feet and an oilskin
To hear the little birds on Mount Victoria
And smell the turds that float in the harbour.

7 Firetrap Castle Song

I tell it the way it happened,—
First I wrote an article
For the *Sunday Times* about the poor of the town
Whom the fuzz are riding like an all-purpose bicycle.

I said maybe I'd have to grab a house
If the City Council couldn't come up
With something better than thirty dollars a week
For a ramshackle derelict hovel.

The Council got worried, they told me to cool it,
I talked to Mrs Campbell and Mr Porter,—
They had no houses, they said, but Mr Carlin
Would write to the Ministry of Works about it.

The Ministry of Works needed some ointment badly
To rub on their eyes, when they looked they could see no houses,
Not a single house in Wellington
Empty and usable for the boobhead and the rouseabout,

And Mr Carlin wrote to the Minister of Works
And I think the poor man suffered from amnesia,
I think he used that letter for arse paper
In between two committee meetings.

So the tribe shifted into Macdonald Crescent,
A three-storey mansion called Wuthering Heights
With no lighting and no water and three smashed grots
And five tons of rubbish as a playground for the rats.

But the roof kept the rain out, and we drove out the rats,
And cooked on the fireplace and wrote slogans on the wall,—
I called on Mr Kuch, our civilized landlord,
To offer him some rent for his firetrap castle,

And he thought it peculiar when I shook his hand,
And he said, 'Mr Baxter, what a card you are!
I don't want to be mixed up in anything religious'—
He wouldn't take the money, which was rather sweet of him,—

Pending an eviction order,—so I followed the tribe to the Labour Bureau
Where the clerks are accustomed to bully the poor
And keep them from getting their Unemployment Benefits
By a game that resembles snakes and ladders.

And I followed the tribe to Number One Police Court
Where Skully sits like Rhadamanthus
Weighing the guts of the poor in his scales
And handing out fines not one of them can pay,

And riding the drunks with a saddle of iron
And treating the Islanders like idiot children,—
I must thank Mr Skully for the opportunity
Of completing my Marxist education,—

Nothing but a bomb will ever cure the fuzz!
It would be nice to plant one just under Mount Crawford,
In the spring it might put out leaves and flowers
To astonish the screws who eat and shit by the clock.

Well, we lived in Firetrap Castle for a month and a half,
Till *Truth* sent round a prudish reporter
Who nearly fainted when she saw
That somebody had written 'Motherfucker'

On the wall of our living room, as a kind of code message
To another friend,—she got out her notebook
And observed that there were flies in the house
And most of us were sleeping on mattresses.

She took a photograph of the scungiest bedroom
Just like a Salvation Army hostel
Or one of the cells down at Central,
And stuck it in her rag, with a long rave on hygiene.

How nice to be nice! But the poor have no money
By definition, and in this country
They flay us for our hides, and tell us to eat asphalt
Unless we can learn to lick the boss's arse.

When they turf us out of that ramshackle crashpad
The ratepayers can support us again
In the clinks and the bins, and I will go back
To knock at the door of Jerusalem.

Roll on the Revolution!

9 New Mood Song

'He nui pohue
Toro raráro'—
The thoughts of a man's mind
Are many and secret,

I must be the old eel
Who hides beside the bank
When the waters of the river
Come down full of mud.

Secrecy, darkness,
Silence, that is
The language of revolution,
To be a friend of all men

But share your soul
With no one except
The one who carries
The same key.

My son opened for me
The Book of *I Ching*,
I tossed three coins
And the Book answered,

'Between the high mountain
And the deep water,
Stand still, meditate,
Go forward gently!'

The branch will flower again
In another spring,
It does not matter
If the cattle tear it down,

And another spring
Will bring the same cattle.

E hoa, let me
Sit in your house for an hour,
We will talk about
The things that concern us both,

And tomorrow the sun will rise
And the day after
Until the day
They bury us.

1971

Song to the Lord Jesus

Lord Jesus, you are like the sun in the sky,
The light shining in our darkness
So that we ourselves can become the light.

Lord Jesus, you died in pain on the cross,
You rose again from the dead.
Now you live within us,
You live our lives and die our deaths with us.

Lord Jesus, all that is in heaven belongs to you,
All things that are on earth.
Send your Spirit like a river of clear water
Flowing through our hearts.

Lord Jesus, you are the house and we are the timber,
You are the vine and we are the branches.
Send your Spirit so that the vine may flower,
Heal in us whatever is at fault.

1972

Song to the Holy Spirit

Lord, Holy Spirit,
You blow like the wind in a thousand paddocks,
Inside and outside the fences,
You blow where you wish to blow.

Lord, Holy Spirit,
You are the sun who shines on the little plant,
You warm him gently, you give him life,
You raise him up to become a tree with many leaves.

Lord, Holy Spirit,
You are the mother eagle with her young,
Holding them in peace under your feathers.
On the highest mountain you have built your nest,
Above the valley, above the storms of the world,
Where no hunter ever comes.

Lord, Holy Spirit,
You are the bright cloud in whom we hide,
In whom we know already that the battle has been won.
You bring us to our Brother Jesus
To rest our heads upon his shoulder.

Lord, Holy Spirit,
You are the kind fire who does not cease to burn,
Consuming us with flames of love and peace,
Driving us out like sparks to set the world on fire.

Lord, Holy Spirit,
In the love of friends you are building a new house,
Heaven is with us when you are with us.
You are singing your song in the hearts of the poor.
Guide us, wound us, heal us. Bring us to the Father.

1972

Song to the Lord God

Lord God, you are above and beyond all things,
Your nature is to love.
You put us in the furnace of the world
To learn to love you and love one another.

Father, we sing to you in the furnace
Like the three Jewish children.
The hope and the doom of the love of friends
Is eating up the marrow of our bones.

Lord Christ, you are the house in whom we live,
The house in which we share the cup of peace,
The house of your body that was broken on the cross,
The house you have built for us beyond the stars.

Lord, Holy Spirit, beyond, within, above,
Beneath all things, you give us life.
Blaze in our hearts, you who are Love himself,
Till we shine like the noonday sun.

Lord God, we are the little children,
The feeble ones of the world.
Carry us for ever in your breast, Lord God,
Give us the power by love to be your holy ones.

1972

How to Fly by Standing Still

1

The circle of the hills contains my house;
The house contains the tribe,

Various, turbulent in their occasions.
I accept the limits of the possible.

The window of my bedroom is mended with cardboard.
After the exchange of many words

Last night I dreamt a demon visited me,
Corpulent, androgynous, the height of a man's body;

My Pentecostal friends would consider exorcism
The right course to follow. Rather it seems probable

I have to be the sponge that sucks up the disordered
Humours of the tribe. Today the cool wind blows gently.

Without the turbulence of new water
The lake of the soul might well grow stagnant.

2

When the spokes fall out of the wagon one has to wait,
Unyoke the horse, hope for the kindness of heaven.

Winter comes to us with a slow drumbeat,
The light is sinking into the earth.

To provide for my people I must go to Wanganui,
And ask the members of the Society of Friends

To send us a few blankets. The nights at Jerusalem
Get colder. I possess a sleeping bag,

But in June and July the fog will last till midday,
And in the small hours some think that they are dying

As they turn to ice under a thin blanket.
Remember, though, Ho Chi Minh said

The cold nights in prison sharpened the axe of the mind,
And when the door opened the great dragon could fly again.

3

They bring me in two eggs and a slice of bacon;
I shout and dance on the floor of the middle room

Like a chimpanzee. Joy is gripping my heart.
Their old koro has to be a madman

For them to feel at home with him. The *I Ching* tells me,
'Joy in movement makes people follow;

'If a man would rule he must first learn to serve'—
Thunder in the middle of the lake,

When the earth goes into winter rest
And we lie down to sleep. They honoured the men of old

With a tomb on the Western Mountain,
And I trust the tribes of the River will give me a tangi

Here at Jerusalem. When our bones rise again
It will be the everlasting springtime.

4

Truth is the bird whose foot shelters the fledgling;
We have to see through the eyes of another man

In order to understand him. Be detached
If you are able. The cock crows in the fowlyard

Beside the house, as light comes over the trees,
But Ricky our rooster cannot fly to heaven.

Words are not enough. I think, brother,
My soul has to be like water

That flows down rapids, through many gorges,
Never losing its cool. The abyss of God above,

The abyss of darkness underneath one's life,
Between the two chasms one might grow afraid

Were it not that daily the sun rises
And there are friends to put their arms around us.

1972

Torso I

These are the days, brother, when they screw the handles
On to the coffins of young men and old women
Who have taken their own lives. I remember Paula's face,
Like a sick dog or cat, the cheekbones of the skull
Jutting through the flesh—'Now Karl is dead
I cannot go on living'—and that bright one,
Weyburn, who shot himself with the twenty-two—

They have to lower them gently into the ground
Because the spirit may trouble us. These are the days,
My friend, when the great shark rises
In the water of the heart. The chestnuts under the tree
Are bursting like bombs. A girl had written on my chest
With an ink pencil—'You are an old bastard'—

None of it matters. If God has forgotten us
One day He will remember. Harder than flames or ice
For a man to endure is the heavy waiting
For a doubtful word. If my limbs tremble
You will understand. The gate in the rock
Is half open. Shut it or go through it.

1972

Sestina to Frank McKay

The winds of spring are starting
Even in June to blow
From a wild sky, and round this house
Where a cat sleeps on a bed
And my friends bring me in some kai,
Goat chops roasted a bit too much

In our family oven. But that's not much
To gripe about. When we were starting
Here we often had no kai
Except onions, and the rain would blow
Through broken windows. Now I lie on a bed
In what the cops would call my house

Though it is in fact a Maori house
Under the wing of the marae too much
For many to like it. The church would give us a bed
Of nails to lie on, the State would like to see me starting
An army borstal. Let the wind blow
From the Maori hill and we will get our kai,

Our houses, our freedom. Tank our friend brings kai
Up from the pa. Father Te Awhitu patched this house
Chopping timber blow by blow
When the pakeha farmers would not have given as much
As a cup of tea. Now the tree is starting
To sprout from its ramshackle seedbed,

The love of the many. I can lie in bed
Under blankets and eat for a kai
The goats my friends have shot, while slips are starting
To block the river road. This old Maori house
Is the mother's lap where the child learns as much
As he is able, and the June rains blow

Harmlessly. I wait for God's breath to blow
Life into the body of a culture on its deathbed
Or else, Frank, for those who have had to bear too much
To make a new start, share their clothes and kai,
Put down mattresses in every meeting house
And build their own canoe. It's difficult starting

Anything new, yet the wind starting to blow
From the house of the sun will tumble the saints out of bed.
It's wise to eat one's kai and not say too much.

1972

from *Five Sestinas*

1 Winter in Jerusalem

The *I Ching* tells me *T'ai*, the sign of peace,
Is what I venture in. The pungas on the hill,
So lately loaded with snow, are green again

Though some branches were broken. Where many men gather
From need or friendship, truth begins to waken
As eels rise in the dark river.

If Heaven gives me this old house by a river,
It is not for myself, but for the purpose of peace,
As the thunder and rain of spring make green things waken,
A fence of poplar leaves between us and the hill
Who is our mother, or the chestnuts we gather
In autumn when the earth is warm again.

In our dreams it may happen the dead return again,
As if the earth spoke to us, because time is a river
On whose bank in ignorance the tribes gather
With emblems of battle, yet desiring peace.
The fathers instruct us from their holy hill
So that the warrior souls may waken.

In winter with a heavy mind I waken
And wait for the sun to lift the fogs again
That bind Jerusalem. Like a bridegroom above the hill
He touches with hands of fire the waves of the river
Like the body of a woman. Our words are words of peace
In this house where the wounded children gather.

We can go out with Maori kits to gather
Watercress, or some tough lads who waken
Early will break the veil of peace
With gunshots, combing the bush again
For young goats, or lift the eel-trap from the river
As fog shifts from the highest hill.

The times are like some rough and roadless hill
We have to climb. I do not hope to gather
Pears in winter, or halt the flow of the river
That buries in sludge the souls who begin to waken
And know themselves. Our peace can't patch again
The canoe that is broken, yet all men value peace.

Peace is the language of the pungas on the hill
Not growing for any gain. These images I gather
As eels waken in the darkness of the river.

3 The Dark Welcome

In the rains of winter the pa children
Go in gumboots on the wet grass. Two fantails clamber
On stems of bramble and flutter their wings
In front of me, indicating a visit
Or else a death. Below the wet marae
They wait in a transport shelter for the truck to come,

Bringing tobacco, pumpkins, salt. The kai will be welcome
To my hungry wandering children
Who drink at the springs of the marae
And find a Maori ladder to clamber
Up to the light. The cops rarely visit,
Only the fantails flutter their wings

Telling us about the dark angel's wings
Over a house to the north where a man has come
Back from Wellington, to make a quiet visit,
Brother to one of the local children,
Because the boss's scaffolding was too weak to clamber
Up and down, or else he dreamt of the marae

When the car was hitting a bend. Back to the marae
He comes, and the fantails flutter their wings,
And the children at the tangi will shout and clamber
Over trestles, with a noise of welcome,
And tears around the coffin for one of the grown-up children
Who comes to his mother's house on a visit,

Their town cousin, making a longer visit,
To join the old ones on the edge of the marae
Whose arms are bent to cradle their children
Even in death, as the pukeko's wings
Cover her young. The dark song of welcome
Will rise in the meeting house, like a tree where birds clamber,

Or the Jacob's-ladder where angels clamber
Up and down. Thus the dead can visit
The dreams and words of the living, and easily come
Back to shape the deeds of the marae,
Though rain falls to wet the fantail's wings
As if the earth were weeping for her children.

Into the same canoe my children clamber
From the wings of the iron hawk and the Vice Squad's visit
On the knees of the marae to wait for what may come.

Sestina of the River Road

I want to go up the river road
Even by starlight or moonlight
Or no light at all, past the Parakino bridge,
Past Atene where the tarseal ends,
Past Koroniti where cattle run in a paddock,
Past Operiki, the pa that was never taken,

Past Matahiwi, Ranana, till the last step is taken
And I can lie down at the end of the road
Like an old horse in his own paddock
Among the tribe of Te Hau. Then my heart will be light
To be in the place where the hard road ends
And my soul can walk the rainbow bridge

That binds earth to sky. In his cave below the bridge,
Where big eels can be taken
With the hinaki, and the ends
Of willow branches trail from the edge of the road
Onto the water, the dark one rises to the light,
The taniwha who guards the tribal paddock

And saves men from drowning. Down to Poutini's paddock
The goats come in winter, and trucks cross the bridge
In the glitter of evening light
Loaded with coils of wire, five dogs, and wood they have taken
From a rotten fence. On the bank above the road
At the marae my journey ends

Among the Maori houses. Indeed when my life ends
I hope they find room in the paddock
Beside the meeting house, to put my bones on a road
That goes to the Maori dead. A gap I cannot bridge,
Here in the town, like a makutu has taken
Strength from my body and robbed my soul of light,

Because this blind porangi gets his light
From Hiruharama. The darkness never ends
In Pharaoh's kingdom. God, since you have taken
Man's flesh, grant me a hut in the Maori paddock
To end my life in, with their kindness as my bridge,
Those friends who took me in from the road

Long ago. Their tears are the road of light
I need to bridge your darkness when the world ends.
To the paddock of Te Whiti let this man be taken.

1972

Sestina of the Makutu

In the dream I am lost in a Maori graveyard
Among the dunes of sand,
And like a wave of black water
The makutu hits me. No terror like this,
Latrines, ovens, graves, a woman's anger
Splitting my skull with a stone axe,

Yet it is Te Whiro who wields the axe
Or else te taipo, the masters of the boneyard
Where I have to walk. Why should the Maori anger
Rise from the roots of the grass and the sand
To choke the soul of this
Old pakeha? To drown in deep water

Is the fate of those who go into the water
Of the marae. I know why the axe
Is raised above my skull. I know why this
Dream comes out of Te Whiro's yard
To flatten a house built on sand
With the storm of an old anger,

And I accept the anger
As drowning men open their lungs to the water
Because the battle among the dunes of sand
Is won by losing it. I know the axe
Of the makutu was made in a yard
Where warriors drank black water before this

For their mother the land. The towns built over this
Black bog of a people's anger,
Sweet-shop, jail and railway yard,
Will fall like leaves into the water
When willows are chopped by the farmer's axe.
Blood swallowed by the sand

Rises again out of the sand.
On an old pakeha's head let this
Makutu break its axe,
Since anger breeds anger.
The one who walked the water
Has no voice in Te Whiro's yard

Except that the yard's dark sand
Should drink down like water this
Old man's blood, and aroha, not anger, blunt the axe.

1972

The Tiredness of Me and Herakles

(a letter to Herman Gladwin)

1

I trapped the great boar,
A Jansenist priest in his lair.
His tusks were longer than the Auckland Harbour Bridge,
His logic pure as the seafoam,
'All men are damned except myself.
The christly do not have erections.'
The occasion of our dispute was a teen-age chick
To whom I had written a poem.
Though he booted me out of his presbytery
We parted civilly enough.
I asked him for a conditional blessing.

2

The cleansing of the stables
Took twelve thousand tons of river water.
The horseshit had hardened in the stalls like concrete.
You couldn't shift it with a pick or shovel.
Ritualism, fetichism, moralism,
Simplicism, angelism, dualism,
Drayload after drayload went swirling out the door.
I was afraid nothing would be left.
But when the floor was wet and cool as limestone
I found wedged in a crack one iron crucifix
And a thin medal of Our Lady.

3

The sky met the earth
To the west of that marae.
Great trees hung over the meeting house.
The earth giant did not greet me gladly.
'Apples,' he grumbled, 'too many apples,
My troubles began with an apple.'
But he let me take the rigid weight
Of the firmament on the strap-hardened shoulder
I got as a city postman long ago.
The apple that he plucked from the oldest tree
Burned in his hand like a sun.

4

In the battle with the shield-bearing women
I got this wound that makes me limp a little,
An arrow lodged one centimetre
Above the right testicle.
They cut one breast off to draw back the bowstring,
The other breast they keep to feed their children.
'Pornographer,' they shouted, 'you have poisoned the wells!'
The dust rose on a desert whirlwind.
Their queen Hippolyta grew amorous
After defeat. I did not like her.
She smelt of dexedrine and cabbage water.

5

All day I ploughed with savage oxen
That snorted and farted like runaway tractors.
That was the labour involving the printed rubbish
Plain men use at evening to wrap up fish and oysters
Or at midday as a table cloth.
The king was gloomy when the paddock had been ploughed,
Though the furrows lay like polished metal.
'You are in danger of becoming vain,' he said,
'With too much exposure by the mass media.'
I noticed that the summer flies
Had laid their eggs in his beard.

6

The bout with Death was a hard one.
He wore a black uniform.
'Why don't you cut your hair?' he asked me.
'Life is filth. I keep the world clean.'
He had come with a pure heart from morning Mass
For a work-out at the police gymnasium
Before supervising the cleaning of a cell
That had some blood and vomit on its wall.
We wrestled in a fog of greyness
Till the swastika pin fell out of his shirt.
I was glad when the boss man called it off.

7

This wet October night
In a house in Auckland
The horseleech's daughter
Is crying, 'Give! Give!'
I have given her my fingers.
I have given her my liver to eat.
I have given her my skull to use as a soup bowl.
The ones who come here stoned on LSD
Forget they had a convent education.
To kill the heads of the hydra
You need a clever branding iron.

8

Three times in twenty years
I have wept a few tears.
I prefer laughter
But it gives me a hernia.
Herman, you old yelling shouting foetus,
Some wisdom has trickled through the cracks in my egg.
The drizzling grief of the town is the swag I carry.
A fist fight would improve the score.
I do not take my compass from Lenin.
My people rarely laugh or weep.
The fear of being hated has turned them into rock.

9

Today I smashed a green hydrangea bush
With a walking stick
At the edge of somebody's private lawn.
Every leaf was the head of a friend.
The meat wagon did not come to the scene.
Five labours still to go.
I am tired already.

1972

The following two poems were written by Baxter on the wallpaper at the home of his friend, the painter Michael Illingworth. They date from around the time Baxter wrote his final poem—'Ode to Auckland'—at Illingworth's kitchen table.

[Moss on plum branches]

Moss on plum branches and
A soft rain falling—no other house
Spread out its arms around me
As this has done—I go
From here with a gap inside me where a world
Has been plucked from my entrails—fire and
Food, flowers and faces
Painted on walls—the voices of two friends
Recalling the always present paradise
We enter and cannot remain in.
Arohanui
Hemi

Hocken Misc MS1631

[A pair of sandals]

A pair of sandals, old black pants
And leather coat—I must go, my friends,
Into the dark, the cold, the first beginning
Where the ribs of the ancestor are the rafters
Of a meeting house—windows broken
And the floor white with bird dung—in there
The ghosts gather who will instruct me
And when the river fog rises
Te ra rite tonu te Atua—
The sun who is like the Lord
Will warm my bones, and his arrows
Will pierce to the centre of the shapeless clay of the mind.
Hemi.

Hocken Misc MS1631

Glossary of Maori words and phrases

Phrases beginning with the introductory words E, he, ka, ko, kua, nga, and te are listed under the second word of the phrase.

a	and
Te Ariki	the Lord
aroha	love, respect, and compassion
arohanui	a plenitude of aroha
ko te aroha i Te Ariki	where love is, there the Lord is
atua	spirit
Te Atua	God
E	O, oh
haere ra	farewell
hangi	earth oven, or, by common usage, a feast
Hatana	Satan
te hau	the wind
he	a, some
hinaki	eel-trap
hine	young woman
Hine-nui-te-po	Goddess of Death
Hiruharama	Jerusalem
E hoa	friend! companion!
Hoani	John, generally referring to Baxter's son
Hone	John
inanga	whitebait; also a pale translucent variety of greenstone
ka	an inceptive verbal particle
kahawai (ka'wai)	species of school fish
kai	food
kaore	no
karaka	a large tree that bears edible, orange-yellow berries
karakia	prayers
nga karaki mo Hemi te tutua	the prayers for James the nobody
kare	ripple
Te Kare	an object of affection (Baxter's name for his wife, as is the next entry)
Te Kare o Nga Wai	Te Kare of the waters
kaumatua	respected Maori elder

kauri	massive cone-bearing forest tree prized for its timber
Te Kawana	the Governor (by extension, the government)
ko te Kawana rite ki a Parao	the government is like the Pharaoh
kea	mountain parrot
kehua	ghost
ki	to, towards
kina	sea egg
kiwi	a species of flightless bird (used colloquially, 'Kiwi' refers to New Zealanders)
ko	introductory particle emphasising the subject
koe	you
kono	woven food basket
koro	uncle, elder relative
kua	introductory word indicating past tense
kuia	revered elderly woman
kumara	sweet potato
kuri	dog
mahi	work
mako	shark
makutu	spell, curse
manu	bird
manuhiri	guest; stranger
he manuhiri au, ko taku haere e te haere o aroha	I am a guest, my coming is the coming of love
manuka	small shrub or tree with slightly aromatic leaves and medicinal properties that often grows in dense clumps
marae	tribal meeting-ground
matai	a species of forest tree
mate	death, sickness
Maui	mythological Maori hero one of whose exploits was to try to kill the Death Goddess by entering her body. (The 'Fish of Maui' is the North Island of New Zealand, hooked and hauled up from the sea bottom by Maui.)
mo	for
nga mokai	Baxter generally uses this term when referring to members of his commune, to mean 'the fatherless ones'; it is usually applied to captives, pet birds, or animals, and often to the youngest members of a family.
moko	facial tattoo

mutu	finished, completed—'Kua mutu' in Maori being the last words of Christ on the Cross
nga	the (plural)
ngaio	a species of shrub or small tree found in coastal regions
ngakau	thoughts, heart (i.e. emotions)
Ngati Hiruharama	the Jerusalem tribe (almost certainly a reference to members of Baxter's commune, as opposed to the literal alternative of a subtribe of the local Wanganui Maori, Ngati Hau)
Ngati Whatua	Auckland tribe
nikau	palm tree
nui	large
he nui pohui toro rararo	a large clematis [tree] stretches downwards towards the ground
o	of
pa	Maori village
pakeha	New Zealander of European descent
parao	Pharaoh
paraoa	bread
pia	beer
piupiu	flax skirt
te po	night
pohue	climbing plant
pohutukawa	an evergreen tree with bright red blossoms
porangi	mad, madman
puha	sowthistle, frequently used by the Maori as a vegetable
pukeko	swamp-hen; bird found on marshlands
punga	tree-fern
pupuhi	blowing
Te Ra	the sun (by extension, God)
te ra rite tonu te Atua	the sun who is like the Lord
rararo	below, underneath
rata	vine or tree with a brilliant red flower
Te Rauparaha	Maori warrior and hero
raupo	bullrush
Te Reinga	In Maori mythology the spirits of the dead are thought to leave from Cape Reinga at the top of the North Island, for their ancestral homeland
rimu	native tree prized for its timber
rite	like

riwai	potato
roimata	tear
roimata ua, roimata tangata	the tears of man fall like the rain
te taipo	the devil
taku	my
taku ngakau ki a koe	I give my heart to you
Nga Tama Toa	Young Warriors, a militant protest group for Maori rights, 1970s
Tangaroa	Maori god of the sea
tangata	man
tangi	(noun) Maori funeral ceremony; (verb) cry
te tangi o te manu	the cry of the bird
taniko	Maori patterns of weaving with coloured thread, especially with cloaks and headbands
te taniwha	spirit or demon
tapu	sacred; forbidden
te	the (singular)
tena koe	greeting
tenei	this
ko tenei te po	this is the night (title of a song)
terakihi	a species of fish
timata	to begin
ka timata te pupuhi o te hau	the wind began blowing
toetoe, toi-toi	a bush with a hollow stalk and whitish-yellow plumes
toro	spread; stretch
totara	species of large forest tree prized for its timber
tuakana	elder brother
tuatara	a New Zealand reptile resembling a large lizard, famous for having a vestigial third eye in the back of its head
tukutuku	woven grass and reed wall panels
tutua	slave, nobody
Wahi Ngaro	the Void, Space (a term used in Maori creation chants)
wai	water; who
ko wai koe?	who are you?
nga wai	waves
waiata	song
He Waiata mo Taku Tangi	Song for my Funeral-ceremony
He Waiata mo Te Kare	Song for Te Kare
wairua	spirit, soul
Te Wairua Tapu	the Holy Spirit

weta	a New Zealand bush insect resembling a large grasshopper
Te Whaea	the Source, the Mother of God
whare	house
wharepuni	meeting house
whiori	tail
Te Whiori o te Kuri	the Tail of the Dog
Te Whiro	Death
Te Whiti	Born in Ngamotu, Taranaki, in 1830, Te Whiti O Rongomai was a religious prophet and leader of the Te Ati Awa Tribe who advocated a policy of passive resistance at the time of the confiscation of Taranaki lands by the Europeans. The community he established at Parihaka was destroyed by British troops in 1881. He died in 1907.

Select bibliography

Major publications by Baxter

Principal volumes and broadsheets of poetry

Beyond the Palisade. Christchurch: Caxton Press, 1944. 2nd edition (ed. Paul Millar), Auckland: Oxford University Press, 1998.

Blow, Wind of Fruitfulness. Christchurch: Caxton Press, 1948.

Hart Crane: A Poem. Sumner: Catspaw Press, 1948.

Charm for Hilary. Christchurch: Catspaw Press, 1949.

Poems Unpleasant (with Louis Johnson and Anton Vogt). Christchurch: Pegasus Press, 1952.

The Fallen House. Christchurch: Caxton Press, 1953.

Rapunzel. Wellington: no imprint, 1953.

Lament for Barney Flanagan, licensee of the Hesperus Hotel. Wellington: no imprint, 1954.

Traveller's Litany. Wellington: Handcraft Press, 1955.

The Iron Breadboard: Studies in New Zealand Writing. Wellington: Mermaid Press, 1957.

The Night Shift: Poems on Aspects of Love (with Charles Doyle, Louis Johnson, Kendrick Smithyman). Wellington: Capricorn Press, 1957.

Chosen Poems. Bombay: Konkan Institute of Arts and Sciences, 1958.

In Fires of No Return: Selected Poems. London: Oxford University Press, 1958.

Ballad of Calvary Street. Wellington: no imprint, 1960.

Howrah Bridge and Other Poems. London: Oxford University Press, 1961.

A Selection of Poetry. Wellington: Poetry Magazine, 1964.

A Bucket of Blood for a Dollar. Christchurch: John Summers Bookshop, 1965.

The Gunner's Lament. Wellington: no imprint, 1965.

The Old Earth Closet. Wellington: Wai-te-ata Press, 1965.

Pig Island Letters. London: Oxford University Press, 1966.

A Small Ode on Mixed Flatting, elicited by the decision of the Otago University authorities to forbid this practice among students. Christchurch: Caxton Press, 1967.

The Lion Skin. Dunedin: Bibliography Room, University of Otago, 1967.

a death song for mr mouldybroke. Christchurch: John Summers, [1968].

Ballad of the Stonegut Sugar Works. Auckland: no imprint, 1969.

The Rock Woman: Selected Poems. London: Oxford University Press, 1969.

Jerusalem Sonnets: Poems for Colin Durning. Dunedin: Bibliography Room, University of Otago, 1970. Reprinted Wellington: Price Milburn, 1975.

The Junkies and the Fuzz. Wellington: Wai-te-ata Press, 1970.

Jerusalem Blues 2. Plimmerton: Bottle Press, 1971.

Jerusalem Daybook (Poems and Prose). Wellington: Price Milburn, 1971.

Autumn Testament: Poetry and Prose Journal. Wellington: Price Milburn, 1972. 2nd edition (ed. Paul Millar), Auckland: Oxford University Press, 1997.

Four God Songs. Karori: Futuna Press [1972].

Letter to Peter Olds. Dunedin: Caveman Press, 1972.

Ode to Auckland and Other Poems. Dunedin: Caveman Press, 1972.

Runes. London: Oxford University Press, 1973.

Two Obscene Poems. Adelaide: Mary Martin Books, 1973.

The Labyrinth: Some Uncollected Poems 1944–72. Chosen by J.E. Weir. Wellington: Oxford University Press, 1974.

The Tree House and Other Poems for Children. Wellington: Price Milburn, 1974.

The Bone Chanter: Unpublished Poems 1945–72. Chosen and Introduced by J.E. Weir. Wellington: Oxford University Press, 1976.

The Holy Life and Death of Concrete Grady: Various Uncollected and Unpublished Poems. Chosen and Introduced by J.E. Weir. Wellington: Oxford University Press, 1976.

Collected Poems. Ed. J.E. Weir. Wellington: Oxford University Press, 1980. Includes a number of previously unpublished or uncollected poems. Reprinted with corrections 1981. Paperback 1988. Reissued in hardback with index, 1995.

Selected Poems. Ed. J.E. Weir. Auckland: Oxford University Press, 1982.

Cold Spring. Ed. Paul Millar. Auckland: Oxford University Press, 1996.

Selected other works

Recent Trends in New Zealand Poetry. Christchurch: Caxton Press, 1951. (Criticism.)

The Fire and the Anvil: Notes on Modern Poetry. Wellington: New Zealand University Press, 1955. (Criticism.)

Aspects of Poetry in New Zealand. Christchurch: Caxton Press, 1967. (Criticism.)

The Man on the Horse. Dunedin: University of Otago Press, 1967. (Criticism and some poetry.)

The Flowering Cross. Dunedin: New Zealand Tablet, 1969. (Prose and some poetry.)

Thoughts about the Holy Spirit. Wellington: Futuna Press, 1973. (Prose and some poetry.)

James K. Baxter as Critic: A Selection from his Literary Criticism. Ed. Frank McKay. Auckland: Heinemann Educational Books, 1978.

Collected Plays. Ed. Howard McNaughton. Auckland: Oxford University Press, 1982.

Horse. Auckland: Oxford University Press, 1985. (Novella.)

Selected studies of Baxter's life and work

Doyle, Charles. *James K. Baxter*. Boston: Twayne Publishers, 1976.
McKay, Frank. *The Life of James K. Baxter*. Auckland: Oxford University Press, 1990.
Oliver, W.H. *James K. Baxter: A Portrait*. Auckland: Godwit Press/Bridget Williams Books, 1994.
O'Sullivan, Vincent. *James K. Baxter*. Wellington: Oxford University Press, 1976.
Weir, J.E. *The Poetry of James K. Baxter*. Wellington: Oxford University Press, 1970.

Bibliography

Weir, J.E., and Barbara Lyon (eds). *A Preliminary Bibliography of Works by and Works about James K. Baxter*. (1979). Christchurch: University of Canterbury, 1979.

Index of poems

Poems from sequences are not individually identified.